Martin Ti—

sundaythoughts.com

Reflections on
Every Sunday of the Year

VERITAS

First published 2001 by
Veritas Publications
7/8 Lower Abbey Street
Dublin 1
Ireland

Email publications@veritas.ie
Website www.veritas.ie

ISBN 1 85390 554 2

A catalogue record for this book is available from the British Library.

Extracts from the work of Jessica Powers are from *The Selected Poetry of Jessica
Powers*, published by ICS Publications, Washington DC. All copyrights,
Carmelite Monastery, Pewaukee, WI. Used with permission.

Designed by Colette Dower
Printed in the Republic of Ireland by Paceprint Ltd, Dublin

Veritas books are printed on paper made from the wood pulp of managed forests.
For every tree felled, at least one tree is planted, thereby renewing natural
resources.

Contents

SEASON OF LENT

SEASON OF EASTER

OTHER FEASTS

Preface

'When I smell the coffee, strong and stale, I find myself again in a small room over a corner coffee house in Oxford. My brain makes a link, and instantly transports me there', wrote the inventor of the World Wide Web, Tim Berners-Lee, in his book *Weaving the Web*. It happens all the time! A piece of music, a particular shade of hair, an unusual smell, the sound of water, the cry of a curlew, can all transport the mind over countries and continents, through time and space, into a world we have known and feel familiar with. In school, it was called 'daydreaming'. The wonderful invention of the Web, so new and so powerful, can be a vehicle for the Word of God. It can connect us to a sacred world, a world of mystery, a world of life. It was in the womb of the World Wide Web that *sundaythoughts.com* was nurtured. It was my invitation to the millions and millions of browsers to 'drop in'. Some did this, usually quite by accident and unannounced.

In 1998 I started a website on which I posted a few thoughts on the scripture readings for the following Sunday. Browsers from exotic places got in touch. On one occasion I ended up giving a talk to a group of visiting students from Russia, the Ukraine and Georgia, arranged by a language school in Norway! They had found the site quite accidentally while browsing. At other times I received searching questions on religion, and on the Roman Catholic Church in particular. This World Wide Web can be a powerful tool for good. After a year of cyberspace, *sundaythoughts.com* returned to earth and the written word. Hence this book. I have tried to make it popular enough to engage the interested lay person, and deep enough to be helpful to priests in providing a spark to ignite their own ingenuity for a Sunday homily.

Most of the reflections are on the Gospel of the day. I have always been conscious of the need to make the connection between the words, parables and miracles of Jesus and life as it is lived at the beginning of the twenty-first century. I am conscious that young people have largely lost the vocabulary of faith. Words like salvation, sanctifying grace, redemption, sin, paschal mystery, have slipped from the lexicon of words that are easily understood by young Catholics. Yet many still want to know: how do I live my life in the light of the Gospel? How do I respond to this or that crisis in a way that is consistent with the words of Jesus? Can I make a connection with this person Jesus, that will influence my life? I have always been inspired by the lives and words of holy men and women, prophets and poets, and so I have tried to include them in *sundaythoughts.com*.

I don't think there is any one way to write or preach a good homily. In writing *sundaythoughts.com* I read the Gospel carefully, asked the Holy Spirit to help, and more times than not, nothing came. There were times when I had to get up and walk around the house, frustrated at my lack of inspiration. 'Why will nothing come?' I asked myself. Occasionally I had to share my frustration with friends. Then a chance remark, an item in the newspaper, an incident in the parish, a radio chat show, ignited a train of thought that opened a door into the heart of the Gospel. There were times when I felt I got a whole new insight into the person of Jesus. I began to understand his humanity, the emotional depth of the man, with a clarity I hadn't got before. I realised that he had deep human needs as I have. I appreciated his empathy and compassion for the 'little people'.

Much of the material is drawn from my own experience of thirty-eight year of priesthood. It is such a rare privilege to have shared the joys, sadnesses, the pain and trauma of so many wonderful people. I offer this book up to the dear friends who have died, to my family and to my special friends who love and support me. I have been blessed, as I know other priests have, by the love and support and friendship of many people. I take this opportunity to thank them most sincerely.

Martin Tierney

Preface

Advent

The Disappeared

Readings: Isa 2:1-5; Rom 13:11-14; Mt 24:37-44

'Home' is taking up where one left off, no matter how long the period away has been. 'Home' is where there is someone to welcome us. Advent is the beginning of a journey home to God's love.

Imagine you are a Jew living in Israel just before Jesus' coming. Imagine that your teenage daughter is beginning to lose faith in the Messiah. She thinks the idea of waiting for a Messiah for thousands of years is just not credible. She says, 'I'm not going to the Temple any more. I don't mind what you or Mammy say!' This imaginary situation is similar to the situation many Catholics find themselves in today.

We have all noticed the dwindling congregations in our churches in recent years. Where have they all gone? Does anyone know why they left? No goodbyes, no tears, no care! How would you feel if some of your family members closed the hall door and walked out into the night? Wouldn't you go and invite them back or ask the reason for their leaving? Wouldn't you think of ways of indicating to them that the door was always open?

As I write there is great joy in the Crennan household in Abbeyleix, County Laois. Kevin hadn't been heard of by his family for seven long years. He didn't even know that his father had died. Then, quite by chance, he turned up in Columbia in South America. His sister Ann rejoiced, 'It is fantastic the way the whole thing happened. We are all over the moon! My mother was especially relieved. She is an elderly person. Maybe she was afraid she would die without seeing her son again.' Home, for a Christian, is being with God, in some way. Home is where too many questions will not be asked. Home is taking up where one left off, no matter how long the period away has been. Home is where we experience warmth. Home is where we are meant to be.

This is a beautiful time of the year in religious terms. Our four weeks of preparation, called Advent, are a looking forward to 'home', as well as a looking at life from a long-term view. Where do I see myself five, ten, years from now? Is my relationship with God growing or do I need to look anew at the spiritual dimension of my life? The readings at this time focus a lot on John the Baptist – the wild man of the desert. Is there anything I can learn from him?

Much of the activity of the Church is concerned with the 'converted'. Many of Jesus' parables, in particular the lost sheep and the lost coin and the prodigal son, invite us to think again. Advent is a time of new beginnings. It is a time for seeking our way home again. Perhaps I am one of the 'disappeared'. Maybe I need to touch base again with my spiritual roots – with the person of Jesus.

During the Pinochet regime in Chile many people just 'disappeared'. The same happened in Argentina. Empty pews give testimony to the 'disappeared' members of the Catholic Church in Ireland. The one time the 'disappeared' tend to return to Church is at Christmas. It is such a festive, family time that most people want to be part of it. Advent can be a gently evangelical sort of time. It is a time to welcome the stranger back to the loving arms of Jesus, back to the Church, who is mother, who desires to nurture, encourage and assist everyone to grow in faith and love of Jesus.

The Gospel today is about the Second Coming and the subsequent judgement. The judgement is not a Tribunal with all the trappings of a court. It is not an adversarial arena where learned lawyers drag over the entrails of your life with a fine comb. Your advocate is also your judge. You can't have a more one-sided structure than that! God's judgement is tempered by love and mercy. Nevertheless, each will have to give an account of his or her life. The only preparation possible and the only preparation necessary is our constant care to live in the light and love brought by our Lord who became like one of us.

Stay Awake

Readings: Isa 63:16-17; 64:1-8; 1 Cor 1:3-9; Mk 13:33-37

People waiting for a heart or liver transplant always have their bags packed, ready for the call that will bring them a renewed life. Today's Gospel asks us to stay awake waiting for the Second Coming.

Lough Derg, the pilgrim island in Donegal, was described by Shane Leslie in 1932 as a 'medieval rumour which terrified travellers, awed the greatest criminals, attracted the boldest of knight-errantry, puzzled the theologian, englamoured Ireland, haunted Europe, influenced the current views and doctrines of Purgatory, and not least inspired Dante!' For me it means staying awake for two days and a very long night! The weariness of the night vigil, begun on a midge-infested summer's evening and ending in the cold chill of a new dawn, is painful. Staying awake isn't at all easy. When I read the Gospels of today's Mass I was haunted by my memories of Lough Derg. The words of Jesus, 'And what I say to you, I say to all: stay awake!', had a very special resonance for me.

This chapter in Mark's Gospel must be read as a whole. Jesus was talking about the destruction of Jerusalem and the Temple, which of course happened in AD 70. It was the beginning of the end of that period of Jewish history which culminated in Masada. He was also warning of persecutions to come. His followers would have to learn that the path of suffering would be part of their Christian journey. Then there are warnings of the last days and the Second Coming of Jesus. If we live in the shadow of eternity, with the possibility of the intervention of God at any time, then we have to be prepared. All of this is enfolded in the language and imagery of the Old Testament.

One thing that has always fascinated me about mountaineers is the meticulous preparation that goes into every expedition. In Chris Bonnington's latest book, *Tibet's Secret Mountain – the triumph of Sepu Kangri*, two preliminary exploratory expeditions were made to the area of the proposed climb before the detailed planning even began. On a hot midsummer evening, Americans were joined by 600 million people around the world to watch in awe as Neil Armstrong, aged thirty-eight, from Ohio, lowered his left foot gingerly into the soft dust of the moon's surface. 'That's one small step for man . . . one giant step for mankind.' It was eight years since President Kennedy had promised to set a man on the moon. Eight years of detailed planning and preparation.

Increasingly the Christian life has been described as a pilgrimage, a journey. The most important staging post on that journey is death. The Gospel today tells us to be ready, to try to live as we would wish to die. I know that people who are waiting for a liver or heart transplant always have their bags packed and remain in touch no matter where they are – always waiting for the call that will bring them new life. We are in a queue waiting for a new life that will last for ever.

Funerals are a regular part of daily life. They are painful events for family and friends. In a very vague sort of way such occasions remind us that we too will follow them – but not yet. Death is always just over the horizon. 'We haven't here a lasting city but seek one that is to come.' The heart that always looks forward will never be truly at peace until it arrives at home. Home is where the heart is meant to be – with God. God, who is infinite love, peace, joy, is the only one who can fulfil our deepest longings and needs.

The fear of death is natural. The journey is from the known, familiar people and ways of life into what? No one has come to tell us what it's like. Faith is the bridge that straddles time and eternity. Perhaps I haven't much of that and I am afraid. We know that He has gone before us. His resurrection is the pledge that we too shall rise again. We don't know when it will be. He will be the one who will beckon and we will go. Life is a preparation for death, the gateway into a new life.

First Sunday of Advent

Waiting

Readings: Jer 33:14-16; 1 Thess 3:12-4:2; Lk 21:25-28, 34-36

Advent is a time of waiting and a time of expectation. We are asked to take a long-term view and look to the Second Coming of Jesus and to our preparedness for it.

We are entering the season of waiting. For some, waiting can be with eager anticipation, for others, it is a matter of daring to hope. This is a letter from Janet who is waiting for a liver transplant.

> Dear Malcolm,
> I never realised how difficult it was going to be to receive a liver. There's a lot of competition out there and many more people are in worse shape than I. I just hope I get one when my liver packs in. I keep strong in the belief that God will provide and that there is a reason for this waiting time. Now that I understand the delay in admittance, I'll put 'waiting' in its place and just be patient. I'm feeling OK but these days I'm more fatigued than ever. At times, I don't have enough energy to sit up. My body feels so heavy. I threw caution to the wind and took an all-day outing (cabin fever gets to me). It took me two days to recover. The outing was so worth it.
> Take care of yourself. You're in my thoughts and prayers.
> Love Janet

The diary of Anne Frank has become one of the bestselling books of all time. Cooped up in an annex for almost four years until betrayed in 1944, Anne had a premonition. She was waiting for something terrible to happen. At the age of fifteen she wrote, 'I hear the approaching thunder that, one day, will destroy us too, I feel the suffering of millions. And yet, when I look up at the sky, I somehow feel that this cruelty too shall end, that peace and tranquility will return once more.'

We are beginning our period of waiting, of looking forward. This looking forward is not just to the coming feast of Christmas but also to the Second Coming of Jesus Christ, the subject of today's Gospel. Cosmic signs and distress on earth are the stock accompaniment of a divine intervention and especially of the divine judgement of humankind. The cloud of the Second Coming will reveal Jesus' hitherto hidden glory, which is the glory of God. He comes in the cloud, the vehicle of God, to effect the divine work of judgement and redemption.

The Second Coming really means that there is a goal to the divine plan working itself out in history, a plan that is accomplished in and through Jesus. God has a plan for our lives and for the whole of humanity. The 'parousia' is the culmination of that plan. We are asked to be alert for the Second Coming of Jesus. That will be the culmination of the redemption. None of us can afford to be presumptuous. Justice tempers God's infinite mercy. There needs to be a time when the scales of justice are balanced. At the beginning of Advent we are being asked to set our sights not on the material preparations for the coming feast but to take a more long-term view of our lives and where we are going in our relationship with God.

I remember when I was a small boy in short trousers attending the annual school retreat. The Jesuit priest, who seemed ancient, began the retreat with the words, 'It is appointed unto man once to die and after death the judgement.' At this stage I had never even seen a dead person, not to mind having little idea of death or judgement! It would be unfortunate if we were never to recall the fact that we will all have to give an account of our lives to the good Lord.

The parousia may be delayed, but it will eventually involve us all. How one lives here and now determines how one will 'stand before the Son of Man'. These words of Luke, apparently so remote, are not at all without reference to our day-to-day lives.

A Powerful Message of Repentance

Readings: Isa 11:1-10; Rom 15:4-9; Mt 3:1-12

There is so much to learn from the remarkable figure of John the Baptist – confession, repentance, humility, self-denial and the power of Baptism.

It's amazing what a 'wild man' can achieve! Mahatma Gandhi was one such person. After the terrible massacre of 400 people by the British at Amritsar in 1919, he undertook a personal fast for three weeks. In defiance of punitive salt taxes, this was followed by leading a 320 kilometre march to the sea to collect salt. He was arrested many times for civil disobedience. His fast, to shame the instigators of communal strife between Hindu and Muslim, helped to avert national disaster. He sought an India free from caste and materialism, always through non-violent means. He reminds me of John the Baptist! The witness of his life was undoubtedly prophetic.

Another modern-day prophet was the late Anton Wallich-Clifford, the founder of the Simon Community, who died in 1963. Through his work as a probation officer, Anton met homeless men and women who were living rough on derelict sites and wasteground in London. He was inspired by other tireless workers for the poor, such as Dorothy Day, who co-founded the Catholic Worker Movement, and Abbé Pierre, who founded the Emmaus Community in France. The work of Mario Borrelli with homeless children in Naples also inspired him. He established volunteer work that has given a new beginning to many people who are usually considered the flotsam of the consumer society. Now Anton was a prophet! Who are the prophets we need to listen to today?

I am not a lover of the word 'prophet'. I think it is used frivolously to describe those who are against the establishment for whatever reason. People are called prophets simply because by their words and actions they invite retaliation from the 'power brokers', whether civil or religious. Nevertheless, the God whom we seek, the God whom John the Baptist was proclaiming, 'spoke through the prophets'. A prophet is one who is called and sent. John was one such person. We cannot ignore his message.

John's message was a tough one. To change one's ways isn't easy. Dietrich Bonhoeffer, who paid the ultimate price for his faith under the Nazis, put John's message in this way: 'Cheap grace is the preaching of forgiveness without requiring repentance, baptism without church discipline, communion without confession, absolution without personal confession. Cheap grace is grace without discipleship, grace without the cross, grace without Jesus Christ, living and incarnate.' (*The Cost of Discipleship*)

When we try to change we usually do so relying on will-power alone. It doesn't have to be like that! There comes a time when we have to 'claim the promises of Christ'. In the Acts of the Apostles we read: 'You must repent, and every one of you must be baptised in the name of Jesus Christ for the forgiveness of your sins and you will receive the gift of the Holy Spirit'. The Holy Spirit is a spirit of power. We need divine power if we are to change our lives. Repentance is a journey towards God. It is a grace rather than an act.

Over the last twenty-five years I have witnessed many, many people turn their lives around through their participation in the 'Life in the Spirit' seminars. I have known people who have had their lives turned upside down. The promises of God are that those who turn to him and receive his Spirit will be changed. They will experience new life. 'The Lord God says this, "I shall pour clean water over you and you will be cleansed. I shall give you a new heart, and put a new spirit in you; I shall remove the heart of stone from your bodies and give you a heart of flesh instead. I shall put my spirit in you. You shall be my people and I will be your God".' People like Gandhi, Anton Wallich-Clifford and John the Baptist turned their lives over to God and a great prophetic work was accomplished through them.

Sin Hurts Others

Readings: Isa 40:1-5, 9-11; Pet 3:8-14; Mk 1:1-8

The existence of sin is hardly recognised any more. Nevertheless, acknowledging sin is the beginning of the path towards wholeness and freedom.

Lloyd Douglas, author of *The Robe*, used to tell how he loved to visit an old violin teacher who had a homely wisdom that refreshed him. One morning Douglas walked in and said, 'Well, what's the good news today?' Putting down his violin, the teacher stepped over to a tuning fork suspended from a cord and struck it. 'There is the good news for today,' he said. 'That, my friend, is the musical note A. It was A all day yesterday, will be A next week and for a thousand years.' I think repentance, mentioned by John the Baptist in today's Gospel, must be put in the context of good news. Repentance is part of a journey towards wholeness and freedom.

What is repentance? Where does it start? It is relational, in the sense that there is an offender and an offended. Sin is a rupturing or damaging of the relationship between myself and God. Only those who know love, know sin. We have all experienced serious family quarrels. We experience pain and hurt when we fall out with someone we love. We play and replay the drama in our minds. The script is analysed for further hurts. Sadness, anger, resentment and longing are the emotions that well up inside us. We try to devise ways of coming together again. Those who are closest seem to hurt each other with a greater intensity than mere acquaintances would. When we know

God's love with the heart rather than with the head we will know immediately what sin is.

A brother said to the Abbot Poemen, 'If I fall into shameful sin, my conscience devours and accuses me, saying: "Why have you fallen?" ' The old man said to him, 'At the moment when a man goes astray, if he says, "I have sinned", immediately the sin ceases.'

We can talk ourselves out of the admission of sin, 'sure everyone's doing it, it couldn't be wrong', or more subtly, 'God will understand', or even self-justifyingly, 'I am not hurting anyone'. The chief danger for anyone seeking a genuine spirituality is the temptation to change the rules. We do it all the time. Adultery is no longer a sin! Or cohabiting, or evading taxation with an offshore bank account, or driving while drunk. We try to escape our imperfection by redefining or lowering the standards necessary for 'perfection' or a full relationship with God. That becomes the slippery slope into amorality.

In the fifth century St Augustine explored the tension between the flesh and the spirit, detailing how in this life everyone is to some extent defective, and he used this point to emphasise that no one is exempt from the need for forgiveness.

The most powerful parables in the Gospels detail the love of God for the sinner. The parables of the prodigal son, the lost coin and the lost sheep dramatise the intensity of God's love for us. God cannot harden his heart against the repentant sinner! First we have to recognise our sin and experience our need for forgiveness and healing. Some people persist in what they know to be sinful and do not experience the need for forgiveness and healing. Their hearts may have been hardened.

Sin damages our relationship with God. In addition, all sin is social in some way. Sin does hurt others. Because sin is an act of selfishness, by that very fact when I sin I make myself less available to love and I harden my heart a little. Therefore, by being selfish, in some way you are hurting, albeit unknowingly, other people.

The joy of today's message from John the Baptist is that there is a forgiveness available for everyone.

Che Guevara Leads The Way

Readings: Bar 5:1-9; Phil 1:3-6, 8-11; Lk 3:1-6

We need heroes, role models. Che Guevara has been such to two generations of young people. Have we been presenting an ersatz Christ to the people?

The year is 2001, the month July; I am walking down O'Connell Street, Dublin's main thoroughfare. Stuck to a number of lampposts I see the picture of revolutionary leader Che Guevara. A caption entices me to attend a meeting of the Young Socialists to air some grievance they have against the system. Now Che Guevara died well over thirty years ago, long before any of these Young Socialists were born. How is it that the image and person of Che Guevara, Latin American guerrilla leader and revolutionary, became and remains a hero to the radical Left? In 1954 he went to Mexico where he joined Fidel Castro. He played an important part in Castro's guerrilla war against the Cuban dictator Fulgencio Batista. He disappeared from Cuba in 1965, reappearing the following year as an insurgent leader in Bolivia. He was captured by the Bolivian army and shot near Vallegrande on 9 October 1967. In Che Guevara is encapusuled the hopes and dreams of people in 'bondage'. He is seen as the revolutionary and redeemer *par excellence*. To the Young Socialists he is a Christ-like figure whose ideology motivates their actions and protests. People need heroes.

The preaching and the actions of Jesus were every bit as radical as those of Guevara. He too preached liberty to the captives and sight to the blind. Che, a doctor, from the Argentinian middle class, crossed the boundaries of acceptability. He did something that made him an outcast from his own class. He took his revolutionary activities deadly seriously. Jesus is the leader to whom John the Baptist points in today's Gospel. His agenda for change is far more radical than that of Guevara's. It starts with a change of heart rather than structures. It starts with leaving behind the old, and taking on the image and the way of Christ. Indifference or apathy where Christ is concerned is not an option.

The dynamic message of Christ has become confused with what people call 'organised religion' or the 'institutional Church'. They seldom see the radicality of the message and the way of life that Christ preached. This is where John the Baptist comes in. We need to see the gospel lived out in its fullness. John the Baptist did this before the gospel had been preached by Christ. He anticipated the message and the way of life that Christ was to point to. He was a person of influence and therefore could lead people to Christ – 'behold the Lamb of God'.

Into the desert of our lives, there occasionally slips a John the Baptist – someone who speaks to us at a deeper level, someone who opens our eyes to something bigger than ourselves. It may be a friend, an inspired teacher or someone who radiates something more than the ordinary. Such a person points us towards the Lamb of God.

When John the Baptist was in the desert he called the people to reform their lives, and he helped them to find the way to God. In today's world we are called to fill this same role with our friends, with our families, and those we meet. This week ask yourself, 'If Jesus should come to my home and my life today, would he find me ready?' John's call for reform and spiritual rebuilding can be your call as well.

Second Sunday of Advent

John Needed Reassurance

Readings: Isa 35:1-6; Jas 5:7-10; Mt 11:2-11

A poet once described faith as 'the loneliness of mystery'. We, like John the Baptist, need to be reassured in our faith in the person of Jesus.

At the time of writing, the *Sunday Times* are running a series of articles entitled 'Skeletons'. In this series people are encouraged to write about skeletons in the family cupboard, about which they were ignorant for years and years. These secrets reveal apparent paragons of virtue to be, in fact, terrible rascals, unknown to family members. Concurrently a television series, *True Lives,* is doing the same about public figures of the past. Florence Nightingale got the treatment last week! There is an iconoclasm, beloved of tabloids, that wants to reduce everyone to the sad and tawdry. No heroes any more!

With Jesus things were different. What you saw was what you got. The man, the life and the message were one and the same. John wanted to be reassured. John was a man used to the wild open places; cooped up in prison his mind may have been playing tricks on him. In Carlisle Castle there is a little cell. Once long ago they put a border chieftain in that cell and left him there for years. In the cell there is one little window, which is placed too high for a man to look out of when he is standing on the floor. On the ledge of the window there are two depressions worn away in the stone. They are the marks of the hands of the chieftain, the places where, day after day, he lifted himself up by his hands to look out on the green dales across which he would never ride again. Prison must have been like that for John the Baptist. He had invested his life in the message. It was important to him. Jesus pointed to the obvious signs that someone very different was here, 'The blind see again, the lame walk, lepers are cleansed and the deaf hear, and the dead are raised to life...'.

There are times when we too need reassurance. When I think of faith, I think of St Thérèse. For about fifteen months she was tortured with doubts against the faith. All she could say was, 'I know that behind the dark clouds my sun is still shining.' If we have the eyes to see, there are signs of faith and of the presence of Jesus in the lives of others: the painful suffering of a cancer patient; the brave acceptance of God's will in bereavement; committed love when a marriage is in difficulty. We also see signs of the transcendent in art, literature, drama and music. We see signs of God in the intricacies of a leaf, or the mottled wings of a butterfly, or the sun dancing on a placid lake. But like John we need reassurance.

Jesus began to talk to people about John. He says, 'A greater than John the Baptist has never been seen'. What a beautiful passage of praise. Here the humanity of Jesus is demonstrated. There are times when we forget to praise others, especially those closest to us. Praise makes the talents of others fertile. We grow when we are praised. There are times when those who exercise authority are unconscious of the power they have over the lives of others. The negative power can be greater than the positive. To withhold, or to neglect to praise the goodness of others, can diminish them. People can shrivel up and lose heart when their efforts go unrecognised. Jesus was so human and knew the complexities of the heart.

Sunday in Hyde Park

Readings: Isa 61:1–2, 10-11; 1 Thess 5:16-29; Jn 1:6-8, 19-28

Like John, there are people who are willing to sacrifice themselves in the interests of the Gospel.

Nearly thirty years ago, whenever I was in London, I visited Hyde Park Corner on a Sunday afternoon. Before more recent developments took place it was a quiet enough spot. Speakers advocating different religious and political viewpoints mounted a soapbox and spoke to the mainly curious bystanders. The speakers were very professional in their presentation, but even more professional were the hecklers. They were witty, knowledgeable and caustic. They tested the speaker's patience to the limits. Every Sunday the Catholic Evidence Guild wheeled out its stall. Actually it was a ladder with a small platform for the speakers. Here in all weathers wonderful men like Frank Sheed and Fr Vincent McNabb withstood the taunts of the hecklers, as they presented the 'good news' of the Gospel. Thirty years ago Catholics had only recently been let out of the catacombs in England into the world of respectable society. Catholicism was a novelty to be explored. At times the arguments became heated and intense. I admired these men, very cultured and literate, in their commitment to the Gospel. They never gave up, even though, in the words of today's Gospel, they were 'voices crying in the wilderness'. To be a voice crying in the wilderness is a very lonely place to be.

The courage of John the Baptist had been fashioned in the wilderness. He was fearless. People are full of fear. The practice of most large hotels to have no thirteenth floor panders to one of the more irrational fears prevalent today. John the Baptist was one of many competing voices seeking attention. There were numerous 'prophets and preachers' around. This did not deter John from warning people to 'make a straight path for the Lord'.

In Retrouvaille, the programme for married couples experiencing difficulties in their relationship, we have found that fear is a mighty obstacle to reconciliation. The fear to trust again after years of pain must be overcome if a relationship is to be rebuilt. When the leap of trust is made, new undreamt of possibilities open out. We have seen how fear has dogged the Northern Ireland Peace Process. The wounds inflicted by one side on the other are still raw, the fear of trusting again too great, and so a spiral of recrimination frustrates the hoped for reconciliation.

There are many people of faith who allow fear to strangle their desire to share their faith with others. Human respect, political correctness, and a fear of not finding the right words, often mute the desires of the heart. We witness most effectively to our faith by the lives we lead. The example of John the Baptist can be an inspiration to us to believe that in a sense 'faith is given to be given away!' I have always thought of faith as a bit like a muscle; the more you exercise it the tougher and stronger it becomes. The more we exercise our faith by prayer, spiritual reading, and above all by sharing it with others, the stronger it becomes.

Third Sunday of Advent

We Cannot Mock God

Readings: Zeph 3:14-18; Phil 4:4-7; Lk 3:10-18

This Sunday John the Baptist is centre stage with a prophetic message to turn from our sinfulness, repent, and turn to God. A timely message for this time of the year.

I tossed and turned in the bed. Sleep wasn't easily coming. Turning to a late night/early morning 'talk-radio' show I was catapulted into a world I knew nothing about. The discussion was on whether the manner in which young women dressed today enticed or encouraged men to sexual violence towards women. 'F..k me! I nearly crashed me car today in the city,' says the first male speaker. 'Je..s, I saw this young one and she had practically nothing on. Bleedin' terrible. Of course it affects men! I wouldn't let my girlfriend out in that sort of stuff. It affected me!' A succession of very angry girls then made the wires fairly sizzle. 'No one is going to tell me what to wear. It's fashion. I'll wear what I bleedin' want! Men are only perverts anyway. They don't have to look.' Married women were on the line supporting their daughters in wearing the skimpiest of clothes. An expletive or the Holy Name prefaced every sentence. 'Where does the gospel fit into all this?' I puzzled. Was I wired to a different planet? The conversation was fruity and without a sliver of moral content. Where do all the nice pious sermons, and bland hymns carefully chosen, and altar boys scoured and clean, and candles and Catholic newspapers, and announcements about the latest novena, connect with the 'vulgarity' of late-night talk-radio? It is the Third Sunday of Advent and the busiest shop in the area is the off-licence!

In Jesus' time the people who lived on the side of the tracks I live on were first of all 'the elders'. They were the lay nobility, the old aristocratic families who owned the land. The Sadduccees came next, people of learning, the academics, living in ivory towers, then as now. The scribes and Pharisees were people of learning too – theologians, lawyers and teachers. In the midst of all this one man stood out as a sign of contradiction. John the Baptist was different precisely because he was a prophet; in a way a prophet of doom and destruction. His style of life, his way of speaking and his message were a conscious revival of the tradition of the prophets. John's prophetic message was a simple one: God was angry with his people and he planned to punish them. He made use of the metaphors of the axe and the winnowing-fan. The forest fire mentioned was an image of hell on earth. God's fiery judgement upon Israel would be executed, according to John, by a human being. John spoke of him as 'the one who is to come', 'He will baptise you with fire'. This was a warning from John that it was time for people to bring order into their lives in accordance with God's plan. If Israel did not change, the consequences would be disastrous.

In an age of exaggerated political correctness, where the most bizarre behaviour is given a benign and approving nod, perhaps it is time for a prophetic voice warning people that defying God's plan has consequences. God's love is tempered with mercy but also with justice. The callers to the radio show need to know that there is a limit to behaviour and there is a time when we need to name sin, acknowledge it, confess and repent. One cannot mock God. The message of the prophet may not be listened to but that is not a reason for remaining silent. The Gospel today has a very serious message that we ignore at our peril.

The Only One To Have Chosen His Own Mother

Readings: Isa 7:10-14; Rom 1:1-7; Mt 1:1-18

Today we are confronted with the loneliness of mystery. To believe demands an act of faith.

If you could have chosen your own mother, would you not have made her the most perfect woman that ever lived, a woman of gentleness and compassion? When God chose to become man, he chose the political system, the country, the village, the time and the place of his coming. He also chose his mother. Never before had this happened. To choose a mother was not just to choose a person but to choose the circumstances of one's birth. And so Jesus was born in Palestine, in humble surroundings, to a mother who had little social status or wealth. But all these details depended on one fact – would the lady say 'Yes' to God's invitation? The 'fiat' of Mary changed the course of human history. The implications of Mary's 'Yes' are as powerful today as they were 2,000 years ago. I am confronted by the need to say 'Yes' to all that Jesus has done, or forever remain a sceptic.

Today's Gospel gives us a glimpse from the wings of the drama surrounding the conception and birth of Jesus. How was it to happen? There was the engagement. At that time, engagements were usually made through the parents, or through a professional match-maker. The engagement was often made without the couple involved ever having seen each other. Marriage was held to be far too serious a step to be left to the dictates of the human heart.

There was the betrothal. The betrothal was what we might call the ratification of the engagement. Once the betrothal was entered into, it was absolutely binding. It lasted for one year. During that year the couple were known as husband and wife, although they didn't have the rights of husband and wife. The betrothal could not be terminated in any other way than by divorce. In the Jewish law, a girl whose fiancé has died during the year of betrothal is called 'a virgin who is a widow'.

This was the stage that Joseph and Mary were at. They were betrothed, and if Joseph wished to end the betrothal, he could do so in no other way than by divorce; and in that year of betrothal Mary was legally known as his wife. Joseph was content to listen to the voice of the spirit, although he had every reason for confusion and doubt.

Both Mary and Joseph had to live with 'the loneliness of mystery', the not-knowing but still trusting, dimension of faith. Supposing it all went wrong? This sort of faith is an adventure that cannot feel the way forward. I heard it once described as looking at the reverse side of a beautiful carpet. What is it? A confused jumble of coloured threads. Only God sees the perfect plan – a plan for good and not for evil. The pattern of our lives is frequently filled with confusion but our faith tells us that there is a plan stretching into eternity.

The mystery of the Incarnation opens us up to other profound mysteries. Christ came as victor and victim, saviour and sacrifice, King of Kings and 'despised and rejected of men'; Christmas is celebrated with joy and yet Jesus was born to suffer and die; the shepherds adored a Christ for the poor, the Three Kings a Christ for the rich.

The Gospel today is at the very heart of the mystery of Christ and his coming. It calls out for supernatural faith rather than human analysis.

Fourth Sunday of Advent

The Virginal Conception

Readings: 2 Sam 7:1-5, 8-12, 14, 16; Rom 16:25-27; Lk 1:26-38

It could be that the story of the virgin birth is more about the power and activity of the Holy Spirit than the virginal conception of Mary.

Jesus is the only one who had the privilege of selecting his own mother. It isn't unreasonable to assume that he chose the most perfect human being that ever existed. She wasn't selected on class, race or popularity, she was selected on virtue. The story of the virgin birth is a powerful one. Some people might be tempted to dwell on the virginal aspect of the story, the fact that Jesus hadn't a father who participated in his conception. Could it be that the point of the story is the activity and the power of the Spirit as much as the virginal conception? Both Matthew (1:18-25) and Luke (1:30-35) state that Jesus Christ was conceived by an action of the Holy Spirit without the intervention of a human father.

It is not the absence of a human father, nor even the co-operation of the virgin mother, that is the important point. From his mother, Jesus was born as a human being, but by the creative act of the Spirit his is a new humanity, the starting-point of a new race, of which we are now part. We share his life through Baptism.

The Holy Spirit is a spirit of power. You remember how Jesus directed his disciples 'to go into Jerusalem' where they would 'receive power from on high and you will be my witnesses in Jerusalem, Judaea, Samaria and throughout the world'. Here we see Jesus himself being conceived through the power of the Spirit just as the infant Church was born through the same power.

The power of the Holy Spirit is for everyone. I can recall in the mid Seventies a man coming to a prayer meeting. He came directly from hospital where he was being treated for chronic alcoholism. After the prayer meeting he asked to be prayed over so that through the power of the Holy Spirit he would be cured of his addiction. From that day until now he has never touched alcoholic drink!

A few weeks ago I was directing a retreat for parents of transition year students in a secondary school. A lady there told me a story about her daughter who for over ten years had been trying to conceive a child without success. They had visited eminent consultants here and in London. She and her husband were distraught. Again through ceaseless prayer and fasting this lady is now pregnant!

There are occasions when we despair of letting go of a habit of sinfulness or overcoming an obstacle in our relationship with God. The power of the Holy Spirit is available to you and me.

I think there is another point to the story – the *'fiat'* or the 'yes' of Mary. Surely this Gospel incident was one of confusion to her? Yet she gave her yes. I believe that there are times when each of us are confronted with the 'mystery of faith', when we have to give our 'yes' without fully understanding. An American poet, Jessica Powers, wrote of the 'loneliness of mystery'. That is what it is at times.

Finally those powerful words, 'Behold the handmaid of the Lord'. That word 'handmaid' can be more correctly translated as 'slave girl'. Of course, at the time of Jesus, the presence and activity of slaves was normal. A slave was owned by and marked with the sign of his or her master. By these words Mary was placing herself at the disposal of the Lord, to use her in whatever way fitted most effectively into his divine plan. She was to be the clay with which the potter was to shape a new vision. We are all called to be saints. 'His will is our sanctification,' St Paul writes. We will become holy through the power of God's Spirit, moulding and shaping us as the potter does.

Fourth Sunday of Advent

A Feast of Fruitfulness

Readings: Mic 5:1-4; Heb 10:5-10; Lk 1:39-45

The story of the Visitation is one of fruitfulness. To do God's will with joy, despite the difficulties, brings blessings in our own lives and in the lives of others.

En Kerem is in the western suburbs of Jerusalem. Jerome Murphy-O'Connor, in his book *The Holy Land,* writes: 'The attractiveness of the site and the fact that it is equidistant to Jerusalem and Bethlehem probably explains the 6 AD tradition which placed here the home of Zachary and Elizabeth, the parents of John the Baptist'.

The Church of the Visitation was one of the highlights for me of a Holy Land visit. As I recall it, the theme of the Church was 'fruitfulness'. The mosaics depicted the whole of nature breaking out in fecundity. Nature was bursting forth in greenery. Deer and other animals bounded from the mosaics on the floor. God the begetter of new life was being celebrated and praised. The appropriateness of this theme for the Visitation story struck me immediately. The meeting of Mary and Elizabeth, whether it is historically accurate or not, is filled with the mystery of the new life; it was a truly sacred moment.

Mary was pregnant. Who knows if she suffered from 'morning sickness' or not? Despite the fact that travel was hazardous at the time, her first thought was not for herself, but Elizabeth. Today, I suppose the prevailing philosophy is 'look after number one' – meaning oneself. The individual is king. In our country, voluntary agencies must go abroad to seek recruits to care for the less fortunate in our society. The mark of whether a society is truly Christian or not is the manner in which it looks after the underprivileged. Mary, often caricatured as a meek and mild person, is in fact a woman of strength. She acted with purpose and set out with 'haste'. The journey was not an obstacle to her. To be chosen by God so often means at one and the same time a crown of joy and cross of sorrow. The piercing truth is that God does not choose a person for ease and comfort and selfish joy but for a task that will take all that head and heart and hand can bring to it. God chooses a person in order to use them. When Joan of Arc knew that her time was short she prayed, 'I shall only last a year; use me as you can.' When that is realised, the sorrows and hardships that serving God may bring are not matters for lamentation; they are our glory, for all is suffered for God. Mary was the sort of person who could rejoice in the Annunciation, although the implications for her were learning to live with mystery and with the shadow of the cross.

There is extraordinary warmth in the greeting between the two women. No shyness or awkwardness here. There appears to have been a bond between them. Everyone needs a friend – an *anamchara*. Could it have been that these two women were spiritual companions to one another? There certainly seems to be a great degree of mutual support and love between them. Both Elizabeth and the child in her womb acknowledge the greater authority of Mary's unborn son. Here were two people who were fitting into God's plan for them, subjecting themselves to his will no matter what that might bring.

This is such a busy time for mothers. A mother so often is the heart of the home and bears so many of the emotional problems associated with what it means to be a family. This is the day to acknowledge the debt of gratitude we owe to our mothers.

Fourth Sunday of Advent

Christmas

The Strangest Christmas Ever

Readings: Isa 9:1-7; Titus 2:11-14; Lk 2:1-14

On Christmas Eve and Christmas Day 1914, the strangest event happened in the middle of a savage war that claimed over ten million victims.

'I think I have seen one of the most extraordinary sights today that anyone has ever seen,' Second Lieutenant Dougan Chater wrote to his mother from the trenches near Armentieres on Christmas Day 1914. 'About 10 o'clock this morning I was peeping over the parapet when I saw a German waving his arms and presently two of them got out of their trenches and some came towards ours. We were just going to fire on them when we saw they had no rifles. One of our men went out to meet them and in about two minutes the ground between the two lines of trenches was swarming with men and officers of both sides, shaking hands and wishing each other a happy Christmas.' In other parts of the line the unofficial truce was signified by the strains of the carol 'Silent Night, Holy Night' coming from the German trenches. The Allied forces joined in the hymn and utter peace reigned on the 'war to end all wars'. Another account of the event from a twenty-five-year-old Lieutenant with the Scots Guards read: 'Detachments of British and Germans formed a line and a German and English chaplain read some prayers alternately. The whole of this was done in great solemnity and reverence'. The peace of Jesus had triumphed, albeit only for a sacred day. Is there any other event, apart from the celebration of the birth of Jesus, that could have made this happen? Christmas is special.

Christmas has other messages – helplessness, poverty, nurturing and family. I cannot think of the first Christmas without remembering that two significant figures could possibly have been within eyesight of one another on that very night – Herod and Jesus. Herod's mighty palace, the Herodian, was visible from Bethlehem. It had everything – saunas and Turkish baths, a marina, huge kitchens, a parade ground, a palace for guests. Herod was filled with fear. He had lined up a whole section of the population who were to be put to death at the time of his own death. He was determined that there would be mourning and tears when he died, even if they weren't for him! Jesus had little — 'the son of man has nowhere to lay his head'. But he was the Prince of Peace. He was born powerless, to a simple Jewish girl, in an outhouse. Herod and Jesus within view of each other! What a contrast: one a saviour, the other a person who put his trust in ephemeral things, like power and money – and they didn't last. Who remembers him?

For some, Christmas is a hellish time. Those who are separated remember happier times full of hope and optimism. At some tables there are absent friends, some killed tragically in car crashes. For those trapped in the prison of addiction Christmas is a burden they could do without. The aged, in the twilight of their lives, may have little of the world's comforts to console them. This is a time for remembering. It is a time also for giving.

The Mystery Of Christmas

Readings: Isa 52:7-10; Heb 1:1-6; Jn 1:1-18

Think of ways to make this Christmas special. Christmas is a time for 'coming home', for family, for celebration.

Freedom is a precious gift. To order one's life in accordance with one's own values is something we take for granted. It wasn't always so. In the twentieth century whole nations were subjugated under Nazism. When final victory came a newspaper reported it like this: 'Suddenly it was all over and Britain took to the streets to celebrate the victory. All at once the drabness and deprivation of five wartime years were forgotten, temporarily at least, in a blaze of multicoloured flags, fireworks and floodlights'. The first reading today celebrates freedom, Israel's release from bondage in Babylon. A day to celebrate, and so opportune to remember at Christmas. Christmas, the beginning of the story of Jesus, a saviour, one who releases us from sin, is a time to celebrate.

As kids we used to sing, 'Christmas is coming, the geese are getting fat. Please put a penny in the old man's hat. If you haven't got a penny a halfpenny will do, and if you haven't got a halfpenny then God bless you.' Simple but profound! Christmas from time immemorial is bound up with celebration and with giving.

Many years ago I recorded the childhood reminiscences of an uncle who was then in his late eighties. He was the last remaining child of a large family. I can remember clearly the vividness with which he recalled Christmastime. This was well before the age of electricity. He told me, 'As little children we stood in wonder looking over the valley at Caheramore, near Kilfenora. We gazed for ages at the twinkling candles in every farmhouse window, the lights stretched as far as the eye could see. The welcoming of the Holy Family was so real to our childlike faith.' In the rural poverty of a small farm Christmas presents were unknown, except on the odd occasion when a rich relative might have sent some money. But Christmas was still special. Isn't it extraordinary how the celebration of Christmas remains so central in our memories when much else has slipped beyond the horizon of our consciousness?

It's easy to complain of the materialism of today. But I believe the spirit of Christmas is so deep in the Irish psyche that it will never be obliterated. From personal experience it is the time people give me money, anonymously, saying quietly, 'You will know who to give it to'. Such gifts help those painfully in need throughout the year.

The crib visually proclaims that 'the Word was made flesh and dwelt among us'. The helplessness of childhood was the guise of the God who came to save. The anonymity of a stable in a crowded town was his birth place. He who made the world was in the world, to save us from ourselves. Love unbeckoned was revealing itself in a child. For me! For you! It was to end tragically – or was it necessary rather than tragic?

The mystery of the crib. What return can I make to the Lord for all that he has done for me? Why not bring your young children on a special visit to the church this Christmas and explain the Christmas story to them as a family? When giving gifts to others, don't forget those in need, and involve your children in the giving, explaining to them what you are doing and why. Why not ask God for the marvellous grace of confessing your sins and experiencing his forgiveness. Do it as a family.

Think of ways to make this Christmas special.

Christmas
A Time of Grace

Readings: Isa 9:1-6; Lk 2:1-14

There is a uniqueness about Christmas. It is a time of grace. The grace of family and the openness to those in need are proper to this wonderful time of the year.

Christmas is indeed a funny time. There is the inevitable frenzy of preparation. People go hyper about buying presents and preparing food. Office parties and carol services and pantomimes clutter the calendar. People come home from the corners of the earth. Children, tense with expectation, wait for Santa. Decorations and Christmas trees are put in place. We wait. Will it ever come? And then bang, it comes, and it is gone again for another year. Is there nothing more?

The coming of the Son of God on this earth is so great an event that God willed to prepare for it over centuries. God foretold him; God announced his coming through the prophets. There was an expectation of his coming. And yet this yearly celebration is so ephemeral. Is it for the feast of a day that we prepare? What then is the intimate grace of the mystery that is Christmas? Christ is born. The grace is that he be born again in our hearts through faith. Faith tells us that this child is God's own Son. He is the Word, the Second Person of the Blessed Trinity. Our salvation is at hand.

The journey from Nazareth to Bethlehem was eighty miles. The accommodation for travellers was indeed primitive. The caravansary was a series of stalls opening out on to an open courtyard. The travellers provided their own food. All the innkeeper provided was fodder for the animals and a fire on which to cook. This was the place where the King of Kings was born.

Christmas is a festival of salvation, when heaven and earth are in communion with each other because the Son of God became 'one like us'. The responsorial psalm proclaims, 'This day new light will shine upon the earth: the Lord is born for us.' This day changed history. Our Western calendar is dated from this day of Christ's birth.

There are two graces proper and unique to Christmas time. These graces are universally recognised. First there is the grace of family. Ideally families are communities of 'life and love'. The family is the first school of giving and forgiving. It is where we learn how to say 'sorry'. Christmas is a time when reconcilation can best happen within the family. It is a time when family members are more open and accepting of the love and forgiveness of other family members. It is a precious time, a time not to be lost.

The other grace of Christmas centres around the most disadvantaged in our society. People give with great generosity at Christmas time. The homeless are housed and fed, albeit temporarily. The St Vincent de Paul Society's Christmas collection is very generously subscribed to. Some people are generous enough to invite a refugee or asylum-seeker to their Christmas table. Others take to the streets to sing carols for charity. How can this grace become a year-long reaching out to those unable to care for themselves?

How can we forget that, for some, Christmas is a time of suffering? Those who have suffered a bereavement during the year feel the pain of absence most intensely at Christmas. The breakup of a marriage renews the ache of what might have been with a rawness that pains. The single and aged feel the loneliness of celebrating an event on their own.

The Birth of our Lord Jesus Christ

Love Is A Decision, Not A Feeling

Readings: Eccl 3:2-6,12-14; Col 3:12-21; Mt 2:13-15, 19-23

Romantic love based on feelings alone promises much but invariably fails to deliver.

American novelist Thornton Wilder has a character called Mrs Antrobus in his book, *The Skin of Our Teeth*. At one stage, Mrs Antrobus says to her husband George, 'I didn't marry you because you were perfect, George. I didn't even marry you because I loved you. I married you because you gave me a promise. That promise made up for your faults. And the promise I gave you made up for mine.' Two imperfect people got married and it was the promise that made the marriage. How strange that must sound in the ears of today's newly weds! We have heard that love is a feeling, and marriage is the road to self-fulfilment. Both statements are only partially true. Feelings come and go. There are highs and lows in every person's life. To base a committed relationship on feelings alone is fraught with danger. No one person can ever hope to fulfil all the needs of another. There will always be a little bit of emptiness in every life. Love is a decision. I decide to love this person today, irrespective of how I feel or whether my needs are being satisfactorily met at this time or not. A decision, built on many considerations, is what underpins all happy marriages.

God created humankind in his own image and likeness, calling them into existence through love. From the beginning man and woman were created for one another. 'It is not good for man to be alone. I will make a suitable partner for him....' 'This at last is bone of my bone and flesh of my flesh....' (Genesis 2) If God is love and we are made in his image, then we reflect or participate in that love. *We are created in love and we are created for love.* For the Christian, loving is the principal expression of his or her faith. We best express our true selves when we love. We most fulfil our true purpose, and that for which God created us, when we are loving.

Marriage, in a providential way, brings two people, who may have been strangers to each other, together for life. They willingly enter into a relationship. This relationship is more than a contract one might make with a builder or an architect; it is a covenant relationship comparable to the relationship God has with his people. It is a relationship of fidelity, where the promise is to 'love, for better, for worse, for richer, for poorer, in sickness and in health all the days of our life'. Because the relationship is one of love and God is love, then when two people are 'in love', God is also present. Because every sacrament is an act of Christ, who is love, when two partners are loving one another, they are administering the sacrament – on a daily basis.

We know almost nothing about the family life of Nazareth, but from what we do know of Jesus, Mary and Joseph from the Gospels, we can be confident that their life together would have been marked by real care and concern for one another. The birth of Christ took place in circumstances of poverty, without many of the comforts we would consider basic, and yet there is a serenity and lack of concern in the Christmas scene. There is a sense of deep joy and peace. We are not conscious of the stark surroundings, but only of the love and tenderness of the three central figures in the story.

God speaks to us in all sorts of ways – through his word in scripture, through the Church, through the circumstances of our daily lives. It is interesting that in today's Gospel he speaks to Joseph through his dreams. Do we listen to our dreams and discern what they are saying to us?

Bringing Out The Best In Your Marriage

Readings: Gen 15:1-6, 21:1-3; Heb 11:8, 11-12, 17-19; Lk 2:22-40

Marriages are under stress. The joy of a happy marriage is worth protecting.

Paul and Joan started off like any other couple in love. They had eyes only for each other. 'He was my knight in shining armour,' says Joan. 'I was a bit of a hippie,' commented Paul. 'I could hardly believe it to be true that someone could love me like Joan did.' Fifteen years later, after the wedding bells were muffled, Paul tried to commit suicide. Everything had unravelled. A deep searing pain had replaced the ecstasy of a young couple in love. Paul and Joan had come to the end of a road that looked full of promise.

I have heard stories like that of Paul and Joan (not their real names) many times. Marriage destined to last for ever comes a cropper. In Retrouvaille (rediscover), a programme for couples experiencing difficulties in their relationships, marriages are being rebuilt. Couples are rediscovering their first love. There are very few cases that are hopeless. Only an unwillingness to begin again can frustrate the hope.

Each of us needs to be special to someone. We grow when we feel cherished and accepted. We blossom when we are loved. God's providence is so much at work in marriage. How is it that people who were formerly strangers, unknown to each other, meet and fall in love? An accident? I think not.

Love is a decision, not a feeling. Every day I decide to love. Feelings are fickle – I'm up and down. Basing one's relationship on feelings alone is dangerous. If love is a decision, then when the hard times come, as come they will, I have more than my feelings to help me through. I have the decision I made; backed up by the promise I gave, to help me through the difficult times.

The love of couples is built on the back of effective communication. So often the woman speaks from the heart; the man from the head – two parallel tracks never meeting. Suppose both get down to the level of feeling? They are both speaking from the same point. This is the point of joy, of pain, even of ecstasy. The struggle is to say, 'I feel angry', 'I feel hopeful', 'I feel irritable and upset'. It sounds so easy. It is not easy because expressing feeling means giving something away that cannot be recovered.

When couples experience difficulties there are two temptations. Firstly, to trawl the past for real or supposed hurts. Secondly, to try to change the other person. In Retrouvaille we say 'the past is past'. It is not possible to unspill spilled milk. Forgiveness is pivotal in a healthy marriage. It is truly healing to say, 'I'm sorry'. To forgive can be a turning point, a new beginning, in a marriage in trouble.

There is only one person in the world whom you can change – that is yourself. When there is a willingness to change on both sides then miracles can happen. On the Retrouvaille weekends, the couples are asked to use the 'I' word. It is understandable to believe that 'if only' the other person would change, then the problem would be solved. Alas, that is seldom the case. When one can articulate one's feelings, and has a willingness to change, everything is possible. Couples who have done a weekend, come away saying, 'I have been married twenty years and I never knew he felt like that.' It happens all the time.

Love is spiritual. When everything else has passed away love remains. God is love. When couples share a spirituality together they have a better chance of succeeding. All the statistics say it! The power of power, who is love, is on tap. Call on his help. He will show you the way when times are difficult.

Families Are To Be Communities Of Life And Love

Readings: Sam 1:20-22, 24-28; Jn 3:1-2, 21-24; Lk 2:41-52

Do we know that purpose for which we were placed on this earth? God's plan for families reveals that they are best fulfilling his purpose when they are communities of life and love.

When I was in the Holy Land in 1993 I bought an icon of the Holy Family that cost me more than I could afford at the time! I was attracted by the apparent physicality of the relationship between Jesus, Mary and Joseph. Joseph has his right arm around Mary in a comforting, affectionate manner. His head rests gently on hers. His other arm embraces Jesus on his mother's lap, and Mary. It seemed to me that the sense of touch was important to the Holy Family. There was a specialness in the relationship between Jesus, Mary and Joseph. I think today's Gospel illustrates the easy familiarity the members of the Holy Family had with one another. I observed this again yesterday at a wedding I attended. The father of the bride, in his speech, spoke in beautiful terms about his wife; his 'best friend', he called her. Such relationships are not easily forged. They are based not on sexual attraction or on mutually agreeable dispositions but on a love that begins with 'the other'. Such intimacy is achieved when, according to St Francis, we realise 'that it is in giving we receive'.

Today's Gospel points to another reality invariably forgotten today, namely that God is a part of every Christian marriage. Where love is God is. If love is in the relationship God is there too. He is there as consoler, healer, encourager and friend. It was in their desire to fulfil the law that the Holy Family had travelled to Jerusalem. They saw themselves as a family not driven by a desire to fulfil their own needs and ambitions but rather to make central to their lives the will of God. His will was the motivating force behind what they did. The same can be seen in the answer of Jesus, 'I must be busy with my Father's affairs'.

There are enormous pressures on the family today. At the wedding reception I mentioned above I was talking to a married man about the responsibilities of raising children. He had six children, ranging from over thirty years of age to early twenties, all of whom have remained faithful, practising Catholics. 'How is it,' I asked him, 'that all of your children continue to practise their religion when the vast majority of young people no longer do so?' 'God was always very important to me and my wife,' he replied. 'My children could see that. We tried to remain close to them on every level and didn't ever leave the spiritual dimension of family life out of the equation.' He continued, 'It really is harder to raise children as Christians nowadays. In fact, everything about Christian family life is getting harder. You cannot talk to young people about a way of life that you are not actually living.' The fact that one family can succeed must be an inspiration to others to know that everything is possible.

A telephone is for communicating, a car for travelling, a knife for cutting. What are you for? What is the purpose of your life? We are conceived in love and for love. It was the love of our fathers and mothers that gave us life. We know from God's Word that his design for our lives is that we lead lives of love. 'Love the Lord your God and your neighbour as yourself.' When we are trying to love, especially within the context of the family, we are best fulfilling the purpose for which God created us. That's a sober thought! The family is intended to be a 'community of life and love'. That is what we are here for.

Feast of the Holy Family

'In The Beginning...'

Readings: Eccl 24:1-2, 8-12; Eph 1:3-6, 15-18; Jn 1:1-18

'Before Abraham was I am.' Before anything was, God already existed. He created us out of love, not out of need.

In the beginning was the Word
and the Word was with God
and the Word was God.

John begins his Gospel with a tremendous statement about Jesus Christ. 'In the beginning was the WORD.' The WORD (Jesus) already was, before the cosmos and the complexity of the world was even formed. It was hardly an accident that John used the term THE WORD for Jesus. To the Jew, a word was far more than a mere sound; it was something that had an independent existence and that actually did things. The spoken word to the Hebrew was fearfully alive. It was a unit of energy charged with power. For that very reason the Hebrew was sparing of words. Hebrew speech has fewer than 10,000 words; Greek speech has 200,000.

By using the phrase 'In the beginning...', John was alluding to the same opening in the book of Genesis. Later, in using the terms 'light' and 'darkness' in opposition, there the connection between Genesis and John. Before anything of creation came about, the WORD already existed. We can recall the words of Jesus here, 'Before Abraham was I am.' Again the revelation of God to Moses, 'I am who I am. I am is my name', emphasises the pre-existence of the WORD before anything came to be. He always was and always will be. Here we are down to the profoundest questions of God and creation.

Poet Jessica Powers has a poem that goes like this:

> God is today.
> He is not yesterday.
> He is not tomorrow.
>
> God is the dawn, waking earth to life
> the first morning ever,
> shining with infinite innocence; a revelation
> older than all beginning, younger than youth....

The Word was made flesh. This WORD was apart from God but was with God, as one. He became like one of us. The Almighty God, who, to put it crudely, 'didn't need us', created us out of love. In the Preface of Sunday we read, 'All things are of your making, all times and seasons obey your laws, but you choose to create man in your own image, setting him over the whole world in all its wonder....' This Word, this loving God, came to his own people and they who were his own gave him no welcome.... 'they treated him like a stranger'.

He who 'enlightened every soul born into the world; he was the true light' was rejected. We are surprised and sad when people no longer walk with us in faith. We find it hard to understand how, knowingly, so many say no to the Lord and choose what we consider less life-loving ways of living. He was rejected before we ever experienced rejection. He was rejected right up to the end.

But there is a promise to those who try to be faithful. 'We have all received something out of his abundance, grace answering grace.' Those who accept Christ become adopted sons and daughters and share in his life. They also experience his grace. St Paul considered knowing Christ as a price worth sacrificing everything else for. 'What is more, I consider everything a loss compared to the surpassing greatness of knowing Christ Jesus my Lord, for whose sake I have lost all things. I consider them rubbish, that I may gain Christ.' (Philippians 3:8)

Second Sunday after Christmas

This Man Was Born To Die

Readings: Isa 60:1-6; Eph 3:2-3, 5-6; Mt 2:1-12

A fifteenth-century painting on the Epiphany illustrates the point that while others are born to live, Jesus was born to die.

A quite beautiful painting, attributed to a fifteenth-century Peruvian artist, Benedetto Bonfigli, presents the visit of the Magi in unusual circumstances. The painting on wood is entitled *The Adoration of the Magi and Christ on the Cross*. The infant Jesus is shown seated on a cushion on the Virgin's lap and he assumes a position of authority as he accepts the gifts and homage of the Magi, who are shown as kings. The eldest of the three kings has taken off his crown and laid it at the feet of the Virgin and child as a gesture of submission. He holds the infant's feet in his right hand, perhaps intending to kiss them with reverence and devotion. Acceptance of the Magi's homage was understood as Christ's prophetic acknowledgement of his destiny to die on the cross. Bonfigli shows the crucified Christ in the middle distance among the hills, his head bowed and blood trickling from his wounds. The painting illustrates the point that Christ was born in order to die for humanity. The two episodes in the one painting illustrate the beginning and the end of the earthly life of Jesus.

It may seem to us extraordinary that those men should set out from the East to find a king, but the strange thing is that, just about the time Jesus was born, there was in the world a feeling of expectation of the coming of a king. The Jews had the belief that 'about that time one from their country should become governor of the habitable earth'. When Jesus Christ came, the world was in an eagerness of expectation.

People were waiting for God and the desire for God was in their hearts. They had discovered that they could not build the golden age without God. It was to a waiting world that Jesus came; and, when he came, the ends of the earth were gathered at his cradle. It was the first sign and symbol of the world conquest of Christ.

The faithfulness of the Magi in following 'their star' and discerning that something more than a mere secular event was here is important. They set out, to where they didn't know; to see what, they weren't sure. They were willing to take the risk. They were willing to let go of reputation, security and home to follow the hunch that God was speaking to them and inviting them to come. When Jesus said 'Come follow me' to the disciples, their positive response was fraught with uncertainty. To follow Jesus is to be willing to walk the path of uncertainty without an insurance policy under one's arm!

Herod's fear was that his power might be challenged. The wisdom of the kings is hearing the voice of God speaking to them in their dreams. The strangers were accepted at the cave of Bethlehem – the first of many Gentiles who were to see, in Christ, a Saviour.

The Epiphany of the Lord

Building A Counter-Culture

Readings: Isa 60:1-6; Eph 3:2-3, 5-6; Mt 2:1-12

Today more than ever, a Christian needs to live within an environment that supports faith. 'Christians supporting one another in faith and love' is the main goal of the pastoral efforts of the Church today.

'When Jesus saw their faith' has always been a special piece of scripture for me. Jean Vanier tells a story of a mentally handicapped girl he came across in a large hospital in Paris. He was being shown around by the medical superintendent when he spotted her seated on a chair facing the wall. She was utterly immobile. She was autistic. The girl, let's call her Mary, had been admitted for treatment for a bipolar condition. While she was in hospital her mother died. It was decided that news of her mother's death would severely aggravate her condition, and that it would be best not to tell her. However, the news seeped in, and through a fellow patient she learned of it and went into a deep depression, refusing to talk to anyone. Vanier describes how he took the girl into his arms and hugged her so that she experienced 'body warmth'. He was given leave to admit her to one of his L'Arche communities in Paris. In the community Mary experienced love, acceptance and support. Little by little she grew in confidence, began to talk and take up her assigned tasks in the community. Finally, over a period of time, she was rehabilitated to such an extent that she was able to take up a job and rejoin the wider community. It was the love and faith of the community that made her well again.

So often Jesus asked for faith from the person seeking a cure. Here he didn't. In this incident it was through the faith of the community that Jesus healed. This healing miracle is saying something to us about community. Most of us live in community. For some it will be the community of the family. Others may live in a looser kind of community, like the parish, a vocational or recreational group, a religious community. A community is formed when people relate to one another in a consistent, regular way. To be a Christian today and to maintain one's basic beliefs and behaviour, almost demands that one relates to a community. I believe that God's purpose, in respect to the human race, was to create a people who were united with him, to create a unity of God with his people, one body, a temple in whom God's Spirit dwells. The goal of the pastoral efforts of the Church today must be to build communities that make it possible for a person to live a Christian life. In other words today, more than ever, the Christian needs a 'counter-culture' that will support him or her. It is within such a culture that one will find healing and happiness, much as today's Gospel story relates.

A community that lives in fidelity to the gospel will be supportive of the 'seeker after truth'. It will help the participant to make the 'hard choices' that the gospel demands. It will provide leadership and guidance. When a society as a whole rejects Christianity, it is necessary to form communities to make Christian life possible.

The Epiphany of the Lord

The Epiphany of the Lord

Follow Your Star

Readings: Isa 60:1-6; Eph 3:2-3, 5-6; Mt 2:1-12

The Magi had a strange vision that they were prepared to follow. Like the Magi, true visionaries are people who can see in the dark.

People still talk of the need to 'follow one's star', meaning that no matter what the obstacles are, we ought not to relinquish our personal vision. Such were the 'wise men from the East' – visionaries. Viktor E. Frankl, the Auschwitz survivor, clung to the vision of seeing his much-loved wife again. This kept him alive in the middle of the bleakest suffering. In his classic *Man's Search for Meaning,* he wrote: 'My mind still clung to the image of my wife. A thought crossed my mind: I didn't even know if she was still alive. I knew only one thing, which I have learned well by now: Love goes very far beyond the physical person of the beloved . . . there was no need for me to know; nothing could touch the strength of my love, my thoughts, and the image of my beloved.' This intensification of an inner life helped the prisoner find a refuge from emptiness, desolation and the spiritual poverty of his existence.

Another seeker with a vision was the anonymous Russian author of that spiritual classic, *The Way of the Pilgrim.* One day the pilgrim attended Mass where the reading was from Paul's First Letter to the Thessalonians, which urges us to 'pray constantly'. The pilgrim asked himself how it could be possible for a person to pray without ceasing, and so began his journey. With no material support he sought spiritual advice in monasteries and from learned people as he travelled across Russia. He wrote: 'For a long time I travelled through various places. I read the Bible and asked for the whereabouts of a spiritual teacher or a

SUNDAYTHOUGHTS.COM

devout and experienced director'. After much wandering, the spiritual classic, *The Philokalia*, was opened for him at the page where the advice of St Simeon was given; 'Sit alone and in silence; bow your head and close your eyes; relax; direct your thoughts from your head into your heart. And while inhaling say, Lord Jesus Christ, have mercy on me, a sinner'. Thus we have the Jesus Prayer, used by many Westerners today, which has gained wide popularity.

The Magi had a strange vision that they were prepared to follow. Their wisdom enabled them to recognise the significance of the star and the royal status of Jesus. They were people of discernment, unwilling to follow anything but what they believed to be an authentic spiritual vision.

The story of the Magi is recounted only in Matthew. The Magi were not Jews. Some believe they were professional practioners of various kinds of magical knowledge, such as dream interpretation or astrology. They stand and pay homage to the King of Kings; Gentiles, representing the whole of the Gentile world, past present and to come. In some representations of this scene the crucifixion is also presented, as in *The Adoration of the Magi and Christ on the Cross*, attributed to Benedetto Bonfigli (1465-75), where the adoration of the kings has been dramatically juxtaposed with the crucifixion to emphasise clearly how from the very beginning of his life Christ was destined to die for all peoples.

Undoubtedly the wise men would have shared the experience of Bethlehem. Perhaps this feast, coupled with Pentecost, has a message in relation to the universality of salvation. It may also speak to us a word of encouragement: introduce others to Jesus your friend. Douglas Hyde, in his book *Dedication and Leadership*, said that when he became a communist his first task was to sell the communist newspaper, the *Daily Worker*, on the street corners of Liverpool during the blitz. As a Catholic he had never been asked to do any more than 'move the chairs in the village hall for Father'. Maybe the Gospel today is inviting us to share the vision of God's overwhelming love with others.

The Baptism of the Lord

Readings: Isa 42:1-4, 6-7; Acts of the Apostles; Mt 3:13-17

Jesus didn't need to be baptised. He was sinless. Everything he did was 'for us'. Symbolically he stepped into the Jordan bearing the sins of all.

The people of Israel were well aware that for three hundred years the voice of prophecy had been silent. They were waiting for some authentic word from God. And in John they heard it. In every walk of life the expert is recognisable. A famous violinist tells us that no sooner had Toscanini mounted the rostrum than the orchestra felt his authority flowing over them. We recognise at once a doctor who has real skill. We recognise at once a speaker who knows his or her subject. John had come from God and to hear him was to know it.

John's message was effective because he was completely humble. His own verdict on himself was that he was not fit for the duty of a slave. He was pointing to someone else. This is a difficult message to understand in our competitive world. Our glossy magazines are full of people who need the limelight as the oxygen of life. We all crave for acceptance and praise. To be recognised, to establish ourselves as a presence in a community, is important to us. A parent told me recently that because her son was now in prison she could hardly leave the house and had to drop out of her former activities. Here was a really good person who felt that the reputation of her son sullied her own reputation!

We have to stop worrying about the neighbours and live not for our reputations, but for God. It isn't easy to 'let go', but that is what John was willing to do. I am certain that he had a big reputation as a prophet and a teacher. He had a level of personal notoriety that reflected favourably on him, and yet his attitude was one of complete humility, 'He must increase, I must decrease.' He was in effect saying, 'If my life does not reflect the goodness of God then it is a failure.'

Jesus became 'one of us' and humbled himself unto death – 'death on a cross'. His live was lived 'for others'. Jesus came to serve rather than be served. Humility acknowledges gifts and talents, but places the praise where it rightly belongs, with God. In the Gospel the humility of the two main players is at the heart of the action. (+ Mary – in her humbless)

Jews didn't get baptised. They were the specially chosen of God and any form of Baptism was not for them! This rite was primarily for converts to Judaism. Even if a Jew were baptised, the one who stood apart would have to have been Jesus. He was sinless and didn't need Baptism for the forgiveness of his sins. He had come to save the lost. So why did he get baptised? Why did he go to a protesting John the Baptist and ask for Baptism? Symbolically Jesus carried the weight of our sins upon himself. He went into the Jordan not as an individual but as a representative of each of us.

'This is my beloved son' is not to be taken as a doctrinal statement as in a Creed. The reference is more probably to 2 Samuel 7:14 in which King David is adopted as God's son, is given the task of upholding justice and is promised an everlasting kingship.

The Baptism of the Lord

Personal Testimony
– Baptism In The Spirit

Readings: Isa 55:1-11; 1 Jn 5:1-9; Mk 1:7-11

The promise of the Gospel today is that Jesus will 'baptise you with the Holy Spirit'. I believe this Baptism is for everyone. This is my testimony of being 'baptised in the Spirit' thirty years ago.

In 1972 I first started attending a prayer meeting in a convent in Mount Street, Dublin. Many elements of those early meetings made a deep impression on me. I marvelled at the familiarity the participants had with the scripture. I had no such familiarity, and I heard many passages of scripture that were fresh to me. The facility people had to pray spontaneously left me puzzled. Up to then, apart from prayers learned by rote from childhood, I always prayed with a book – a lectionary, the Divine Office, the Ritual. I wasn't used to the practice of praying over people while imposing hands upon them. The hymns were new and powerful. After a few weeks I heard people speaking about 'Baptism in the Spirit', or some called it 'the release of the Spirit', but I didn't know what it was. One evening I asked to be prayed over for 'the Baptism of the Spirit'. I was told I wasn't ready!

About a week after I was lying awake in bed one morning when quite spontaneously I found myself praising God. This wasn't an intellectual exercise; it seemed to come from the gut or core of my being. The words weren't premeditated, they just came. I caught a glimpse of the goodness of God and the showering of his gifts upon all humanity and upon me. His love seemed to touch me – almost in a physical way. I recall getting up and dressing, all the while praising God. Something was happening that I felt I had no control over. It was as if

God had embraced me in a giant bear hug and I was filled with an overwhelming sense of the presence, power and love of God. Then I started to praise God in words and syllables that were unknown to me. This again was spontaneous and not premeditated. My first desire was to share the love of God with everyone. I wanted people to ring the doorbell or phone me so that I could tell them about the glory and goodness of God. This was the Baptism in the Spirit.

Of course Baptism in the Spirit does not mean another sacrament. Some theologians have described this experience as the breaking out into human consciousness of the power of the Spirit already received in Baptism and Confirmation. The Baptism in the Spirit in terms of its fruits is an experience with God that produces in the person a new or greater desire for prayer; a substantial increase in the person's hunger for an understanding of scripture; a greater awareness of the presence of God, an increase of love and the ability to express that love. The experience is a deep and lasting one. Although the intensity of the experience is long gone, something intangible remains. A greater facility and desire to pray, an attraction towards the prayer of praise and the spirit of love are some of the elements of the experience that I think have remained with me over the years.

The Baptism of the Lord

Why Did Jesus Get Baptised?

Readings: Isa 40:1-5, 9-11; Titus 2:11-14; Lk 3:15-16, 21-22

Jesus didn't need to get baptised. He was sinless. He may have come to John as a gesture of solidarity or to identify with the message of repentance that John was preaching.

There are some people who shoot across the kaleidoscope of history leaving a deep impression. In the religious context John the Baptist was one such person. Jesus did not need to be baptised! He was sinless. Many scholars speculate on his decision to come to John for Baptism. Some suggest it was a movement of solidarity. Jesus wanted publicly to identify himself with the preaching of repentance. Jesus had been brought to the Temple by Mary and Joseph earlier in his life and identified with Temple practices. Nevertheless, there is no evidence whatsoever that, after he left the Jordan and the desert, he ever baptised anyone or sent anyone to be baptised by John or anyone else. Many thought of him as the successor of John the Baptist, but, successor or not, Jesus did not baptise.

Jesus saw his ministry as different to John's. His outreach was to the 'lost sheep of the house of Israel'. The ministry of Jesus was focused on the poor, the blind, the lame, the cripples, the lepers, the hungry, the miserable, prostitutes, tax-collectors and others who were downtrodden. His ministry was one of compassion. His ministry was like the instructions he gave to his own disciples to go out and 'to preach and to heal'.

John stood out as a sign of contradiction. He was different. John prophesied doom and destruction for Israel. There had been no prophets in Israel for a long time. The spirit of prophecy had been quenched. God was silent. The silence was broken by John the Baptist. John's message was simple: the people had turned from God; God's punishment was at hand. He used the images of the axe and the winnowing-fan.

John's Baptism was directed towards a change of heart involving the forgiveness of sins. Undoubtedly Jesus was highly impressed with John the Baptist. He spoke of him in highly praiseworthy terms. John was seen by Jesus as the voice of God warning his people of an impending disaster and calling for a change of heart. By allowing himself to be baptised, Jesus was making a statement about where he himself stood.

But in Jesus' Baptism something happened. Before he could take this tremendous step he had to be sure that he was right and in the moment of Baptism God spoke to him. What happened in the Baptism was an experience proper to Jesus. The voice of God came to him and told him that he had taken the right decision. God said, 'You are my beloved Son, in whom I am well pleased.' 'You are my beloved Son' is from Psalm 2:7 and was accepted as a description of the Messianic King.

John was unique. The readiness with which he was willing to subsume his ministry into that of Jesus' was an act of humility. Undoubtedly he drew great crowds and gained a high degree of notoriety and yet he was willing to lay this down. He recognised in Jesus someone greater than himself. It isn't easy to 'let go'. We all like to think that we are indispensable people. We are full of our own importance. John gives us an example of how we ought to see the decisions we make and the things that we do in the light of eternity.

The Baptism of the Lord

Lent

The Real World

Readings: Gen 2:7-9, 3:1-7; Rom 5:12-19; Mt 4:1-11

References to the so-called 'real world' litter everyday conversations. Where is this real world?

Chat shows are liberally sprinkled with reference to 'the real world'. Our own Prime Minister constantly refers to it. Where is it? What's it like? If the real world is the place where people fiddle and cheat, I am not sure if I like it! If it is the place where infidelity in marriage and over-indulgence in alcohol is the norm, can I stay in the unreal world please? Using the term 'the real world' is an effort to convey the impression that it is the only world there is, and that intemperate behaviour is the norm. For the phrase 'real world' substitute 'in this day and age'. These interchangeable terms tell us that if we don't agree with the speaker we are the Neanderthal people of the twenty-first century, the dinosaurs left behind when the forces of conservatism ebbed away.

I think there is another world, equally real. This second world is the world where people try to love God and their neighbour. This is a world where a fall is followed by repentance; where an argument is followed by an apology. This is the world where 'looking after number one' is not the only priority. It is a world where people pay tax, a fair wage, and do an honest day's work. It is a world where people try to be faithful in marriage and where one's word is one's bond.

Let's face it – these two worlds are in competition with one another. How can a Christian live in the so-called 'real world' with integrity? Here are some pointers that may help.

Firstly, strengthening the will to withstand temptation: St Paul wrote about the evil that he didn't want to do but kept doing and the good his mind was set on doing was harder to accomplish. Bad habits, sin if you like, are only driven out by the grace of God and by repeated good habits. The good habits can be simple ones – like getting out of bed when the alarm goes or helping my wife with the child-minding responsibilities in the family. It could be a decision to pray as a family or to seek out a person to befriend, maybe someone who is sick or feeble. It could be a decision to forego some pleasure in order to contribute a little to charity. It might be refusing the second drink in the pub or offering to do the shopping. Can you think of other ways? The Jesuits used to call this *'agere contra'* – acting against oneself. It is a good way to strengthen the will.

Secondly, faith-fullness. How do I remain faith-full to God? The faith-full journey begins with small practical steps of piety. Faith-fullness is relational – it has to do with growing in a deeper relationship with the one who loves us. This happens through prayer, through little acts of piety like saying the Stations of the Cross or Grace before and after meals; through nourishing our souls with a little spiritual reading or time spent before the Blessed Sacrament; one day at a time

The line of scripture, 'He who think himself to stand let him take heed lest he fall', is ever present to me. Too many great people have fallen from grace in recent years to be presumptuous of oneself continuing in virtue. The alcoholic pledge to refrain from alcohol 'just for today' is a wise one. With God, my walk is a daily one, belonging to a counter-culture. Perhaps the Christian community, now more than ever, needs to be a vibrant counter-cultural community. This is a milieu, where like-minded people draw strength and support from God and one another. The rise of vibrant lay Catholic communities in recent years on the Continent is evidence that people are experiencing the need to gather together in order to remain faithful. Have another thought – why not try to make the world of virtue the 'real world'? Why not try to win over those who live in the 'real world'? Tell them about Jesus Christ, and the message of liberty and peace and salvation he delivered to us while on earth. The 'real world' can be changed.

Temptation

Readings: Gen 9:8-15; 1 Pet 3:18-22; Mk 1:12-15

For too long we lived with a model of spirituality that urged 'be perfect as your heavenly Father is perfect'. The reality is that only God is perfect.

Bill Wilson, the founder of Alcoholics Anonymous, never did 'get religion'. But he did retain and maintain lifelong sobriety. How did he stay sober? The struggle of the addicted to break through the apparently impenetrable barrier of craving has been the subject of many books and films. Bill Wilson didn't feel that organised religion could help him because of its fixation with the minutiae of commandments and canons. At the same time he knew he couldn't do it on his own. He needed the help of a higher power. He claimed that 'we alcoholics had to find some spiritual basis for living'. He added 'else we die'. Bill operated within a 'spirituality of imperfection' which begins with recognition that trying to be perfect is the most tragic human mistake. It is only by ceasing to play God, by coming to terms with hideous mistakes and shortcomings, and by accepting the inability to control every aspect of their lives, that alcoholics can find peace and serenity.

Western Christianity has been obsessed with a linear kind of thinking – everything is either right or wrong, black or white, good or bad. In this spirituality there is little room for shades of grey. The motto or slogan driving this model of spirituality is, 'be perfect as your Heavenly Father is perfect'. But only God is perfect! The reality is, of course, that God loves imperfect beings, like you and me. He is not waiting for us to be perfect before he loves us.

The 'spirituality of imperfection' is based in the lived acceptance of human limitations and powerlessness. It is rooted in the path of self-knowledge. It is lived on a daily basis. St Teresa of Avila wrote that 'this path of self-knowledge must never be abandoned nor is there on this journey a soul so much a giant that it has no need to return often to the stage of an infant and a suckling … self-knowledge and the thought of one's sins is the bread with which all palates must be fed no matter how delicate they may be'. (*The Book of Her Life*)

The Gospel today is about the temptations of Jesus. Temptation itself is a daily experience. The daily temptation to selfishness, lust, envy, greed, is the daily baggage of the pilgrim. Many people abandoned the struggle of the Christian life because they had tried and failed repeatedly to succeed. The white flag has been run up.

A brother said to Abba Poemen, 'If I fall into shameful sin, my conscience devours and accuses me saying: "Why have you fallen?" ' The old man said to him, 'At the moment when a man goes astray, if he says, "I have sinned," immediately the sin ceases.' The chief danger in dealing with temptation is to change the rules. That is what many people do. The modern person's attempt to deal with temptation is to deny the reality of sin. We have tried to airbrush the reality of sin from human experience. The lived admission of failure is the beginning of the journey.

First Sunday of Lent

Lent Is A Good Time
To Begin Again

Readings: Deut 26:4-10; Rom 10:8-13; Lk 4:1-13

We think we are free. But are we? Jesus came so that we 'might have life and have it to the full' and yet we frustrate his plan by our waywardness. Lent is a good time to begin again.

I was brought up in a world where everything was black or white, right or wrong, good or bad. There was no greyness. There were few ambiguities to life. Everyone knew their station, their position in life, and stuck to it. Voices from above, whether government, schoolteacher, parents or Church, regulated every moment of our lives, but we were not unhappy. We thought this was how it was meant to be. There weren't any voices from radio, or television, or the Internet, telling us anything different. Today's Gospel centres on temptation and the possibility of sin. Unlike in the time of my youth, these are words that would not be clearly understood today.

Jesus came for a purpose. 'I have come,' he said, 'so that you might have life and have it to the full.' We were to have this life in this world through following his example, and in the next through his suffering and death. Jesus was single-minded. He wouldn't allow himself to be deflected from the plan laid out for him. In the Gospel Jesus is being enticed to a life of power and success, whereas the path he had chosen was one of solidarity with the poor, a path full of pain and suffering, and ultimately the cross. Jesus stuck to his chosen path.

I don't think people commit sin because they want to offend God or hurt others. They do it because they say to themselves, 'This is going to make me happy, or rich, or successful.' They think, 'I need to be fulfilled to be a whole person, and this will provide that fulfilment.' Whether it is cohabiting before marriage, failing to pay one's taxes, being unfaithful to a spouse, or lying to get out of trouble; at the time they are seen as 'good'. They are actions that will help or assist me in some way. They may be recognised as sin but chosen anyway because I need that little bit of happiness. True freedom is freedom to choose the 'good', but it is also the freedom to say 'no'. Not many people have that freedom, and it is seldom achieved by will-power alone. Maybe that is why alcoholics are advised to 'look to a higher power, however you envisage it'. People see the Churches and Commandments as inhibiting them from acting as they wish. In fact, the law of God is the law of love, because it helps us to be free. To choose God before my own desires is to choose life rather than decay.

Temptation, then, is the mirage that tells us that putting 'number one' first, even before God, will bring us happiness. Temptation presents a counterfeit version of happiness and tries to allure us into following. It's not often one sees an unhappy monk. Why? Because they choose what they are doing freely. Sin is a free decision to choose the superficial attractiveness of acting contrary to God's will. To presume that God will rescue us from the consequences of our own recklessness is to 'tempt the Lord'.

We have lost the sense of sin. But it is not possible to have a sense of sin if one has no idea of the infinite love of God. We suffer when we hurt those whom we love. I don't deliberately thwart the wish of a loved one. Most sinners haven't experienced God's love and, therefore, neither do they experience the pain of thwarting that love. Conversion is a turning towards the love of God and walking away from all that can come between us and God's love. Lent is a good time to begin again.

First Sunday of Lent

A Mountain-Top Experience

Readings: Gen 12:1-4; Tim 1:8-10; Mt 17:1-9

There are times when our relationship with God can bring overwhelming consolation. There are also times when we walk the valley of dryness and despair. At both times God is present.

In the Charismatic Renewal many people did have a 'mountain-top experience'. Through the Baptism in the Spirit, the Spirit, already received in Baptism and Confirmation, burst forth into their conscious experience. They didn't just know God with their heads, they knew him with their hearts also. Scripture came alive for them. The gifts of the Spirit, about which they knew little before, became active in the community. Gifts like wisdom, knowledge, teaching and healing were expected and exercised. People spent long hours in prayer and days of renewal were a regular feature of most prayer groups. For thousands of people a 'mountain-top' experience was a reality.

The following testimony is typical of the experience of many charismatics:

> Then it hit me – total submission to Him! All of a sudden my hands went up as though I had no control – all the way up! At the same time the Lord Jesus baptised me in his Holy Spirit. When I raised my hands it was like diving into water. I could feel God's presence from the top of my fingertips, coming down over my arms, over my head – complete immersion in the Lord. Praise in the gift of tongues flowed freely up to God. More satisfying than all the accumulated honours of many years. God's love that

night surpassed anything I had ever known. Ever since that night, the Bible and Prayer Book have become living words to me as well as the desire to serve my Lord in my local parish or where He places me. To love and serve Jesus Christ is fulfilment, joy unspeakable, and real life.

One cannot stay all the time on the mountain. Peter, James and John, too, had to come down from the mountain. The drudgery of everyday life, the occasional monotonous boredom, the frictions and tension of life meant that serving God was not always accompanied by spiritual 'highs' but by persevering fidelity. When one comes down from the mountain that's when one needs good Christian friends who will help one grow to a deeper love of God that does not rely on the 'consolations of the Lord' but on faith.

Did Jesus bring his friends up to Tabor to console, reassure and help them? To give them a glimpse that there was something more to come? All of us need signs of God's presence. We see it in the miracle of birth, in a new dawn, in springtime, in a healing miracle.

Moses and Elijah represented the two major parts of the Old Testament, the Law and the Prophets. By their presence they showed that all was fulfilled in Jesus. Peter wanted tents to be put up, to make the experience last. But that was not the point. The Transfiguration confirmed the rightness of the way Jesus had chosen. It pointed to the glory that would one day be his. But before that time he had to die on the cross. This was the topic of conversation with Moses and Elijah – Jesus' 'exodus'. But the disciples did not understand this until after the Resurrection.

Not Guilty!

Readings: Gen 22:1-2, 9-13; Rom 8:31-34; Mk 9:2-10

Jesus is pleading our case before the right hand of the Father. An acquittal is the most likely verdict because of what Jesus has done for us.

On a number of occasions I have gone to court to give a character reference on behalf of a defendant whom I knew and wanted to help. I found the whole atmosphere of the courtroom intimidating. On every occasion, I felt I wasn't listened to. The judge seemed aloof and inaccessible. I wasn't allowed to speak freely but only at the behest of a barrister. It is a task I dislike performing. I can relate to the woman who ran from the Four Courts in absolute joy. She had just been acquitted of the murder of her husband. She was really speechless. Her mother spoke to the press on her behalf. For her, a new life was just beginning, She was a free person.

God has acquitted us. Who then can condemn us? The answer is that the Judge of all people is Jesus Christ. He is the one who has the right to condemn – but is so far from condemning. He is at God's right hand interceding for us, and therefore we are safe. 'God for us did not spare his own Son; surely that is the final guarantee that he loves us enough to supply all our needs.' The words used of God are the very words God used of Abraham when Abraham proved his utter loyalty by being willing to sacrifice his son Isaac at God's command. God said to Abraham, 'You have not withheld your son, your only son, from me.' (Genesis 22:12)

Paul seems to say, 'Think of the greatest human example in the world of a man's loyalty to God; God's loyalty to you is like that.' Just as Abraham was so loyal to God that he was prepared to sacrifice his dearest possession, God is so loyal to us that he is prepared to sacrifice his only Son. Surely we can trust a loyalty like that for anything. In our difficulties and pain there is a deep aloneness. We think nobody cares. We struggle alone, or so we think. But it is not so. God is with us – closer than we can think or imagine. The author is saying four things about Jesus. He died. He rose again. He is at the right hand of God. He is interceding for you and me. It is as if Paul said, 'You think of Jesus as the Judge who is there to condemn; and well he might for he has won the right. But you are wrong; he is not there to be our prosecuting counsel but to be the advocate to plead our cause.' That is a fantastic thing. He is more effective than the most learned of lawyers. He is more articulate, more persuasive, more compelling, more powerful, than the greatest barrister. Isn't that a wonderful consolation? Together we will win any case. I will be acquitted through what Jesus has done and is doing for me.

Transfigured

Readings: Gen 15:5-12, 17-18; Phil 3:17-4:1; Lk 9:28-36

Many scripture commentaries have little to say about the Transfiguration. Some confine themselves to presenting the arguments on the location of the event – Mount Harmon or Mount Tabor.

This was a remarkable 'mountain-top' experience. The contrast with what went before is striking. Jesus had tried to explain that he had to go up to Jerusalem where he would suffer many things and ultimately death, 'and on the third day he would rise again'. This upset the disciples, who really didn't understand what this meant.

Why did Jesus choose a mountain? There is something inherently sacred about mountains, which is not confined to one religious tradition. There are so many mountains in the Himalayas, revered by both Buddhists and Hindus. The massive mountain of Ixtaccihuatl in Mexico was considered by the Aztecs to be the home of the gods. The mountain of the Holy Cross in the Colorado Rockies is seen as a sign and promise of God. Croagh Patrick, Ireland's holiest of mountains, where St Patrick's is reputed to have prayed, is a sacred place, attracting thousands of pilgrims annually. The mountain is the place of struggle, of mystery, of isolation and peace. The mountain is the place of silence, where the voice of God can be heard.

Jesus chooses his three special friends, Peter, James and John, to accompany him. Jesus' relationships were in concentric circles. At the core was Peter, James and John, then the twelve, then the seventy-two, then the ministering women, and finally those who followed him and interested bystanders. Jesus never really touched the multitude. He confined his activities to a relatively small geographical area. Is there a message here for us? Someone once said that evangelisation is 'eyeball to eyeball', meaning there is no substitute for personal contact in sharing God's love. Jesus shared the most intimate moments of his life, Gethsemane and Tabor, and the raising of the daughter of Jairus, with just Peter, who would be the leader of the apostolic Christian community, James the first martyr, and John the 'beloved disciple'. With these three men Jesus shared a special friendship.

On the mountain he prays. When Jesus begins to pray his disciples fall asleep. How wonderfully human. What did the transfigured appearance of Jesus mean? Was it a glimpse of the future resurrected life? Was it a reasurrance that the suffering and the cross that Jesus had previously foretold should not trouble their faith because there was something else on the other side of suffering and death? Jesus wishes to strengthen the faith of the disciples by the Transfiguration.

On the mountain the divinity shines out through the veil of Jesus' humanity. Moses the law-giver and Elijah the prophet appear with Jesus. The Transfiguration confirms the faith of the apostles. It is a mysterious participation in the knowledge that God has of himself. And the Father declares that the babe of Bethlehem, the youth of Nazareth, the preacher of Judaea, the victim of Calvary is his well-loved Son.

'It is good for us to be here.' There are times when the presence of God is tangible. We sense that he is near. There are other times when our pilgrim journey is through light and darkness and there is 'the darkness of the soul'. This is a time of consolation and hope. It is well to remember that even when we walk in darkness we can believe like St Thérèse that 'behind the dark cloud my sun is still shining'.

Aids And The Samaritan Woman

Readings: Ex 17:3-7; Rom 5:1-2, 5-8; Jn 4:5-42

Jews and Samaritans were bitterly divided. Jesus speaks with love to the woman at the well and things begin to happen!

'One of these days I'm going to have a lot to tell,' filmstar Rock Hudson once promised a friend. The day never came, and when Hudson died of AIDS at his home in Beverly Hills in 1982 his story, as he alone might have told it, died with him. But it was clear that the role he played in life was more dramatic, and infinitely sadder, than any of the parts he had assumed in sixty-five movies and several TV series. For thirty-seven years he had led a double life: in public he was a romantic star, adored by millions of women, admired by millions of men; in private he was a homosexual who bitterly resented the lies and deceptions that he felt had been forced upon him. That was the first we heard of AIDS. A ripple of fear went through the industrialised world. 'Could you drink out of a cup that had been used by an AIDS victim without getting the disease?' Firefighters and police, nurses and paramedics, prison wardens and social workers, began to wear rubber gloves. Dead AIDS victims were immediately put in body-bags, for fear of contagion. Big names died and their deaths were mourned in whispers. A 'cordon sanitaire' was drawn around the sufferers. Family, friends and churches rejected some. Some said, 'Serves them right. It's God's way of punishing them for their promiscuous or drug-taking lifestyle.' They were pariahs.

Now maybe you know how Samaritans were treated at the hands of the Jews at the time of Jesus! There existed an extremely violent hatred between the Jews and the Samaritans. There was a proverb common at the time of Jesus, 'A piece of bread given by a Samaritan is more unclean than swine flesh'. When Jesus wished to make the Jews blush for their hardness of heart and ingratitude, he held up a Samaritan as an example to them. No wonder the woman said, 'How can you, a Jew, ask me, a Samaritan, for a drink?' It was unthinkable. She recognised Jesus as a prophet. Jesus met this woman where she was. He struck up a conversation with her. He took an interest in her life; without condemnation or blame. Through her contact with Jesus she herself became a witness to her own people. They also responded to Jesus and invited him to stay. Sometimes we are unaware of the influence we have through our words and actions. A word of hope and consolation and encouragement may entice someone to go deeper and find the Lord. Evangelisation begins with a smile. It is interesting that in his document on evangelisation (*Evangelii Nuntiandi*) Pope Paul VI said, 'The sure sign that a person has been evangelised is that they in turn become evangelisers.' This is exactly what happened in the case of the Samaritan woman.

Sacred Places

Readings: Ex 20:1-17; Cor 1:22-25; Jn 2:13-25

Do we find the sacred space we yearn for in our church buildings? Is our worship of the heart or just of the lips or head? Here we have a Gospel to challenge us to make our Sunday worship a spiritual milestone in the week's activities.

There are places that are especially sacred to all of us. Around the town of Kilkee, in County Clare, where my family went on holiday every year, are numerous places that are sacred to my childhood. Wandering around the coastline and peninsula evokes memories of joys, sorrows and yearnings which continue to give direction to my life.

At the end of the six days war in 1967, battle-hardened Israeli troops, having broken through the Arab lines, rushed to the Wailing Wall, the last remnant of the Second Temple. This Wall is the most sacred spot in the world for a Jew. These gnarled and weary men touched and prayed and stuck their petitions into the cracks in the Wall, with tears streaming down their dust-stained faces. They were home at last.

All over the world, whenever Jews stand in prayer, they face Jerusalem. Every synagogue in the world is built with its ark on the side of Jerusalem. Jerusalem was the place of sacrifice and the place of the ark in the holy of holies. A person standing in Jerusalem to pray would face the Temple grounds. Jerusalem was also the chief location of schools where the Torah (the Word of God) was taught. The holiness of Jerusalem pertains to God's presence. When a Jew says 'next year in Jerusalem', it is more than just a prayer that he or she may visit the Holy City or even settle there, it is a prayer for the entire future of the Jewish people.

It was an enormous tragedy for the Jewish people when the Temple was finally destroyed by the Romans in the year AD 70. The prophet

Zechariah saw the return to Jerusalem as the beginning of the total renaissance of the Jewish people. 'I will bring them, and they will dwell in the midst of Jerusalem; and they will be my people and I will be their God in truth and righteousness.' The action of Jesus in throwing the money-changers and merchants out of the Temple has a real relevance for today. Jesus acted as he did because God's house was being desecrated.

In the Temple there was worship without reverence. Reverence is an instinctive thing. Worship without reverence can be terrible. The walls of our parish churches are seeped with prayer of joy and pain, sorrow and happiness. Here we met Jesus in the sacrament of his love for the first time. Here burden was lifted from our backs with the absolution of Jesus ministered by the priest. Here we have a place holy to many people.

The most dignified prayers on earth can be read like a page from an auctioneer's catalogue. It may be worship that does not realise and appreciate the holiness of God. It may be the use of the house of God for purposes and in a way whereby reverence and the true function of God's house are forgotten. Perhaps today our irreverence takes on a different form than that of the money-lenders in Jerusalem. It might take the form of the installation of stained-glass windows, the obtaining of a more sonorous organ, the lavishing of money on church furnishings, while real worship is far away. It is not that these things are to be condemned – far from it. They are often the lovely offerings of the loving heart. When they are aids to true devotion they are God-blessed things; but when they are substitutes for true devotion they make God sick at heart.

I believe this Gospel has implications in regard to how we celebrate the Liturgy. Do we pray with our lips or our hearts? Is the stranger (Gentile) welcomed by the parish community? Are all the congregation participating in what happens in church? Is there anything in our church life – a snobbishness, an exclusiveness, a coldness, a lack of welcome, a tendency to make the congregation into a closed club, an arrogance, a fastidiousness – that keeps the seeking stranger out? If so, this Gospel is for us!

The Doctrine Of
The Second Chance

Readings: Ex 3:1-8; 1 Cor 10:1-6; Lk 13:1-9

The parable of the fig tree has many lessons for us, not least that God is always willing to give us a second chance.

There are people who are free, yet imprisoned. Nelson Mandela was one such person. He spent eighteen of his twenty-seven years in prison in Robben Island Penitentiary. His spirit was unbowed and free. The prisons of the world are full of prisoners of conscience. They are people who refuse to change their mind. The Church tried force to bend the wills of medieval reformers. The Spanish and Roman Inquisitions became a cruel reign of terror – all in the interests of having people recant their errors and conform. But fear or force are not effective tools for bending minds or hearts, at least in the long term. Turning is a free decision. In this Gospel Jesus is trying to say, 'There is another way to freedom'.

The Jews were involved in intrigues, rebellions, plotting and political ambitions. Jesus saw this as a form of national suicide. Rome was powerful and would eventually step in to crush the Jews. This is precisely what happened. Jerusalem was destroyed. The Temple was razed to the ground and the Jews crushed. Jesus, in an oblique way, was trying to tell them that kingdoms of this earth have their place, but the Kingdom of God comes first. 'Choose God freely and walk in his ways if you want to be a truly free people.' The path of love must be freely chosen.

The fig tree occupied a specially favoured position. It was not unusual to see fig trees, thorn trees and apple trees in vineyards. The soil was so shallow and poor that trees were grown wherever there was soil to grow them; but the fig tree had a more than average chance, and it had not proved worthy of it. Repeatedly, directly and by implication, Jesus reminded people that they would be judged according to the opportunities they had. There are times when our faith is not seen as the tremendous gift that it is. We have been given this gift. It is designed to grow within us and bring us closer to the all-loving God. How have we used it?

The parable teaches that uselessness invites disaster. It has been claimed that the whole process of evolution in this world is to produce useful things, and that what is useful will go on from strength to strength, while what is useless will be eliminated. The most searching question we can be asked is, 'Of what use were you in this world?'

The fig tree was drawing strength and sustenance from the soil; and in return was producing nothing. That was precisely its sin. In the last analysis, there are two kinds of people in this world – those who take out more than they put in, and those who put in more than they take out. Am I a taker or a giver? We can use and abuse those closest to us for our own ends. We can sap the energies and resources of those around us; we can wallow in self-pity, without a thought for those worse off.

'Die when I may,' said Abraham Lincoln, 'I want it said of me that I plucked a weed and planted a flower wherever I thought a flower would grow.' Once a student was being shown bacteria under the microscope. He could actually see one generation of these microscopic living things being born and dying and another being born to take its place. He saw, as he had never seen before, how one generation succeeds another. 'After what I have seen,' he said, 'I pledge myself never to be a weak link.'

To be given a 'second chance' is to be given a new life. It is always Jesus' way to give a person chance after chance. But there is a final chance and this is the point of decision – for or against.

Jesus Heals On The Sabbath

Readings: 1 Sam 16:1, 6-7, 10-13; Eph 5:8-14; Jn 9:1-41

We all want to be healed. Jesus healed, not to manifest his power, but out of love and compassion for those who suffer.

A sure-fire way to gather a crowd is to advertise a 'healing service'. In the twenty-first century, charlatans, in every country and religion, know that the experience of suffering – physical, mental and spiritual – is no longer tolerable. Everyone wishes to be healed, and believes that suffering can and should be eliminated. In the past we thought that physical suffering was what needed healing most. Now people talk of 'inner healing', 'healing of memories' and 'healing of the family tree'. Without meaning to be cynical, one could say that a whole industry has grown up around healing. National budgets for health care are continuing to spiral and have become a major topic of political controversy.

In the time of Jesus, sickness and sin were considered closely intertwined, and so the question of the disciples: 'Who sinned, this man or his parents, that he was born blind?' For most of the Old Testament period there was no belief in the afterlife: death was final and nothing of the human person, except memories and a name, survived. Therefore, if God was truly just, virtue should be rewarded with long life, children, health, prosperity, riches and honour. Conversely, sin should be punished with illness, poverty and shame. Here we have a man born blind and conclude that either his parents or he himself has sinned. Jesus rejects the equation of sin with misfortune.

Jesus was filled with compassion for those who suffered. His healing miracles were not designed to manifest his power, or to elevate himself in the eyes of those healed, but to show forth his compassion and love. If Jesus is the 'same yesterday, today and the same forever' then his healing power is available to us today. The Church believes that this healing power is available to us, especially in the sacraments, which are 'meetings with Christ', but also through prayer and healing ministry.

The miracle itself made a deep impression on those who witnessed it and raised the question of whether the person who performed it might not be a prophet sent by God. In St John's eyes the very miracle itself was an invitation to faith. Towards the end of the chapter the man born blind makes his own personal profession of faith.

The fact that a miracle had taken place could not be denied. It was called into question by the Pharisees but placed beyond doubt by the blind man's parents, who were, however, reluctant to be involved in an argument with the Pharisees. The man himself was convinced that Jesus must have been sent by God since he had the power to work such a miracle and this was the basis of his own personal faith. The Pharisees tried to avoid the same conclusion by a theological argument that was not without some validity: God will not choose a sinner to be his spokesperson and representative. Now this man is clearly a sinner because he has violated the law of rest of the Sabbath. Therefore he is not God's spokesperson and representative. But Jesus maintained that it was not necessarily a sin to use his power to relieve suffering on a Sabbath. The precept of love could take precedence over the cultic law of Sabbath rest. The moral and ethical principles which held sway during the week were not to be thought of as suspended on the Sabbath. Hence his claim to be God's messenger could not be dismissed a priori.

He Died So That
We Might Live

Readings: Chron 36:14-16, 19-23; Eph 2:4-10; Jn 3:14-21

*In human terms the execution of Maximilian Kolbe in Auschwitz gives us a
glimpse of the enormous love of God for each one of us.*

It is said that four million people died in the Auschwitz gas chambers.
No one knows how many others were shot or hanged, or died through
torture, disease, starvation or medical experiments. It was a monument
to the power of hate. One man who might well have been forgotten for
all time but for an act of exceptional heroism was a Polish priest named
Maximilian Kolbe. Kolbe suffered terribly at Auschwitz. On one
occasion he was savagely beaten by a violent anti-clerical Kapo named
Krott. After the beating a young prisoner who was there described his
appearance: 'His face was covered with bruises, his eyes were glazed
and his temperature was so high that his tongue was stiff and rigid and
his words died in his throat'.

A few days after this beating one of the prisoners from Maximilian's
block was missing at the evening roll call. The Lagerführer had
threatened that if anyone escaped, ten of his fellow prisoners would be
condemned to starvation in his place. Now he was about to put his
threat into operation. Lagerführer Fritzsch walked slowly along the
ranks of emaciated prisoners. He savoured to the full his power of life
and death. He quite arbitrarily selected his victims, one by one. No
sound came from them except a cry of despair from one of them,
Francis Gajowniczek, lamenting the fact that he would never see his
wife and children again. Something utterly unexpected happened at
that point. A prisoner stepped out of the ranks, pulled off his cap and

stood in front of Fritzsch. It was Maximilian. 'I am a Catholic priest,' he said, 'I am old. I want to take his place, because he has a wife and children.' For a moment Fritzsch was nonplussed. Then he said one word – 'Out' – and Maximilian joined the condemned and Gajowniczek rejoined the ranks. Maximilian, after two weeks of starvation, was injected with carbolic acid. The date was 14 August 1941.

Maximilian died so that Francis Gajowniczek might live. Not only did he live but he attended the canonisation of Maximilian many years later in Rome. If you want to know what Jesus did, the example of Maximilian helps. Jesus died so that I might live. 'God so loved the world that he sent his only begotten Son so that everyone who believes in him may not be lost but may have eternal life.' Jesus stepped forward and took my place. He took my sins and the sins of the world upon himself and stepped forward to crucifixion and death. His act was a free act of love. One act of will would have been enough. That we might know and understand the depth of his love, he died a horrible death, slow and painful, but eminently acceptable to the Father. How can we ever know the depths of God's love for us?

Fourth Sunday of Lent

A Story Of Estrangement And Reconciliation

Readings: Josh 5:9, 10:12; 2 Cor 5:17-21; Lk 15:1-3, 11-32

The story of the Prodigal Son can never be taken for granted. Each reading brings fresh insights into what has been called a 'gospel within a gospel'.

Leaving home, even if a family is dysfunctional, is always a wrench. It is a cutting of the umbilical cord, with everything that is and was familiar. It is leaving a part of one's history behind. Why did the son do this? The word that came to me very strongly was 'estrangement'.

Estrangement is the source of much suffering. So many sons are estranged from their fathers whom they see as cold, uncaring and indifferent. I learned of Jews after World War II, wandering the face of Europe, cut off from everything – country, home, family, love, a place to call their own. Arabs, too, feel estranged from their land and the Jews who inhabit it. I learned that there is a literature of estrangement, which includes authors as well known as Miller, Camus, Capote, Beckett and others.

Could the son have been estranged because he just wasn't getting his own way? There can be a truculent type of estrangement – sullen, resentful, bitter and self-pitying. Is this what the son suffered from? Things weren't working out according to his plan. There is a certain heartless callousness in his request. He said in effect, 'Give me now the part of the estate I will get anyway when you are dead, and let me get out of this.' The father did not argue. He knew that if the son was ever to learn he must learn the hard way; and he granted his request. I am sure the son left a hurting father behind.

The 'prodigal' was at the bottom of the pile. 'Feeding pigs' for a Jew was the end. This was a task that was forbidden to a Jew because the law said 'Cursed is he who feeds swine'. I have seen the 'prodigal son' on the streets of Dublin. These are youngsters who have left home vowing never to return. Times get hard. A drug culture smothers them. They end up sleeping rough with little hope of a future. I offered to make the path easy for them to return home, by offering to make contact with parents or guardians. This offer was always refused. No matter how great the destitution, none could admit failure and seek the solace of home.

The key phrase of this parable is 'when he came to himself'. Jesus believed that so long as a person was away from God he was not truly himself. He was only truly himself when he was on the way home. The father must have been waiting and watching for the son to come home, for he saw him a long way off. When he came, he forgave him with no recriminations. Once Lincoln was asked how he was going to treat the rebellious southerners when they had finally been defeated and had returned to the Union of the United States. The questioner expected that Lincoln would take a dire vengeance, but he answered, 'I will treat them as if they had never been away.' It is the wonder of the love of God that he treats us like that.

The elder brother was actually sorry that his brother had come home. He stands for the self-righteous Pharisees who would rather see a sinner destroyed than saved. His attitude shows that his years of obedience to his father had been years of grim duty and not of loving service. He utterly lacks sympathy. He refers to the prodigal, not as 'my brother' but as 'your son'. He deliberately distances himself from his own brother. He has a peculiarly nasty mind – there is no mention of prostitutes until he mentions them.

Once again we have the amazing truth that it is easier to confess to God than it is to many a person; that God is more merciful in his judgements than many even good people; that the love of God is far broader than the love of people; and that God can forgive when human beings refuse to forgive. In face of a love like that we cannot be other than lost in wonder, love and praise.

Friends

Readings: Ezek: 37:12-14; Rom 8:8-11; Jn 11:1-45

Bethany for Jesus was a 'safe place'. It was a place of friendship, where there was a partnership of hearts. And now Lazarus is dead!

There used to be a poster that said 'Strangers are friends you haven't yet met'. This is only partly true. There is a uniqueness about true friendship that cannot be easily replicated. In true friendship there is a partnership of hearts. The place of friendship is a sacred space, filled with the confidences, good and bad, that bring consolation to the soul. The place of friendship is 'home', a place of recreation, of safety, of shared laughter and pleasure, for 'in the dew of little things the heart finds its morning and is refreshed'.

Poet Kahil Gibran wrote:

> and let there be no purpose in friendship save the deeping of the spirit.
> For love that seeks aught but the disclosure of its own mystery is not love but a net cast forth: and only the unprofitable is caught?

Bethany was a place of friendship for Jesus. Martha, Lazarus and Mary were his friends. And now Lazarus is dead!

By his account of the raising of Lazarus St John intended to emphasise and illustrate Christ's statement, 'I am the resurrection and the life', and to indicate that faith in him is the necessary condition of achieving a share in this life. The necessity of faith is suggested early on in the narrative when Thomas shows himself willing, as a consequence of his friendship with Jesus, to be brought into a situation in which he would be in real danger of death. Lazarus was allowed to die in order that Christ might be glorified. Jesus, by his delay and his words and subsequent miracle, was leading them to a deeper faith in himself as 'the way, the truth and the life'. This was all done in the context of his friendship with Lazarus and his sisters.

Mary obviously had a deep faith. I am sure this was as a result of her friendship with Jesus. She believed that the just will rise on the last day, that Jesus had the power of working miracles, that Jesus was the Christ, the Son of God, who had come into the world. Of course John was writing for a believing Christian community and the Gospel must be seen in that context.

The Gospel today brought to my mind the words of a great hero of mine, Martin Luther King. On 3 April 1968, the day before he was killed, Martin Luther King delivered an eerily clairvoyant speech:

> Like anybody, I would love to live a long life. Longevity has its place. But I'm not concerned about that now. I just want to do God's will. And he has allowed me to go up to the mountain and I've looked over, and I've seen the Promised Land. I may not get there with you. But I want you to know that we, as a people, will get to the Promised Land. And so I'm happy tonight. I'm not worried about anything. I'm not fearing any man. Mine eyes have seen the glory of the coming of the Lord.

I find in these words a sort of echo of what Mary was saying in the context of the raising of Lazarus – that sure faith that 'we haven't here a lasting city', that 'there is more to come'.

What We Have
And What We Need

Readings: Jer 31:31-34; Heb 5:7-9; Jn 12:20-30

Losing control of one's own destiny and putting it in the hand of God may for many seem like suicide. Yet the Gospel tells us that it is in losing our lives that we gain something immeasurably greater.

How many influential people have forged their greatness on the anvil of suffering? George Frideric Handel, the composer, suffered intensely. His biographer wrote that 'his health and fortunes had reached a lowest ebb, his right side had become paralysed, and his money was all gone. His creditors seized him and threatened him with imprisonment, and for a brief time he was tempted to give up. But then he rebounded to compose the greatest of his inspirations, the epic Oratorio, *The Messiah*'.

Martin Luther King, at one stage of the civil rights struggle in America, was imprisoned on a trumped-up charge. Cockroaches were crawling all over his narrow cell. The food he was given to eat consisted of acidic black-eyed peas, beans and greens. Hungry, numb from the cold, worn down from tension and lack of sleep, he caught a terrible cold and lay shivering and hacking on his bunk. The wardens were brutal and abusive and he was alone. Today one of America's most recently instituted public holidays is Martin Luther King Day.

But greatness is not confined to the famous. Carl Hammerschlag, in his wonderful book *The Theft of the Spirit*, tells the story of Dan who was a social worker; 'eager and bright, he was also severely spastic from cerebral palsy'. Carl received a letter from Dan; one extract reads as follows: 'In the old days, I cried for my losses in a voice that was so shaky it would never be lifted up in a church choir to sing glory to God. I cried for the loss of my hands that so often I could not control. Hands that would never draw, paint, or create. Hands that I desperately tried to conceal. I cried for my legs that lacked grace. I walk like a goose or like a falling-down drunk. I cried for ballets I would never dance and mountains I would never climb. Now what I hear is a voice that can soothe and heal. I touch people with my sounds because they feel my caring and I think now that God hears my laboured song and welcomes it!'

Jesus is saying in John 12:23-26 that only by death comes life. A paradox. It is because people have been prepared to die that the great things in history have happened. It is only when a person buries their personal aims and ambitions that he or she begins to be of real use to God.

The tyranny of control is what moves so many of us. We want to dictate the course of events both in our own lives and in the lives of others. To open one's hands and ask that they be filled only with the desires of the Lord is a type of suicide – or so we think. But it is there that greatness lies. I remember Martin Luther King writing about how he knelt down at the kitchen table in his home in Alabama. A hail of stones had just come through the window. His wife and children were in danger. He was already a skilled preacher and a highly qualified academic. Did he need this additional worry and danger? It was at that time he decided to put the will of God and the welfare of the Negro people first. Greatness grew from that decision. We have only to think of what this world would have lost if there had not been people prepared to forget their personal safety, security, selfish gain and selfish advancement. The world owes everything to people who recklessly spent their strength and gave themselves to God and to others. No doubt we will exist longer if we take things easy, if we avoid all strain, if we look after ourselves as a hypochondriac looks after his or her health. No doubt we will exist longer – but we will never live.

This Gospel poses a terrible paradox in an acquisitive society. Very often it is through suffering that we experience life. We are moulded and shaped through suffering. We are being directly challenged about what we have and what we need. It should cause us to pause and think.

Fifth Sunday of Lent

Adultery

Readings: Isa 43:16-21; Phil 3:8-14; Jn 8:1-11

Adultery is as old as humankind. The example of Jesus in dealing with the woman caught in adultery is a model of gentleness and compassion.

A man running for President has a weekend off. He spends it entertaining a part-time actress from Miami. A newspaper stakes out his home, reports his interlude, and overnight his private life turns into a public obsession. In the relentless glare of the cameras, he testily denies that he had a sexual affair with the woman, and bristles over questions about adultery. Stories of other liaisons surface. The candidate, the clear front-runner for the Democratic nomination, describes himself as a hunted quarry and withdraws from the field, denouncing the political process. The man was Gary Hart. The year was 1987.

The scribes and Pharisees brought a woman along who had been caught committing adultery. Making her stand there in full view of everyone, they said to Jesus, 'Master, this woman was caught in the very act of committing adultery. Moses ordered in the law to condemn women like this to death by stoning. What have you to say?' This was 2,000 years earlier but the two situations are not dissimilar.

In the twenty-first century, trial is by media for a whole range of misdemeanours and crimes. In the first century the Pharisees wanted to test Jesus to see if he passed muster in his application of the Mosaic Law. The rabbis said, 'Every Jew must die before we will commit idolatry, murder or adultery.' Adultery was one of the three gravest sins, punishable by death. In Leviticus, the law is quite clear: 'If a man commits adultery with the wife of his neighbour, both the adulterer and the adulteress shall be put to death'.

Jesus was being presented with a dilemma. His ministry was primarily focused on the poor, the outcast, the prostitutes and tax-collectors. His parables had emphasised this point again and again. If he said she shouldn't be stoned he would be encouraging others to break the law. If he said the woman should be stoned his reputation for love, mercy and forgiveness towards all would be in tatters. In addition, he knew and they knew that under the Roman law the Jews did not have the authority to put anyone to death. He was between the proverbial 'rock and a hard place'.

He stooped down and wrote with his finger in the ground. Was he playing for time? Looking for an appropriate response? One can imagine the taut silence as everyone waited. What would he say? I suppose one of the most famous lines of scripture, remembered even by unbelievers, is, 'Let him who is without sin cast the first stone'. It may even mean 'the person who is without sin in his heart' or 'the person who never thought of committing the same sin'. Let that person cast the first stone. It is a wonderful answer. If it were decreed that each of us was to wear our past sins pinned to our backs we wouldn't leave the house in the morning!

We are asked not to praise or blame but only to seek to understand. It is not what people do, but why, that is important. I recently read a newspaper account of a policeman who murdered his wife and children and then committed suicide. The tabloids were having a field day. But why? Who knows the force of the temptation under which any person acts?

The gentle words of Jesus, 'go in peace and sin no more', are evidence of the desire in his heart to reclaim the sinner to a life of love rather than selfishness. 'There is no condemnation in Christ Jesus.' Jesus just wants to love us back to life. That is what he did with the woman who committed adultery.

Living the Paschal Mystery on a Daily Basis

Readings: Isa 50:4-7; Phil 2:6-11; Mt 21:1-11 or Mt 26:14-27, 66

In his passion, death and resurrection, Jesus gives us an example of how he wants us to live. Do we want to continue the journey beyond the shouting and cheering and palms into the 'letting go' of Jesus?

Veronica O'Brien, a long-time envoy of the Legion of Mary in wartime Europe, always enters my mind on Palm Sunday. She collaborated with the late Cardinal Leon Joseph Suenens in bringing the gospel to many people of influence, through faith-sharing groups called Fiat. I visited her late in her life when she was confined to bed. On her bedside locker she had a little stuffed toy donkey. 'That's me,' she explained weakly. 'I always considered myself a donkey bringing Christ to others as happened on Palm Sunday.'

The procession of palms is full of Messianic overtones. Jesus is the one 'who comes in the name of the Lord'. The people had heard of his teaching and his works and were hoping that he was the one who would liberate them. They cheered in expectation that he would fulfil their wishes. They would disappear into the mists of anonymity as soon as the passion journey begins. The exultation would turn either to silence or to taunts and jeers. Many of us are fair-weather friends of Jesus. We find it easy to judge the actions of those who don't conform to the gospel. We lament the sins of others, unable to see our own shortcomings. I know that some people who are most condemnatory of abortion, when an unplanned or unwanted pregnancy happens within their own family circle, are willing to compromise. There is much truth in the phrase, 'There, but for the grace of God go I', or as the Bible warns 'He who think himself to stand let him take heed lest he fall'. When we 'put our hands to the plough' the Bible urges us not to look back.

Palm Sunday sets the scene for the week ahead. Today we can enter into union with Jesus as we begin a pilgrimage of faith through his passion, death and resurrection. How can we live the paschal mystery on a daily basis? How can we follow the way of Jesus? Firstly, there was the 'letting go' of Jesus. He was willing to let go of everything that was humanly important – his friends, his reputation, his popularity, the manifestation of his divinity, his disciples and his mother. What have we got in our lives that we are holding on to? What is the thing or person that we feel we cannot do without? Just offer that up to Jesus at the beginning of this week. Secondly, there was the 'letting be' of Jesus when he hung suspended between heaven and earth. He could no longer influence events. All was silent. There are times in our lives when we don't know where to turn or what decision to make. That could be a time for 'letting be', just remaining peacefully in his presence until the way becomes clearer. Finally, there is the 'letting grow' of Jesus, the bursting forth of new life in the Resurrection. Such moments are part of every human life. These are times when we discern talent or ability in ourselves or others and we 'go with it'. We move when God prompts us. Don't hesitate. Looking on at new life as a spectator, fearful that something might go wrong, is not the 'letting grow' that Jesus wants of us. Harry Truman, the thirty-third President of the United States, learned a prayer as a boy and said it throughout his life. It contains Palm Sunday sentiments: 'Oh! Almighty and everlasting God, Creator of heaven and earth and the universe. Help me to be, to think, to act what is right, because it is right; make me truthful, honest and honorable in all things; make me intellectually honest for the sake of right and honour and without thought of reward to me. Give me that ability to be charitable, forgiving and patient with my fellowmen – help me to understand their motives and their shortcomings – even as thou understand mine! Amen. Amen. Amen'.

Palm Sunday

Symbol And Tradition

Readings: Isa 50:4-7; Phil 2:6-11; Mk 14:1-15:47

The wonderful season of Easter with its symbols and traditions is put back to the periphery of the Catholic consciousness. This decline must be arrested, otherwise we are allowing ourselves to be robbed of the spirit.

Today we set out on an Easter pilgrimage. It moves from the raucous shouts of the crowds on Palm Sunday to the quiet poignancy of the Holy Thursday meal. The betrayal, by a friend, is full of sadness. Jesus becomes a spectacle, an object of curiosity and derision, until he ends up at Calvary. An eerie silence fills the earth until the surprise and joy of Resurrection. This is a pivotal moment in history. The implications of this even on a personal level and for the whole of civilisation are enormous. And yet we are filled with sadness. Easter, the high point of the Christian year, is now a time for hiking in the hills, for festivals and sunshine holidays.

We have forgotten that rituals and symbols can provide the structure by which life experiences and yields new meaning. It is through rituals that we separate our ordinary selves from our extraordinary possibilities and create the sacred time necessary to address important questions with the attention they deserve. Rituals have most power and meaning when they are shared in groups that reinforce the unity and community we need to sustain ourselves. The core of a culture is a package of beliefs learned from childhood that make the world coherent. When we lose or jettison the core of the Easter mystery we allow ourselves to be robbed of the spirit. We put up monuments to fallen heroes to try to encapsulate a spirit of times past that we feel needs to be kept alive. Commemorations and anniversaries try to do the same. When we abandon these traditions we relinquish a part of who we are and we suffer the consequences. The passion, death and resurrection of Jesus have been celebrated for thousands of years. When we link in with this 'remembering' we become part of the Communion of Saints, all who have gone before us.

The fact is that Jesus did not save us from suffering in this present life. Rather, he saved us by suffering. The cross cannot be removed from the human life like a cataract from the eye. At this time we confront the mystery of suffering, the 'why' of it all. We hide suffering behind walls. We struggle frantically to find a place for our parents or grandparents who are now suffering from Alzheimer's disease. The slow and the sluggish interfere with our pace of life. It is in the passion and death of Jesus that we find a meaning to what we see as meaningless suffering. He has gone through the veil of suffering before us. We will hardly be asked to bear more than he bore on our behalf. We join in solidarity with Jesus and all the suffering people of this world when we celebrate the paschal mystery.

Palm Sunday

Defeat Is Turned Into Victory

Readings: Isa 50:4-7; Phil 2:6-11; Lk 19:28-40

Sometimes the journey is painful. We are wounded people, but the sun of the Resurrection is already breaking the horizon.

In every Jewish house at the celebration of the Passover a question is asked of the father of the house. 'Why is this night unlike all other nights?' In response, the story of the deliverance of the Jewish people from the tyranny of the Egyptians is read from the book of Exodus. This has happened for thousands of years. The same question will be asked this year in the homes of the Jews. Can I ask a question? 'Why is this week unlike all other weeks for Christians?' Holy Week is not so much a holy time as a time to be kept holy. I know the supermarkets will be open, commerce will continue and money-making will go its merry way. This is all the more reason why those who profess to love Christ should be different.

In preparation for Jubilee 2000, Pope John Paul said an unusual thing. He said, 'The Christian has a duty to sanctify time.' Time is God's – none of us knows whether he or she will be alive tomorrow. The breath that is in us is God's. It is his creative power that is keeping each of us in existence. We make time holy by tithing time to God, giving back to him what is already his. This week in our ceremonies we will tithe time back to God as we listen to his Word in scripture, celebrate his presence and meet him in the sacraments. We will journey with him as the final drama of our salvation is played out in word, song and sacrament.

We are all Good Friday People. We are people on the pilgrimage of life. On the way we invariably meet the cross. Sometimes it is in the nature of things that we meet God in the desert, in sickness, in prison, in bereavement or some other desolation. God often lets his people fall sick and lets every prop on which they lean be knocked from under them. These are the Good Friday People who have shared in Christ's sufferings and know what it is all about. These are people who have suffered during the year. Christ has been through the gateway of suffering before you. He knows all about it and suffers along with you.

'Come down from the Cross if you are the Son of God,' taunted some people standing around the Cross of Christ. He didn't. The rising sun of the Resurrection was already breaking the horizon. The cross was not the end. It will be the same for us. We join with Christ on his final journey through pain, suffering and the cross to the glorious Resurrection.

Palm Sunday

Easter

Why Did Jesus Die?

Jesus took my place before the Father. He died so that I might live.

In the early hours of 24 July 1943, in Operation Gomorrah, 791 RAF bombers hit the centre of Hamburg with incendiaries and high explosives, creating the war's first firestorm. People in shelters were turned to ashes; others were sucked into the flames by the gale-force winds following the escalation of temperatures of 1500 degrees Fahrenheit. The RAF dropped a stupendous 8,344 tons of bombs that night. About 50,000 people died.

On 22 July 1995 Louise Branson, a reporter with the *Sunday Times*, filed this report: 'The prisoners, estimated to number 4,000, were separated from their families when Srebrenica fell last weekend. They were taken to the nearby town of Bratunac and were placed in three detention centres, including a football field and a school. One woman said her husband, who is in the Bosnian Serb army, had told her of mass shootings in the stadium; she believed the number was 3,000. The motive was largely revenge, she said, for Muslim killings of Serbs both earlier in the war and more recently. One man said "insiders" had told him that the total number of detainees was 4,000. The sound of constant gunfire from the football stadium was explained as celebratory gunfire. One woman said her friends told her they had seen several buses taking bodies to a field to be burned'.

In April 1987 Ivan Boesky, who said, 'greed is all right; everyone should be a little greedy', left a federal court for jail after he admitted paying for advance knowledge of mergers and takeovers – in the illegal Wall Street practice known as 'insider trading'. He then spilled the beans on others. Boesky got four and half years in jail for his greed.

On 15 August 1998 a massive bomb blast rocked the town of Omagh in Northern Ireland. Twenty-nine people died, most of them women and children. Both Catholic and Protestant were among the dead. The youngest to be killed, Breda Devine, was eighteen months old. Maura Monaghan was twenty months old. The bomb was the work of an IRA splinter group, which called itself, provocatively, the 'Real IRA'.

The above are only a tiny glimpse of the evils of which human beings are capable. Multiply these many thousands of times and still we only get a peep at evil. A single human heart is only a microcosm of the universal heart of all peoples. My heart contains within itself the possibility of evil greater than those mentioned above. It also contains the potentiality for holiness. I cannot dismiss the sins of others, thinking, 'I may be bad but I would never do that!' There is little that I am not capable of. How can I be reconciled to God for my own evil? How can I, a simple human being, make adequate satisfaction to God for my own wrongdoing?

The old Negro spiritual asks, 'Were you there when they crucified my Lord?' The answer of course is 'Yes'. Jesus is crucified daily when greed, murder, lust, envy and passion encrust the human heart. But it is through the passion, death and resurrection of Jesus that there is hope in the midst of evil. Jesus became a human being so that he could represent me, another human being, before the face of the Father. He was 'like me' in all things except sin. But he was more than just a human being, he was God. Jesus took my sins upon himself. He took the sins of the world upon himself. As God, his passion, death and resurrection were infinitely pleasing to the Father. His paschal mystery was to make infinite satisfaction to the Father for the sins of the whole world. He thereby gained for me the possibility of eternal life. It is through what Jesus did that I have another chance, and another chance, and another chance. He took my place and died so that I might live.

'God so loved the world that he gave his only son, that whoever believes in him should not perish but should have eternal life.' (Mark 9:7) He came not only to reconcile us to the Father but that we might know the extent of his love for us. He came and gave us a model of holiness.

The Indispensable Nature of Light

Readings: Acts 10:34, 37-43; Cor 3:1-4; Jn 20:1-9

Without a helmet light, pot-holing in County Clare would have been absolutely frightening. The light was indispensable. Without Christ, 'the light of the world', we struggle in darkness.

Many years ago, driving from Dublin to County Clare, I picked up two hitchhikers. They were university students on their way to spend a weekend pot-holing near Lisdoonvarna. They invited me to join the student group they were to meet up with. In what looked to me like an ordinary green field, a stream trickled from the hillside. There was an opening large enough for a human body. I was given a wet-suit, and a helmet with an attached torch, and invited to 'follow the leader'. The leader was crawling on his stomach through the opening. I was none too happy. I crawled after him, with the water gurgling around me. After what seemed an interminable and frightening time the little tunnel opened out into a big cavern. It was inky black. The blackness was broken only by the thin pencils of light on the top of each helmet. It was both awe-inspiring and frightening. I was already thinking of how I was going to get out of there!

In St John, the theme of light and darkness is always prominent. 'I am the light of the world' on the face of it seems a fairly innocuous statement. I was never stunned by the profundity of it. But down in that cavern I was utterly dependent on the light from my helmet. Without that there was no going backwards or forwards. By 'light', John means not just the blinding radiance of Christ's presence, but truth, purity, moral perfection. No one who has access to him can live in darkness. The searchlight of God's presence shows us up.

Down in that pot-hole that light on my helmet may have meant the difference between life and death. What about God's light? God's light is not the merciless light that only exposes and does not heal. We are called to submit to God's light, to relax and be at home in it, and to share our lives with others who have come along the same path. When that happens there is a common energy and purpose running through us all. We become part of one another. And the effect of the death and resurrection of Jesus continually works through all our lives, purifying and changing and renewing us, like a body being healed.

St Paul recognised the pivotal role of the resurrection of Jesus in God's plan of salvation. Writing to the Corinthians he says:

> But if it is preached that Christ has been raised from the dead, how can some of you say that there is no resurrection of the dead? If there is no resurrection of the dead, then not even Christ has been raised.
>
> And if Christ has not been raised, our preaching is useless and so is your faith. More than that, we are then found to be false witnesses about God, for we have testified about God that he raised Christ from the dead. But he did not raise him if in fact the dead are not raised. For if the dead are not raised, then Christ has not been raised either. And if Christ has not been raised, your faith is futile; you are still in your sins.
>
> Then those also who have fallen asleep in Christ are lost. If only for this life we have hope in Christ, we are to be pitied more than all men. But Christ has indeed been raised from the dead, the first fruits of those who have fallen asleep. For since death came through a man, the resurrection of the dead comes also through a man. For as in Adam all die, so in Christ all will be made alive.

The Resurrection is a blinding ray of light illuminating the way to the Father and to eternal life. It is not a memorial to be celebrated but a power to transform us.

Easter Sunday

There Is No Need For Alarm

Readings: Rom 6:3-11; Mk 16:1-16

The Resurrection of Jesus meant that the disciples had to change. Things would not be the same again.

There are people whose faith is as credible and true to them as the ground they walk on. It used to be called a simple faith but I am not so sure. There is a passage in John Steinbeck's novel, *The Winter of Discontent,* that illustrates what I mean:

> Aunt Deborah read the Scripture to me like a daily newspaper and I suppose that's the way she thought of it, as something going on, happening eternally but always exciting and new. Every Easter, Jesus really rose from the dead, an explosion, expected but nonetheless new. It wasn't two thousand years ago to her; it was now.

This same faith explodes with newness and excitement each year. These people of 'simple faith' relive the mysteries of Jesus. They have never heard of 'hermeneutics', nor would they want to. They know Jesus has risen. They know too that the Resurrection was not a return to a former life but a quantum leap forward into a higher life. In other words, the body that rose on Easter Sunday morning was radically different from the body that was buried on Good Friday afternoon. They know that the resurrection of Jesus is a pledge that they too shall rise again with him in glory. How, they can't fathom, but they know!

Women played a significant part in the life of Jesus. Women work from the heart out. They often see with the heart, rather than with the eyes. Martha and Mary knew intuitively that the ministry of Jesus was life-giving. Their home was a place of refuge and comfort for him. It was the women who stood around the cross comforting the dying Jesus. Once again they were first to minister to the dead body of Jesus. On the occasion of the Fourth World Conference on Women in Beijing in 1995, Pope John Paul wrote a letter to women in which he pointed out that 'Jesus treated women with openness, respect, acceptance and tenderness. In this way he honoured the dignity which women have always possessed according to God's plan and in his love'. Today's Gospel bears this out. These women loved and respected Jesus in return.

The beginning of new life is a daunting experience. A mother carrying her first child waits with eager anticipation but with some fear for the birth. 'New beginnings' can be frightening. Things will change. The disciples and the women in today's Gospel will learn to relate to the risen Christ in a new way. Their listening will be different. That sort of change is frightening. Like us, they were more secure with things as they always had been. The new life of the Resurrection will demand of the disciples a willingness to change. Pentecost will put the seal on their mission.

It is so easy to fool oneself. I worked for a short time with a colleague who prided himself on his ability to delegate. He spoke about it often and urged his priest friends to do the same. This same man was experienced by others, particularly the parishioners, as controlling. At the end of the day everyone had to 'ask Father' no matter how trivial the task. The Resurrection was an explosion into a new way of being. It demanded a new way of responding. The apostles were up to the task.

Look for 'resurrection signs' around you, and go for it. 'There is no need for alarm' is the message from the empty tomb. 'He is risen, he is not here.' When we relive the mysteries of Christ in our own life, the paschal mystery of the passion, death and resurrection of Jesus is a 'letting go', 'letting be' and 'letting grow'.

The Resurrection

Readings: Rom 6:3-11; Lk 24:1-12

The Resurrection is not the product of fevered minds. It is a historical reality that straddles time and eternity.

Up near the King David Hotel in Jerusalem there is an excavated ruin of a tomb from around the time of Christ. In 1993 I was staying in the Pontifical Biblical Institute close by the park where this tomb is situated. I had plenty of time to examine it in detail. The tomb was a sculptured hole in the side of a hill. A very large stone, the size of a large tractor wheel, was fitted upright into a groove, which was the length of the entrance and beyond. The wheel-like stone could easily enough be rolled aside to expose the entrance. I am sure it would take at least two or more people to do this. Inside, there was an antechamber that then led into a small shelved room. A newly buried corpse would be placed in the antechamber until decomposition happened and then it would be moved into the inner chamber where it would remain. In this way many bodies could be accommodated in the same tomb. In today's Gospel 'they discovered that the stone had been rolled away'.

Many years ago, in a book entitled *Who Moved the Stone?*, the evidence for the Resurrection was examined forensically. When examining the crux of the problem, the author Frank Morison wrote:

> It is not that one or two emotional women who had been specially identified with the closing scenes of the Crucifixion received a presentiment that Jesus had risen and persistently

asserted it in the teeth of hostile denials and the half-expressed doubts of their friends. Such a view of the situation will not stand a small part of the historic strain which has to be placed upon it. It is that the whole party, including the nine men who fled at the arrest, and certain independent persons who have not previously come into the story, were convinced that something had occurred which changed their entire outlook. It turned their dejection into triumph and their sorrow into an intense joy.

Of course, the significance of the Resurrection is not just that it is a historical fact, but that this event is one around which the whole of the Christian message and its authenticity depend. 'If there is no resurrection from the dead, then neither has Christ been raised. And if Christ has not been raised, then empty too is our preaching; empty too, your faith . . . if the dead are not raised neither has Christ been raised.' (1 Corinthians 15:12) In addition, it is a promise and pledge that there is more to come: 'If we have been united with him like this in his death, we will certainly also be united with him in his resurrection'. (Romans 6:5)

Easter, then, is the celebration of new life. Christ remained, but in a new way. The risen Lord was no phantom or hallucination. He was real. The Jesus who died in truth was the Christ who rose again. Christianity is not founded on the dreams of disordered minds.

Easter Sunday

Emigrant Faith

Readings: Acts 2:42-47; I Pet 1:3-9; Jn 20:19-31

The leap into the world of mystery and the world of the Spirit demands the gift of faith.

Some 22,000 prospectors made it from Alaska over the Chilkoot, one of the main trails into the goldfields of the Klondike in western Yukon territory, Canada, where gold was discovered in 1896. They had to slog it out, often in temperatures of 70 degrees below zero, with six weeks of total darkness. Many were drowned in the Yukon, some froze to death, others drifted into alcoholism in Dawson City. The story has been documented in *The Hard Road to the Klondike* by an Irish emigrant, Michael MacGowan. He detailed the squalor, the faction fighting, the cold and the pain, but he said 'the hardest thing we had to bear was being without a priest'. To those rough Irish fortune-seekers, being without Sunday Mass was their biggest hardship. This surely was an extraordinary faith! They felt they needed the presence of Jesus in their midst as a consolation and a joy. The Gospel today is about faith.

The *Constitution on the Liturgy* of the Second Vatican Council says that 'before people come to the Liturgy they must be called to faith and conversion'. The story of Thomas the doubter gives us an opportunity to reflect on issues of faith. Today, we live with a cacophony of media voices, directing messages that challenge the very idea of the existence of a supernatural faith. There is a real battle for the mind going on in the world. Much of what we hear and see on the airwaves is not sympathetic to supernatural faith or religion in general. In this environment faith needs to be protected.

The *Catechism of the Catholic Church* makes two important statements about faith. Firstly, 'faith is a personal adherence of the whole person to God who reveals himself. It involves an assent of the intellect and will to the self-revelation God has made through his deeds and words'. It also says that 'faith is a supernatural gift from God. In order to believe, man needs the interior help of the Holy Spirit'.

Our daily lives focus on the empirical world, the world of see, touch and feel. Faith deals with the world of mystery, the world of the spirit. While we can say that 'religion is reasonable', it is the 'gift of faith' that allows us to make the leap from one world into another.

The Old Testament, in particular, abounds in examples of people who possessed a deep faith and who lived and died accordingly. They all looked forward to the time when God would fulfil his promise, but none of them lived to see it. Abel demonstrated his faith – and was killed. Enoch walked by faith – and lived. Noah's faith saved his whole family. Abraham's faith took him away from his settled life at home and made him an alien and refugee. Faith made him willing to offer up his only son, trusting that God would bring him back to life. Isaac, Jacob and Joseph in turn all demonstrated their belief in God's promise. Faith determined Moses' choice to leave the Egyptian court and throw in his lot with a nation of slaves. Jericho was taken by faith, not superior force. Jeremiah was beaten and imprisoned. Isaiah, it is said, was sawn in half. Zechariah was stoned.

Jesus often demanded faith as a prerequisite before he performed a miracle, but there were times when the faith of the community was sufficient for the miracle, as with the man let down from the roof. The mysterious nature of faith can often be seen in the conversion of such saints as Francis of Assisi or Ignatius of Loyola.

The gift of faith is a precious gift. It provides meaning and direction to the human person. It offers pointers to the deeper questions of life. Faith can and needs to grow. It grows through exercise – prayer, spiritual reading, the sacramental life. Other voices compete for the allegiance of the human heart – which is made for God.

Second Sunday of Easter

The Resurrection, Cookham

Readings: Acts 4:32-35; 1 Jn 5:1-6; Jn 20:19-31

A remarkable painting, recently on display in the National Gallery in London, teaches many lessons about the resurrection of Jesus.

At the National Gallery in London, a stunning exhibition entitled *The Image of Christ – Seeing Salvation* drew huge crowds. One person described it to be 'better than any retreat'. In the exhibition there was a quite extraordinary painting by Stanley Spencer (1891-1959) entitled *The Resurrection, Cookham*. This painting was received enthusiastically when first exhibited and Charles Marriott of *The Times* newspaper wrote that 'in all probability this is the most important picture painted by an English artist in the present century'.

Spencer's painting is a composite between the Resurrection and the Last Judgement. He does not portray Christ as a threatening judge but rather as a loving and merciful maternal figure, who nurses two babies cosily in his arms. This painting, more than any other I have viewed, portrays the 'fruitfulness' of the paschal mystery. This fruitfulness is seen in the nurturing by Christ of the two infants as he comes from the tomb. It is also seen in the acts of reconciliation featured in the painting – one woman enjoying an intimate reconciliation with her husband as she brushes down his jacket, and another delighting in smelling a flower. Here the maternity of God is vividly illustrated.

The painting is set, not in far off Jerusalem, but in Cookham Parish Church, thus rooting the power and fruitfulness of the Resurrection in the 'now' rather than in the 'then'. Perhaps we look at the Resurrection as a mystical or historical fact without working out the implications and the power flowing from the resurrected Christ. The fact that Spencer located the Resurrection in a final judgement setting is also assuring us that the Resurrection is the merciful pledge that 'we too shall rise with him in glory' on the last day.

The fruitfulness of Christ, portrayed in the painting by the two children cradled in Christ's arms, is also illustrated in the Gospel today by the promise of the forgiveness of sins, the giving of the Holy Spirit, the gift of peace, and the strengthening of faith. All these effects flowing from the Resurrection are possible in the daily lives of the Christian believer. Jesus Christ can and does make a difference in the lives of those who are open to him. There are wonderful implications attached to a relationship with the 'pilgrim God who speaks'. The Resurrection is good news to be shouted from the rooftops.

There was a report in the newspaper recently of the Good Friday ceremonies in a large working-class Dublin parish where only fifty-eight people turned up. All but six of these were women. Why is it that the life of Jesus and the power flowing from it isn't seen as good news to be celebrated liturgically? How is it that the paschal mystery isn't seen as life-giving to so many baptised people? I think the Resurrection is not a personal mystery of faith to be celebrated and rejoiced in but one to be shared. The great mission of the Church is to 'share the good news of Jesus Christ' with everyone – believer, skeptic, agnostic and atheist.

Thomas The Doubter

Readings: Acts 5:12-16; Apoc 1:9-13; Jn 20:19-31

It is not doubting that is the problem, rather it is a failure to seek the truth.

There was an attractive impetuosity about some of the disciples. Peter, always ready to make the big gesture, is one such. Surely Thomas is another? When Jesus had proposed going to Bethany, after the news of Lazarus' illness had come, Thomas' reaction had been, 'Let us also go, that we may die with him'. Thomas never lacked courage. There can never be any doubt that he loved Jesus. He loved him enough to be willing to go to Jerusalem and die with him when the other disciples were hesitant and afraid. When the death of Jesus came it seemed to Thomas like a tragic end to an inspiring friendship. He was broken-hearted, so broken-hearted that he could not meet the eyes of people, but wanted to be alone with his grief.

So it happened that when Jesus came back again Thomas was not there; and the news seemed to him to be too farfetched to be true. He refused to believe. Belligerent in his pessimism, he said that he would never believe that Jesus had risen from the dead until he had seen and felt the print of the nails in Jesus' hands and thrust his hand into the wound that the spear had made in Jesus' side.

Jesus came back again; and this time Thomas was there. And Jesus knew Thomas' heart. He repeated Thomas' own words, and invited him to make the test that he had demanded. And Thomas' heart ran out in love and devotion, and all he could say was, 'My Lord and my God!' Jesus told Thomas, 'There is another way. The way of faith. Blessed are those who have not seen and have believed.'

Our culture is indifferent to matters of faith. 'Technology contains all the answers we need' says the post-modernist mentality. But in the end it was the death and resurrection of Jesus that challenged Thomas to look for the ultimate proof that life has a deeper meaning than the 'now'. It is the same today. It is in the face of death, particularly the death of a dearly beloved, that we are challenged as Thomas was challenged. Nothing has changed!

Thomas absolutely refused to say that he understood what he did not understand, or that he believed what he did not believe. He would never still his doubts by pretending that they did not exist. He was not the kind of man who would rattle off a creed without understanding what it was all about. Thomas had to be sure – and he was quite right. 'There lives more faith in honest doubt, than in half the creeds.'

There is more ultimate faith in the person who insists on being sure than in those who glibly repeat things that they have never thought out, and that they may not really believe. Think of St Thérèse who suffered severe doubts against faith in the last months of her life. All she could say was, 'I know that behind the dark cloud my sun is still shining.' It is not doubting that is the problem, rather it is a failure to seek the truth. The genuine seeker will never be lost.

The Pilgrim Journey

Readings: Acts 2:14, 22-33; 1 Pet 1:17-21; Lk 24:13-35

*What happened on the road to Emmaus changed everything for the disciples.
That experience is not for the privileged few but for all God's people.*

In his biography of a remarkable First World War chaplain, Fr Willie
Doyle, Alfred O'Rahilly tells the story of a Dublin Fusilier who
happened to be home in Dublin on leave at the time of Fr Doyle's
death. Meeting a friend who told him the news, he kept repeating
incredulously, 'He's not dead. He couldn't be killed.' When at last he
was shown a paper describing the padre's death, the soldier
spontaneously knelt down on the pavement and began to pray. Then,
to the crowd that had gathered round him, he recounted how, when he
was lying wounded in an exposed position and expecting every
moment to be killed by a shell, Fr Doyle had crept out to him and
carried him to a place of safety. I am sure the two disciples on the road
to Emmaus had similar feelings of confusion, sadness and desolation at
the death of Jesus.

The two men needed to tell their stories of how they remembered
Jesus. They had been impressed by Jesus the man; they hoped for a
divine intervention while he was alive; but their hopes had been
shattered by his death. They had obviously remained tied strongly to
the Jewish expectation of the Messiah and had no idea of the divinity
of Christ. But after Jesus had explained all that the scriptures taught
about the coming Messiah they gained a deeper insight into the
revelation of God that is Christ. In the plan of God the cross was the

necessary road to glory. The stranger had put meaning on the event they had witnessed and participated in.

The conversation between Jesus and the two disciples in which they discuss recent events is a clear outline of the primitive preaching in the Acts of the Apostles. Luke has used the terms of the traditional catechesis to describe a real conversation of which he had no record. As a teacher of the good news, he notes the main facts of the primitive kerygma – Jesus lived, died and was raised by God from the dead, a fact that is witnessed in the scriptures and proved by the testimony of the apostles.

By the time this story had reached Luke it had been influenced and modified by the eucharistic liturgy. For the story follows the sequence of the liturgical celebration: the reading and explanation of scripture and the 'breaking of bread'. Further, Luke has placed the story in a liturgical setting. The 'breaking of bread' can hardly have been the Eucharist, nor would the disciples have understood it as such. But Luke describes the actions of Jesus as precisely as at the Last Supper. It appears he wants to suggest the Eucharist to his readers so that they may learn that it is in that celebration that Jesus will be truly recognised.

There is a lot of all of us in the two disciples. There is a poignancy in the companionship of the two disciples travelling together. This companionship is important. In our pilgrim journey we need spiritual friendship to encourage and support us in good and bad times. There is the vitality that is always contained within the experience of a meal shared. Most of the significant events of our lives are celebrated within the context of a shared meal. Baptisms, First Communion, anniversaries, weddings and so on involve mutual sharing. There is a sacredness attached even to the most mundane of family meals. The Mass is such a shared occasion. It is not a private devotion. It is a family, a community occasion, where we appreciate that those celebrating with us are our brothers and sisters.

Faith, God's Gift To His People

Readings: Acts 3:13-15, 17-19; 1 Jn 2:1-5; Lk 24:35-48

The Resurrection tests our faith. 'Blessed are those who have not seen and still believe' are the reassuring words that come from the heart of Christ.

I can still remember that day in 1958 when my family gathered in what was then called Collinstown Airport (now Dublin Airport) to say goodbye to my sister who was emigrating to America. We weren't sure if and when we would see her again. My sister's journey took nine hours and involved a refuelling stop at Gander in Newfoundland, Canada. The journey by Concord can now be made in just over three hours! Today, over forty years later, messages can be bounced from a satellite in the sky, to enter our homes a fifth of a second later as news pictures. This is the IT revolution. This is the world of see, touch and feel. This is the world where the latest buzz word is 'globalisation'. This is the information age. This world *appears* to have little time for faith, but it has. Buy a car and you get a twelve months' guarantee. How do you know that the car dealer will deliver on the guarantee? You just take it on faith. You fly in an aeroplane 30,000 feet above the ground. How does it happen? How do you know you are safe? You just have to believe it on the airline's say so. You send your child to school, thereby putting your faith in the teacher and the school. It's a risk but you do it.

I have always seen religious faith as that special gift or power from God that allows me to make the jump from the see, touch and feel world into the world of the spirit, the world of mystery. Let's face it, the resurrection of Jesus stretches the credulity even of the IT generation to the very limits and beyond! Without the gift of faith,

Third Sunday of Easter

122

SUNDAYTHOUGHTS.COM

rising from the dead is difficult to believe! Jesus rebuked Thomas, 'Because you have seen me you believe. Blessed are those who have not seen and believed. All the prophets, all the scriptures, and all the miracles should have been enough for you to believe that I am the Son of God.' Thomas had all this evidence that is unavailable to us and still he doubted! The seed of faith is sown in Baptism. It is nurtured in the heart and in the home. It flowers when an adult choice is made to say 'yes' to Jesus.

The risen Lord had a word of encouragement for all future believers when he said, 'Blessed are they who did not see, and yet believed.' Faith is a person's response to God, who reveals himself through Jesus Christ. Faith involves the human faculties that allow us to come to a knowledge of the existence of a personal God. To believe, our intellect and will are aided by grace. However, in order to enter into a real relationship of intimacy with God we need the grace of being able to welcome this revelation.

Like all gifts we can barter it away by failing to live up to the obligations of faith. Our faith can and is strengthened by prayer, spiritual reading, Mass and the sacraments. Faith, like a muscle, grows as it is exercised. If we fail to exercise our faith it grows weak and dies. We can in some sense 'lose the faith'. It is our faith that gives meaning and direction to our lives. Jesus, by his many bodily appearances, was anxious to convince the disciples that he was truly risen. He went to the trouble of inviting them to touch his risen body and explore the wounds of his crucifixion. In this touch the pain of the cross and the triumph of the Resurrection were united. Without the cross there could have been no resurrection.

Peter – 'Master Of The Universe'

Readings: Acts 5:27-32; Apoc 5:11-14; Jn 21:1-19

The beauty of Peter's character is fully revealed in the incident by the lakeside when he and the others had breakfast with Jesus.

For a number of years I was the chaplain at Dublin Airport. Christmas time is a wonderful time at airports – at least for the curious bystander. Planes are flying in from all over Europe: France, Zurich, Rome, Berlin, Frankfurt; and from further afield: San Francisco, New York, Atlanta. Mothers and fathers and other eager relations wait for the sons and daughters, husbands and wives, and friends they haven't seen for some time. When the awaited face is spotted the transformation in the faces of the waiting people is instantaneous and joyful; they run to be the first to hug or kiss the returned emigrant. This image immediately struck me when I read in today's Gospel: 'at these words "It is the Lord" Simon Peter, who had practically nothing on, wrapped his cloak around him and jumped into the sea'. There was something very special about his relationship with Jesus! Peter had an exuberance and spontaneity about him that wouldn't be thwarted by anything – even his shameful denial of Jesus not so long before. Of course, Peter had shared the 'highs' and the 'lows' with Jesus. He was there at the Transfiguration and again at Gethsemane. In the garden he fell asleep and got a mild rebuke from Jesus: 'So you could not stay awake with me even for one hour'. He followed as far as the courtyard and his courage failed. Immediately, at one look from Jesus, he realised his ghastly blunder, repented and went out 'and wept bitterly'. Nowadays, there is a lot of talk about the need for males to develop their 'feminine side' – Peter certainly had it!

Peter also had strength of character, which influenced the others. When he said, 'I'm going fishing', the others said immediately, 'We'll come with you.' Invariably, there will be dissenters when any plan is mooted. They wanted to be with Peter!

They had been out all night fishing and undoubtedly they were tired and hungry. Jesus had already started a charcoal fire and had fish cooking on it. The simplicity of the scene by the lakeside is remarkable. Jesus just says, 'Come and have breakfast.' The first and simplest aim of this story is to make quite clear the reality of the Resurrection. The Lord was not a vision. It was Jesus, who had conquered death and was with them. His resurrection was not a restoration of life, such as happened to Jairus' daughter, the son of the widow of Nain, and Lazarus. With Jesus, it was not simply a case of restoring life to a body. It was a quantum leap into a higher life. Paul compares the body before resurrection to a seed planted in the earth; the body after resurrection differs as a seed does from a plant. He is in what theologians call a 'glorified state'.

Then Jesus challenges Peter. 'Simon, son of John, do you love me more than these?' It is unclear whether 'these' refers to his boat and tackle, or the other apostles. But it appears Jesus is challenging Peter to put him before everything else in life. It is also part of a healing process, offering Peter the opportunity to be healed of the ache that his denial must inevitably have left behind. Peter is given the role of shepherding the Church.

Third Sunday of Easter

The Priest

Readings: Acts 2:14, 36-41; 1 Pet 2:20-25; Jn 10:1-10

Much has changed in the life and ministry of the priest in the last thirty years. The fundamentals, of modelling his life on the 'good shepherd' of today's Gospel, remain.

The priesthood is in trouble. Since the Second Vatican Council well over 100,000 priests have left the active ministry. In the meantime, our world has been increasingly secularised. For those priests who remain, the societal supports that were so important in the past have largely gone. Serious wrongdoing within our own ranks has been demoralising. The polarisation of views on a whole range of fundamental moral and doctrinal issues has caused confusion. Many priests feel isolated and alone. The result in many cases has been a lessening of apostolic zeal. Perhaps it is not over-dramatic to quote George Bernardos, in *The Diary of a Country Priest*, when he writes: 'We pay a heavy price for the superhuman dignity of our calling. The ridiculous is always so near to the sublime. And the world, usually so indulgent to foibles, hates us instinctively.'

Such a situation is not uncommon. Catholic France, after World War II, was described by Masie Ward in a groundbreaking book, *France Pagan*, as follows: 'A continually encroaching paganism, a Catholicism tied to all appearances to the old regime, a Catholicism losing bit by bit its property, its support from the state, its authority over education, its religious orders – perhaps its fervour?' It was into this context, sprang, albeit briefly, a courageous pastoral experiment of priest-workmen. These priests lived and worked a regular life alongside fellow workers, the vast majority of whom had no faith. They sought to live a life in a brotherhood of mutual affection and religious interdependence. They gathered around them little clusters of newly converted people who sought to cling to Christ, the living vine. Abbé Godin, one of these heroic priests, wrote: 'The priest is a living sacrament, a source of life throughout his life. There is a mysticism of action in the priesthood. The priest must be both a mystic dwelling with God and a man in the midst of men. He must go out and cry the Gospels from the housetops. The priest must constantly, by his exercises of piety, be keeping company with God'.

Today's Gospel of the Good Shepherd is a time for reflecting on the priesthood. If the priest is an 'alter Christus' his life is modelled on the life of Jesus, the Good Shepherd – who is willing to lay down his life for his sheep. In Ezekiel 34 we read: 'I myself will be the shepherd of my sheep and I will make them lie down, says the Lord God. I will seek the lost and I will bring back the strayed and I will bind up the crippled and I will strengthen the weak'. Thankfully, the priest still has a privileged access to the pained and broken people of our world. He still has the possibility, like Simon of Cyrene, of helping to carry the cross behind Jesus 'in his distressing disguise'. He can still demonstrate the patient love of the 'good shepherd' in his ministry.

The priest has the opportunity of representing all peoples before the throne of God when he offers the Mass or recites the Breviary. Through the prayers of the priest, constant intercession is being made to God for those in distress, the sick, the weak, the lame and the confused. The forgiveness of Christ, his healing, his life-giving Body and Blood, are ministered through the priest.

The Good Shepherd

Readings: Acts 4:8-12; Jn 3:1-2; Jn 10:11-18

It is difficult to convince oneself that you are the object of the infinite love of love.

Those who follow Gaelic Games played in Ireland must be familiar with the scripture John 3:16. Over the last five or six years a person has situated him or herself behind the goalposts at the headquarters of the Gaelic Athletic Association in Croke Park in Dublin. On the day of a big hurling or football match the stadium bulges with sixty- or seventy-thousand people. Televised games go worldwide to Irish emigrant viewers. When a goal or point is scored, the cameras zoom in on the goalposts, and there the banner reading John 3:16 is held aloft for all the world to see. This new form of evangelism proclaims the scripture, 'God so loved the world that he gave his only begotten Son that whoever believes in him should not perish but have eternal life'. Martin Luther called John 3:16 'the heart of the Bible', the Gospel in miniature. It is so simple a child can understand it; yet it condenses the deep and marvellous truths of redemption into a few words, echoed in today's Gospel: 'I lay down my life for my sheep'.

Human love is like a magnet buried deep within the heart of the loved and the beloved. They are drawn together with compelling force. Their desire is not to be two but one. Apart they are incomplete. This poem, 'Love Finds a Way', illustrates what I mean:

> Love finds a way home,
> Nothing but nothing can restrain its desire
> To be at the heart of everything

Into our resentment and our hate,
Into the cancer of our self-neglect
Love finds a way

Into our guilt and our shame,
Into the paralysis of our fear
Love finds a way

Into our mania and our make-believe
Down through the tunnels of our escapes
Love finds a way

O yes love finds a way in where love has been locked out
For love is a fire, love is a blade
Love breaks open our hearts to each other
And stays.

It is difficult to be convinced that God loves me. All of us are so conscious of our sinfulness. There are so many things we have done for which we feel ashamed. How can God love me? Many of the parables of Jesus are a plea from him to acknowledge and accept his love. Pause a while. Reflect on your uniqueness. You are the beginning and end of an assembly line. There is no one in the whole wide world exactly like you. And God knows your name – 'I know my own'.

God is solicitous for our well-being. The life of the shepherd is totally bound up with the sheep. God's love is not static. He is more than solicitous, he identifies with us in our struggle, in our weakness. He is with us as we walk and as we sit. The shepherd led (not drove) his sheep to fresh grazing and guarded them from wild animals by lying across the entrance to the sheepfold at night, so becoming its 'door'. In the Old Testament God is often called the shepherd of Israel. And his chosen leaders are also the nation's 'shepherds'. In this parable, Jesus chooses to describe himself as the true shepherd. The phrase sums up so much: the close, personal relationships between himself and each of his followers; the absolute security they can have in him; his leadership and guidance; his constant company; his unfailing care; his sacrificial love.

Sheep And Shepherds

Readings: Acts 13:14, 43-52; Apoc 7:14-17; Jn 10:27-30

Until the recent outbreak of 'foot and mouth' disease we took the shepherd and his sheep very much for granted. Jesus, in the image of 'shepherd', gives us an insight into the loving care he has for each one of us.

In early 2001, nightly images of blazing pyres flickered across the television screens of the British Isles. Infected sheep and cattle were being torched, to halt the spread of the dreaded disease of foot and mouth. For a city dweller this didn't mean that much to me. Then one evening a sheep farmer from an infected area telephoned me to ask for prayers. His entire flock of pedigree sheep, bar six sheep, had been culled. He was distraught as he described how his life's work looked like coming to an end. If the final six sheep were killed everything he had lived for would be gone. With a breaking voice, he begged me to ask our Church congregation to pray for him. It was only then that the relationship between the shepherd and his sheep and the message of today's Gospel struck me.

Judaea was a pastoral country; its shepherds were among its best-known figures. The shepherd was responsible for the entire flock of the village. His life was arduous, his work never finished. There was always a shortage of good grazing, no walled fields, as we know them, and danger from wild animals. He needed qualities of patient endurance, constant watchfulness and courage. His relationship with the sheep was more than that of an animal carer. He knew each of them and usually had named them. In our country, sheep are reared for their meat. In Palestine, in contrast, sheep are reared for their wool. This means that the same sheep spend many years with the shepherd. He comes to know them more closely than we would be familiar with.

In the New Testament Jesus is the Good Shepherd. He is the shepherd who will risk his life to seek and to save the one straying sheep (Matthew 18:12; Luke 15:4). He has pity upon the people because they are as sheep without a shepherd (Matthew 9:36; Mark 6:34). His disciples are his little flock (Luke 12:32). When he, the shepherd, is killed, the sheep are scattered (Mark 14:27; Matthew 26:31). He is the shepherd of the souls of people (1 Peter 2:25), and the great shepherd of the sheep (Hebrews 13:20). The image of the 'good shepherd' is of one who is compassion itself; a person who deals tenderly with each individual sheep.

At night the sheep which belonged to the various villagers were left in a sheepfold. There was a gate and a guard. In the morning the shepherds came in by the gate and led their sheep to pasture. Jesus uses the images of the shepherd and the gate of the sheepfold and refers them to himself. It is in their shepherd that the sheep find security; the shepherd is the one who will protect them. It is the same with Jesus. When we are alone, frightened or isolated, Jesus is always there with love, compassion and forgiveness. He is also the way to the Father. It is through Jesus, the shepherd, that we come to new life. The sheep enter and leave for pasture lands through the gate; so, too, entry into God's pastures and into the Church is through Christ.

Fourth Sunday of Easter

'I Am The Way, The Truth And The Life'

Readings: Acts 6:1-7; 1 Pet 2:4-9; Jn 14:1-12

How can we find meaning in our lives? The Gospel today proposes that it is in Jesus that the human life finds true and lasting meaning.

In his intriguing book, *The Theft of the Spirit*, author psychiatrist Carl Hammerschlag proposes the theory that without faith in a believable ethic we suffer. The theft of the spirit destroys us at every level – the individual, the family, the neighbourhood, the culture, the nation, the fate of the world. He claims that the Native American people have suffered the theft of the spirit. Their totems have been stolen, ending up in antique shops or museums throughout the world. Their rituals have been lost. Rituals and symbols can provide the structure by which life experiences yield new meaning. In many cases, Native Americans have been reduced to running casinos or falling into alcohol addiction on their reservations. Can it be that 'the theft of the spirit' is happening here in Ireland?

Can life have a meaning? Is there a purpose in the daily routine, punctuated only by the occasional holiday or family celebration? How is it that so many young people commit suicide today? Addicts in search of a fix prowl our cities. Our modern glass-fronted cathedrals are peopled by financial gnomes feverishly following the markets. For some, meaning can be following their favourite football team with passionate intensity. The words of Thomas in today's Gospel must find an echo in the heart of many. 'Lord, we do not know where you are going, so how can we know the way?' How can we know the way?

There is a search for meaning in today's world. Life is only tolerable and fruitful, even happy, when it has a deeper meaning. When I have made as much money as I can and my future is secure, I ask, 'Is that all there is?' When I have exotic holidays and come home burnished by the sun, I ask, 'Is that all there is?' When my children are reared and have flown the family nest, I ask, 'Is that all there is?'

In the Gospel today Jesus says, 'There is more, there is a greater meaning to life than the immediate provable reality.' He says words that echo down the centuries – I AM THE WAY, THE TRUTH AND THE LIFE. This is a promise to you and me. He says 'I am the way', not 'I will show you the way'. He is not the signpost or the map or the guide. He himself is the way. When we hold his hand we have the assurance that we cannot get lost. This does not mean that we will not have to live with mystery, or in darkness, or experience a homelessness, but it does mean that we can repeat with St Thérèse of Lisieux, 'I know that behind the dark cloud my sun is still shining'.

The Western word has lost confidence in truth. What is truth? My truth has equal validity with yours! What is true for me is true! But Jesus is saying 'I am the truth'. There is an objective truth outside of yourself. You can have confidence that in following Jesus you walk with truth.

Jesus is the life. Life is so precious. This week I attended someone who had attempted suicide. Life was no longer worth living. Life was cheap, disposable. Jesus is like oxygen to a dying person. He is life. If I am feeling dead or listless or apathetic, Jesus is the kiss of life. When I live close to him I participate in his life. Am I a life-giving person? Are people the better for having met me? If Jesus is life and I participate in that life through grace, I too can be life-giving.

What It Means To Be The Body Of Christ

Readings: Acts 9:26-31; Jn 3:18-24; Jn 15:1-8

The world could be transformed if we lived out the doctrine of the Body of Christ on a daily basis.

As a young person I was always intrigued when people told me, 'you are the splitting image of your mother'. Others saw something that I didn't see. Yet at times the similarities between parents and their children are easily detected. Some carry the father's prominent nose or the mother's eye colour. Usually the colour of the hair is the same as one or other of the parents. Frequently athletic prowess or intellectual ability are carried over into the next generation. When the seed and the egg meet and fuse to form the foetus we are made up of a bit of both parents. The wonder of conception means that the traits or genetic history are carried forward into the next generation. We have often heard of a person being described as 'Christlike'. This person is compassionate, kind, understanding. How is it that the image of Christ shines through in many people's lives? Baptism is also a type of conception. We are reborn into a new life. In Baptism the life of Christ is infused into the person in whose image we are made. We carry that likeness to Christ throughout our lives. It isn't at all peculiar that Jesus says in today's Gospel, 'I am the vine, you are the branches.' Both vine and branches carry the same life within.

The dignity of the human person comes not from fame, popularity or money, but from being a child of the Father. Mother Teresa used to talk of the poor as 'Jesus in his distressing disguise'. How true this was. We share the life of Christ and participate in his divinity through our Baptism.

But if the baptised carry within them the image of Christ and his inner life, that makes us related to one another! The Christian carries the indelible mark of Christ. This is where the whole idea of the Body of Christ comes from. A body is a unified system of separate parts. My hand is not my leg, my nose is not my ear, yet they belong to and are utterly part of the one body. The implications of this doctrine are awesome. If we Christians were to live as the one body (of Christ), would we have poverty, discrimination, prejudice? If we lived as brothers and sisters of one another, wouldn't the healthy members of the body rush in to help the diseased? I suppose as in a human family selfishness is always a factor. Original sins and human weakness naturally prevent the Body of Christ from shining in the world as the witness it ought to be. As we look back on our pilgrim journey we naturally ask how much fruit have we borne. There is no doubt about it, overcoming our sinfulness unaided by grace is impossible. Alcoholics Anonymous recognised this years ago; the twelve-step programme looks to 'a higher power', whatever name one puts on that. Jesus said, 'You shall receive power from on high.' As with electricity, one needs to turn on the switch to receive the power. The Christian needs an open heart and a willingness to change to receive this power. One needs to 'remain in me' as Jesus invites us. We can produce spectacular results on the surface without this power. These works may deceive a lot of people, but like the seed falling on rough ground, the fruit soon withers away and little remains. The danger is that the desire to be admired, thought well of, impress one's superiors, is ever present. These are temptations to which many of us easily succumb.

The challenge today is to live out the doctrine of the Body of Christ. The temptation is to give in to negativity, a carping spirit, a dis-spiritedness and apathy, which is counter to the Gospel of Jesus.

Fifth Sunday of Easter

I Am Your Brother Joseph

Readings: Acts 14:21-27; Apoc 21:1-5; Jn 13:31-33

We need models for living. One cardinal, who died in 1995, was a true model for the priest.

In November 1995 one of America's best-loved priests, Cardinal Joseph Bernardin, died peacefully. He was no ordinary man. Bishop Goedert announced his death like this: 'Our brother Joseph is at peace. As Christians, we believe that Cardinal Bernardin at long last begins a new life, an everlasting life, with our Lord Jesus. We believe that today he will meet his Redeemer face to face . . . . He was our friend. He was our priest. He was our bishop. But most of all, he was truly our brother Joseph, whom he promised to be when he first came into our midst in August 1982. We loved him deeply. We will miss him dearly'.

Shortly before he died, this priest, who had been unjustly accused of sex abuse, who was severely criticised by his fellow bishops for being too liberal, prayed with and offered reconciliation to his unjust accuser. It was he who, rather than isolate the abortion issue, developed the 'seamless garment' philosophy of respect for life from 'the womb to the tomb'. He tried to initiate a 'Common Ground Project' to bring diverging viewpoints in the Church together.

Just before he died Cardinal Bernardin wrote to his priests as follows: 'I have never understood what it means to be a priest more than I do now. People look to priests to be authentic witnesses to God's active role in the world, to his love. They don't want us to be business managers; they are not interested in the petty conflicts that may show up in parish life. Instead, people simply want us to be with them in the joys and sorrows of their lives. No matter how significant our other work might be, the people want something different from their clergy. The things people remember most are small acts of concern and thoughtfulness. Years later, that is what they tell you about their priest'.

On the evening of his funeral the Dunkin Donuts across Chicago Avenue reported that their coffee sales were eight times what they usually sold in the late evenings. The local McDonald's, which carried a sign reading 'Gentle Joseph, rest in peace', started distributing coffee free of charge. The London *Tablet* magazine described him as 'the most influential American churchman since Martin Luther King Jr'. He was a model for every priest.

Today has been designated as Priesthood Sunday. A priest is one who tries to bring 'God to people, and people to God'. He is a wounded healer always conscious of his own frailty. He knows his unworthiness to be a channel of God's love and mercy. He has no power of his own right. His only power is the power of God working in and through him. The world needs signs of the transcendent. As someone said recently, 'We need people to keep the rumour of God alive!' Such a person is the priest. A priest cannot fulfil his calling without the prayers and support of the people; together we make up 'the People of God'. Please pray that young people may begin to hear once more that call of Jesus to 'Come follow me'.

Fifth Sunday of Easter

If You Love Me ...

Readings: Acts 8:5-8, 14-17; 1 Pet 3:15-18; Jn 14:15-21

There is a big 'if' in today's Gospel. There is a price to be paid for friendship with Jesus and receiving his Spirit.

Dietrich Bonhoeffer was an extraordinary human being. If he had belonged to a Church that made saints, he would be one. He was martyred by the Nazis in 1945. As early as 1933 he was publicly denouncing a political system that corrupted and grossly misled a nation. He left Germany for London where, as a pastor, he ministered for nearly two years. On the eve of war some friends got him to America, but he would not stay there. His heart belonged to his poor oppressed and persecuted fellow German Christians. He was arrested by the Gestapo in 1943 and was finally executed on the personal orders of Hitler in 1945. It was he, I think, who coined the phrase 'cheap grace'. 'Cheap grace is the preaching of forgiveness without requiring repentance, baptism without church discipline, absolution without personal confession. Cheap grace is grace without discipleship, grace without the cross, grace without Jesus Christ.'

We long for cheap grace. We long for the soft option. Love without giving. Comfort without cost. Much of what we observe in the New Age movement is the fulfilment of the desire for cheap grace. Many of those who flocked to the Bhagwan Shree Rajneesh, the free-love guru of the Seventies, and the forerunners of the New Agers of today, were looking for 'cheap grace'. Most of the New Age movement is concerned more about how one feels than about how one acts. But the desire for cheap grace is within us all.

What has all this to do with today's Gospel? The Gospel of today opens with the conjunction 'if'. It's a big if. Jesus says 'if you love me . . . I will ask the Father'. In this passage Jesus seems to make the gift of the Spirit conditional upon the disciples' love of Jesus and keeping the commandments. This is covenant language reminiscent of the great 'if' of the book of Exodus. 'If you hearken to my voice, and keep my covenant, you will be my special possession, dearer to me than all other people'.

God cannot force himself into our lives. He has given us the gift of free will. He has to be, warts and all, invited into our lives. The gift of the Spirit cannot be given, because it cannot be received in one who does not love Jesus and try to live according to his word. In other words, there is no such a thing as 'cheap grace'. There is a price to be paid in this life. There are demands placed on us in our friendship with Jesus.

In working with married couples we say that love is a decision, not a feeling. When love is a decision there is a price to be paid! We decide to love despite our feelings. We don't base the most important relationship in our lives on how we feel today. It is in overcoming one's feelings of apathy, disinterestedness, that one grows in love. True love is a demanding path. Love is its own reward, for it is in paying the price that we reap the reward. The 'if' of today's Gospel is a reminder that keeping the commandments must be at the heart of our relationship with God. The Gospel today is alerting us to the wonderful feast of Pentecost. Pentecost is coming. The gift of the Spirit is available to all. We are being invited to prepare for this great gift by being open to obeying God's commandments. The gift of the Spirit is costly because it calls us to follow, and it is grace because being called into friendship with Jesus is a gift.

Sixth Sunday of Easter

The Courage To Change

Readings: Acts 10:25-26, 34-35, 44-48; 1 Jn 4:7-10; Jn 15:9-17

If the early Church had lacked the courage to change and adapt, it is unlikely that it would have spread so rapidly. In accepting Cornelius for Baptism Peter demonstrates that following the prompting of the Spirit means leaving human considerations to one side.

On 1 October 1979 Pope John Paul visited Drogheda. He came to a country rocked by violence, its soil stained with the blood of both Catholic and Protestant. There was little hope for peace. On that occasion the Pope spoke directly to the people of violence, pleading with them in these powerful words: 'On my knees, I beg you to turn away from the path of violence and to return to the ways of peace. You may claim to seek justice, I too believe in justice, and I seek justice. But violence only delays the day of justice'. His voice went unheeded at that time. Yet now we have a peace process with those on the Republican side decommissioning their weapons and those on the Unionist side sharing power with former 'terrorists'. Who could have ever thought it possible? What changes had to come in the human heart to make this happen? Change is torturous and often painful but it is possible.

I was struck by the huge, even seismic shift that the apostolic band had to make to detach themselves from Judaism. Not only that, but to receive non-Jews like Cornelius into the womb of the infant Church must have been humanly difficult. People naturally resist change. The tried and tested paths are the comfort zones of life. Even parishes are slow to change. Time and time again what the former parish priest did is quoted. A problem in the Church today is its unwillingness or inability to change and adapt to the utterly changed circumstances we now find ourselves in. I believe that this reading from the Acts of the Apostles gives us encouragement not to be afraid. It is said that the Church always arrives on the scene 'breathless and late'. This is hardly good enough any more.

In this reading we have human courage aided by the Holy Spirit. Up to this point the gospel has been preached only to Jews, converts to Judaism (proselytes) and Samaritans (who observed the law of Moses). Now God steps in to make it plain that the message is for all people (34-35). He prepares Cornelius, and he prepares Peter. Three times the vision and message come – apparently instructing Peter to break the Jewish food-laws. This must have frightened Peter. How he must have doubted his own discernment to disregard what he was hearing.

But when the men from Cornelius arrive, he is quick to realise the far deeper human implications of his dream. Cornelius, a centurion, was one of those who formed the backbone of the Roman Army. This in itself must have been seen as a stumbling block to Peter. Nevertheless, a second Pentecost – the coming of the Holy Spirit on the Gentiles – follows his teaching. No one could then deny Baptism to those who had received such an obvious mark of God's favour.

Sixth Sunday of Easter

Link In To The Power

Readings: Acts 15:1-2, 22-29; Apoc 21:10-14, 22-23; Jn 14:23-29

Did you know that you have access to the source of spiritual power? You are not alone in the struggle to do good and avoid evil.

We live in the future. The body is in the 'now', but the mind and heart take wings in joyful anticipation, or in expectation of the worst. We circle around what is going to happen; the next holiday, a wedding, a homecoming, a graduation. And then the dread! A loved one dying, death itself, a potential business failure, loss of a job, falling out of love. Like greyhounds in traps we are straining to be released into the future. Who isn't looking forward to a summer holiday? Here is Jesus promising that there is more to come: 'The Advocate or helper, the Holy Spirit whom the Father will send in my name will teach you everything'. What are we to look forward to?

When speaking about the coming of the Holy Spirit Jesus said to his disciples, 'Go into Jerusalem and wait for the promise of the Father and you shall receive POWER from on high.' I suppose most of us experience a sense of powerlessness over our own lives, especially when it comes to doing good or avoiding evil. But we are not powerless. The life of Jesus demonstrated the power of the Holy Spirit.

This power had been active and evident in his Jesus' life. The Holy Spirit descended upon him at his Baptism in the river Jordan. He was led by the Spirit into the desert where he was tempted by the devil. And at the beginning of his public life Jesus declared that he would carry his mission out through the power of the Spirit. John the Baptist declared that Jesus would baptise people with the Holy Spirit. And Jesus himself promised his disciples that after he had left them he would send the Holy Spirit to be with them all the time. It is a matter of faith that the power of the Spirit is available to you and me every day. I can be different. I can change. I can be a new person. Not through will-power alone, but through the power of the Holy Spirit. That is the promise of today's Gospel. How often do I ask for that power? How often do I experience it?

> Come Holy Spirit
> fill the hearts of the faithful
> and enkindle in them
> the fire of your divine love.

The Gospel today prompts us to look forward to the feast of Pentecost and to a new outpouring of the Holy Spirit. Jesus speaks of his ally, the Holy Spirit, and says two basic things about him.

Firstly, the Holy Spirit will teach us all things. To the end of the day the Christian must be a learner, for to the end of the day the Holy Spirit will be leading the Christian deeper and deeper into the truth of God. There is never any excuse in the Christian faith for the shut mind. Christians who feel that they have nothing more to learn are Christians who have not even begun to understand what the doctrine of the Holy Spirit means.

Secondly, the Holy Spirit will remind us of what Jesus has said. This means that in matters of belief, the Holy Spirit is constantly bringing back to us the things Jesus said. We have an obligation to think, but all our conclusions must be tested against the words of Jesus. It is not so much the truth that we have to discover; he told us the truth. What we have to discover is the meaning of that truth. The Holy Spirit saves us from arrogance and error of thought. The Holy Spirit will also keep us right in matters of conduct. Nearly all of us have this sort of experience in life. We are tempted to do something wrong and are on the very brink of doing it, when back into our mind comes a saying of Jesus, the verse of a psalm, the picture of Jesus, words of someone we love and admire, teaching we received when very young. In the moment of danger these things flash unbidden into our minds. That is the work of the Holy Spirit.

Sixth Sunday of Easter

The Glory Of The Final Promise

Readings: Acts 1:1-11; Eph 1:1-17-23; Mt 28:16-20

As Jesus is about to leave this earth, he gives his final mandate to his apostles and to us!

> So the eleven disciples went into Galilee, to the mountain where Jesus had instructed them to go. They saw him and worshipped him; but some were a little sceptical and not sure. Jesus came and spoke to them. 'All power,' he said, 'is given to me in heaven and upon earth. Go, therefore, and make all nations my disciples, baptising them in the name of the Father and of the Son and of the Holy Spirit, and teaching them to keep all the commandments I have given you. And, look you, I am with you throughout all days until the end of the world.'

So often we feel powerless, especially in the face of temptation and in times of difficulty and pain. If we are struggling with an addiction, a wrong relationship, or a habit we just don't seem to be able to break, we experience the frustration of powerlessness. Or we want to make Jesus known and loved, but human respect prevents us from speaking of him – even to our friends. Is that because we rely too much on our own power? We can go it alone; or so we think. In relation to the coming of the Holy Spirit Jesus promised the apostles that they would 'receive power from on high'. Again, that promise is being made implicitly when he says, 'All power is given to me in heaven and on earth. Go, therefore. . . .' The truth is that we do not have to rely on our own power.

We are in the midst of a spiritual warfare but we are not fighting with our hands tied behind our backs. The power of God is with us. Nothing was outside the power of him who had died and conquered death. In today's reading we come to the end of the Gospel story; here we listen to the last words of Jesus to his men. It is a poignant moment; full of sadness but full of hope. Jesus gave them the great commission: they were to go out and make all the world his disciples. It may well be that the instruction to baptise is a development of the actual words of Jesus. That may be argued about; the salient fact remains that the commission of Jesus is to win all people for himself. This mandate is for you and me, who share in the priesthood of Christ through our Baptism and Confirmation. We are all being asked to bring others to the knowledge and love of Christ.

There are times when the love of Jesus is obscured by the Church, with its controversies and its many failings. But religion is a relationship. It is a relationship with the God who loves us. The Church exists for one purpose only – to know God and to make God known. The Church is there to help us to know God and to inspire us to bring others to God's love. Jesus also promised them a presence. It must have been a staggering thing for eleven humble Galileans to be sent forth to the conquest of the world! Even as they heard it, their hearts must have failed them. But, no sooner was the command given, than the promise followed. They were sent out – as we are – on the greatest task in history, but with them there was the greatest presence and power in heaven and on earth. He would be with them, no matter what. Jesus is with us. He dwells within us. That is our strength.

Ascension of the Lord

If The News Is 'Good' Why Don't We Share It?

Readings: Acts 1:1-11; Eph 1:17-23; Mk 16:15-20

The courage to witness to our faith, and to the person of Jesus, is an integral part of what it means to be a Christian.

I can recall reading a description of how a young Catholic student of Notre Dame University, Indiana, by the name of Patti Mansfield became involved in the Charismatic Renewal. She and a number of student companions decided to go on a weekend retreat. This wasn't unusual and they weren't expecting anything significant to happen. But something extraordinary did happen! During the retreat most of the participants were touched by God in a deeply moving way. They experienced a new outpouring of the Holy Spirit. The scriptures became alive for them and they began to experience the Gifts of the Spirit, including the gift of tongues. Patti said that herself and her companions had 'news too good to keep'. From then on the desire of her life was to make God, and his love, known to all those with whom she came into contact. Patti, now in her fifties, is still witnessing to the power and love of God.

Today information can be transmitted with ease from even the most inaccessible parts of the globe. It wasn't always that way. At the time of the Roman Empire, when Jesus lived, the task of bringing back the good news of victory in battle to the home city was assigned to a slave. As a reward for undertaking what was frequently a perilous journey the slave was given his freedom. The bearer of the good news of victory thus became a free person. This is where the whole notion of 'evangelisation' comes from. An evangelist is the bearer of good news

– the good news of Jesus Christ, who has set us free through his passion, death and resurrection. Jesus called on people 'to go out to the whole world; proclaim the good news to all creation....' He was calling on them to be evangelists – bearers of good news to the world.

We have recently celebrated the twenty-fifth anniversary of the encyclical *Evangelii Nuntiandi* of Pope Paul the VI. In that document he said some direct and startling things. He claimed that the proof that we are in a relationship with Jesus, that our own conversions are authentic, is that we become bearers of the good news to others. 'Finally, the person who has been evangelised becomes himself an evangeliser. This is the proof, the test of the genuineness of his own conversion. It is inconceivable that a man who has received the word and surrendered himself to the kingdom should not himself become a witness and proclaimer of the truth.'

The way I see it is this: through our Baptism we share in the priesthood of Christ; this means, by saying yes to our Baptism, we also say yes to bringing God to people and people to God – that is the function of a priest. The Pope talks about evangelisation as 'a duty which will rebound to the benefit, not only of the Christian community, but of the whole human race'. Baptism imposes duties, one of which is to proclaim Jesus.

How is it that secular forces are continually gaining ground? Perhaps it is because the lives of Christians do not reflect the joy of the Lord. Do people ask themselves of Christians, 'Why are these people different?' Can they see the fruit of our relationship with Jesus in our lives? I can recall a song of the Beatles that went 'Let me introduce you to a friend'. Evangelisation is introducing people to our friend, who is Jesus. There are many ways whereby we can make the love of God known: by not being afraid to witness – to defend the truth and live it in our lives; by entering into and playing a full part in the community of the Church of which we are members; by actively engaging in apostolic work and making God known – through teaching, music, street theatre, retreats and so on. The way may be different according to personality, charism and opportunity.

Ascension of the Lord

What About Those Who Have Left?

Readings: Acts 1:1-11; Eph 1:17-23; Lk 24:46-53

Over the last two decades many people have quietly left the practice of the faith. Could it be that going to church wasn't a life-giving experience for them?

When I heard that 'young people had lost the vocabulary and language of faith' I knew we had a crisis. Fr David Tuohy, SJ, a lecturer in UCG, did a year-long survey of young people between the ages of eighteen and twenty-five and this was the finding that most surprised me. Words that I take for granted, like sanctifying grace, salvation, redemption, liturgy, evangelisation, mean little or nothing to young people. There would be a greater possibility of being understood speaking Swahili in Red Square than using this type of religious language with young people today. If we are transmitting on a different wavelength, what possibility is there that we will be received? Is it any wonder that so many young people say Mass is boring? If the language we use is 'churchy' or 'super-spiritual' it is highly unlikely that it will be understood. We might be better going back to the Latin Mass – at least it had the aura of mystery about it! Maybe it's not their fault but ours! Jesus said to his disciples and to us, 'You shall be my witnesses.' Have we fallen down in the way we have witnesses to the faith by word and example?

In another life I frequently received phone calls enquiring as to how an individual might leave the church. It wasn't enough to stop practising, they were looking for a more formal process! People do alienate themselves, they exclude themselves, they no longer want to be counted in the official parish body or to be considered as members of the congregation. However, most people just lapse. This is a case of not fulfilling the obligations that Church membership requires. Someone has said this is not so much a question of losing the faith as of losing the parents' faith. Everyone needs to create their own faith. Attempts have been made to invite people back. But back to what? If they come back, will they find the life that Jesus promised – 'I came that you might have life'? The more the parish community is a life-giving community, the more people will find the urge to return.

Ascension of the Lord

Prayer – Who Am I Lord And Who Are You?

Readings: Acts 1:12-14; 1 Pet 4:13-16; Jn 17:1-11

Many books have been published on prayer. The stumbling prayer of the half-believer must be music in the ears of God.

I have been amazed that people who claim no longer to believe in God still use God's name. It still surprises me that the name of Jesus continues to be used as a profanity in a post-Christian era. It has been said that 'there are no atheists in foxholes'. The author Brendan Behan described himself as 'a daytime atheist'. I think of the struggle of the whiskey priest in Graham Green's *The Power and the Glory,* as he attempted to make his final confession to himself and to God. 'What an impossible fellow I am, he thought, and how useless. I have done nothing for anybody. I might just as well have never lived . . . he felt only an immense disappointment because he had to go to God empty-handed, with nothing done at all.' I cannot help believing that deep within the human person there is a longing to be in touch with the transcendent without knowing the 'who' or 'what' of it. When I think of prayer, the first prayer of St Francis comes to mind: 'Who am I Lord and who are you?' I remember the simplicity of what St Teresa said: 'I just do what children have to do before they learn to read; I tell God what I want quite simply without any splendid turns of phrase, and somehow he always manages to understand me'. I have read many fine books on prayer and I have studied methods of prayer, but I wonder if prayer isn't a struggle to reach beyond experience to that Somebody or Something who has life and death in his hands. Here in today's Gospel we have the priestly prayer of Jesus. Perhaps this Sunday is an opportune time to speak about prayer.

I suppose there will be no prayer in a person's life unless one experiences a need to pray. Somehow prayer begins with a hunger or a longing to reach out beyond myself to the one I call God. Prayer begins with the desire to get in touch with God. This may only arise, in the beginning, at particular times and moments – times of trouble and pain are the most usual. We ought to act on these promptings and, like St Teresa, 'tell God what I want'.

God speaks to us in all sorts of ways. He speaks to us through the Bible, through nature, through the Church. He also speaks to us through the circumstances of our daily lives. For the ordinary person, that is where they are most likely to hear the voice of God. Everything that happens to us, good or bad, is self-revelatory. It tells us something about ourselves. It is in ordinary events of life, like an argument, an anniversary, a disappointment, a friendship, that God will speak to us. 'What are you saying to me through this incident or happening?' I ask, continuing 'Show me what it reveals to me about myself'. When we look at the events of life through the eyes of God we look at things from a different perspective. The futile alternative is to play and replay these events, an activity that often reinforces prejudices, fears and dislikes.

Others have found the 'Jesus Prayer' both profound and simple at the same time. I like it because at each saying the emphasis can be put on a different word or phrase, thereby encompassing a breath of Christian vision that cannot be grasped by quickly saying the prayer over and over. 'Lord Jesus Christ, – Son of the living God, – have mercy on me, – a sinner.' All this is personal prayer. The prayer of the Body of Christ, the Church, in the Eucharistic sacrifice is the supreme prayer because it is the prayer of Jesus.

Seventh Sunday of Easter

Idolatry Gets In The Way Of Love

Readings: Acts 1:15-17, 20-26; 1 Jn 4:11-16; Jn 17:11-19

It was in the South Bronx that I saw unselfish love in action. The idols that we have in our lives are often obstacles to love.

There are some people who believe with absolute certainty. For them dogma has been 'idolised'. Idolatry makes love impossible. It is safer to love an idol than a real person who is capable of surprising you, loving you, even changing you. Our Church comes across as unloving and lacking in compassion. In our defence of dogma we are seen as staunch and uncompromising. Perhaps we have lost the flexibility to love? When people are appointed to leadership positions in the Church they must adopt a 'persona' that is often at variance with the real person. They, in a sense, must become idolaters.

It's not just Churches that practise a form of idolatry. Many years ago a very distraught person, we will call her Mary, came to me for help. She was imprisoned in the 'idolatry' of a jealous husband. He met her off the bus from work every day. He insisted on accompanying her on every shopping trip. Every phone call was followed by enquiries as to the caller. Even visits to her family were monitored. He wanted to possess her. She was 'his' wife. Real love needs space to grow. It seems that many men and some women cannot give up the illusion of possessing another person. The 'idol' becomes more important, more potent, than the actual living creature.

The second reading today is about love – a most confused word. Some time ago I read the report of a rape trial in the newspaper. I was horrified to see the action of an accused rapist described as 'making love'. Marriages break up because couples buy into, unwittingly, an ersatz version of love. This is a love that promises self-fulfilment to the nth degree. No one person can completely fulfil the needs of another so completely that nothing else is lacking. I recall visiting a married couple, very good friends of mine, whom I assumed had a very happy marriage. In the course of conversation the woman told me how desperately lonely she was. Her husband's job demanded a lot of international travel, which meant she was at home alone for long periods. This was her 'unfilled' space, which he was unable to fill. Other couples, with the hectic lifestyle of today, drift into the unhappiness of a 'married single' lifestyle. They discover, hopefully not too late, that their needs are unfilled.

Love is a stance towards life. It is a way of being that is open, always conscious of the 'other'. Love is not a feeling, it is a decision. I can recall staying for a few days in the South Bronx in New York with a new Order of Augustinian Friars. This was the truly depressed area so vividly illustrated by Tom Wolfe in *Bonfire of the Vanities*. Fat, overfed rodents scampered over the derelict sites. Burnt-out cars and debris scatted the area. A pall of hopelessness hung in the air. The Brothers ran two soup kitchens, one for men and another for women. The flotsam of society came to be fed. It is in a place like this that you see, touch and feel love. Those who are in need are rightly treated as equals. They are given their dignity as sons and daughters of the Father. It is here that one can apply the words 'greater love than this no man hath than he should lay down his life for his friends'. This is a love that begins with a 'you'. This is giving where there is unlikely to be any return. This is unselfish love.

Seventh Sunday of Easter

Dead Man Walking

Readings: Acts 15:1-2, 22-29; Apoc 21:10-14, 22-23; Jn 14:23-29

The Holy Spirit is described as an 'Advocate'. It is he who helps, consoles and supports us. In human terms the example of Sr Helen Prejean, on whom the film Dead Man Walking *was based, is the best example of an effective advocate.*

Sr Helen Prejean was the Sister around whom the very successful film *Dead Man Walking* was made. It focused on her relationship with a man on Death Row who was preparing for the climax of his life in the electric chair. She remembers: 'I said to Pat, "I will be there with you. I cannot bear the thought that you would face death without seeing at least one loving face." I remembered the crucifixion of Jesus, and the women who were there. Not that this criminal was Jesus – not that he was innocent. But the most profound moral question of our violent society is not what to do with the innocent, but what to do about the guilty. We ask, "Don't they deserve to die?" But the real question should be, "Do we deserve to kill them?" '

In a talk some years after the film she said: 'I come to you from Louisiana, as one who has been into the valley of death and accompanied three people to execution and watched them die in the electric chair. I come to you as one who has accompanied murder victims' families in their sorrow and their grief. I come to you as one who has spoken with and counselled prison officials whose job it is to kill their fellow human being. I come to you as one who has confronted governors and heads of departments of correction, legislators and others who in the halls and assemblies of law enact legalised death. I come to you as your sister. I come to you as one who is alive and shining with hope that in our country violence does not have to be the way'.

I am using this story today to focus on the Holy Spirit as Advocate. A forgotten quality of the Third Person of the Blessed Trinity. Life is invariably a struggle. It has its highs and lows. During life we frequently experience a sense of need. Being alone without help and guidance is an empty place to be. But we do have help. The Holy Spirit is our Advocate, our Helper, and our Guide. Sr Helen Prejean, in a human sense, best illustrates what being a helper, an advocate, means.

Those who slip through the net are accompanied by a sense of hopelessness and helplessness. Rising a little from the pit is too painful to contemplate. Besotted with drugs, alcohol or ill from depression, the journey back again isn't attractive. Recently a man was pulled dead from the River Liffey. No one even claimed his body. He was special to no one. It was only by his spectacles that he was finally identified. These people are God's people. Something can happen.

At the first prayer meeting I ever attended, a passage from Ezekiel 37 was read. The dry bones in the desert were described as lifeless, scattered, and bleached by the sun – without hope. 'Son of Man, can these bones live?' was the question. Then the Lord spoke to the bones: 'I will cause breath to enter you, and you shall live. I will lay sinews upon you and cover your skin and put breath in you, and you shall live; and you shall know that I am the Lord'. What is the Spirit but the breath of God? I have seen it happen.

On one occasion I was walking up Abbey Street when I saw a young man approaching me. He had a Walkman glued to his head. He was smartly dressed. His distinguishing feature was his smile. He kept looking at me and smiling. 'Do I know this man?' I asked myself. I stopped him and asked, 'Do I know you?' 'You mean you don't recognse me! Do you not remember I used to sleep in the church porch at night? Up to my eyeballs in drugs, I was.' Then I recognised the face – now transformed. 'I'm clean,' he said with triumph. A 'dead bone' brought to life again by the breath of the Spirit. God can and does do wonderful things.

Seventh Sunday of Easter

The Feast Of Pentecost

Readings: Acts 2:1-11; 1 Cor 12:3-7, 12-13; Jn 20:19-23

Evangelisation is the primary responsibility of the Church. The message of Jesus spread throughout the world only because a small group of people responded to the power of the Holy Spirit with enthusiasm and generosity.

Douglas Hyde, a lapsed Catholic, in his book entitled *Dedication and Leadership*, recalled how, when he joined the Communist Party in the early 1940s, he was sent to sell the communist newspaper, *The Daily Worker*, on the street corners of Liverpool. 'Here I was,' he recalled, 'endangering my life for a cause I had learned to believe in, whereas when I was a Catholic I had never been asked to do more than move the chairs in the village hall for "Father"!' In the Gospel today the apostles, new recruits, if you like, are being told by Jesus, 'As the Father has sent me so am I sending you'. Like the communists of Douglas Hyde's time they are being given the toughest assignment.

Jesus had come to redeem us through his death. He had come with a message for all people and now he had gone back to his Father. He relied upon the infant Church to spread his message. The Church was to be a mouth to speak for Jesus, feet to run his errands, hands to do his work. Today, Jesus is dependent on you and me. The gospel of love may never be heard unless I am willing to bring it to the market-place. This is my vocation. Of course, I will not be entirely alone. God's grace and power will be with me. I can recall going on 'Peregrinatio pro Christo' with the Legion of Mary over forty years ago. We undertook difficult assignments to make Jesus known and loved. One of the first assignments I got was in Soho in London. In those days Soho was a warren of strip joints, pornography shops, restaurants and outdoor markets. It was a difficult assignment and it was only the prayer beforehand in St Patrick's Church on Soho Square that made it possible. We felt that all evangelisation began with personal contact.

> You asked for my hands
> That you might use them for your purpose.
> I gave them for a moment, then withdrew them
> For the work was hard.
> You asked for my eyes
> To see the pain of poverty.
> I closed them for I did not want to see.

People who are to be sent out need someone to send them; they need a message to take; they need a power and an authority to back their message; they need someone to whom they may turn when they are in doubt and in difficulty. Without Jesus, the Church has no message, no power, no support. As a baptised person, Douglas Hyde already had a mandate, but like so many other people then, and today, the obligation and responsibility to make Jesus known and loved was not consciously recognised.

Jesus breathed on his disciples and gave them the Holy Spirit. There is no doubt that, when John wrote in this way, he was thinking back to the old story of the creation of humankind: 'And the Lord God formed man of dust from the ground, and breathed into his nostrils the breath of life; and man became a living being'. This was the same picture as Ezekiel saw in the valley of dead, dry bones, when he heard God say to the wind: 'Come from the four winds, O breath, and breathe upon these slain that they may live'. The coming of the Holy Spirit is like the wakening of life from the dead. When the Holy Spirit comes upon the Church she is recreated for her task. The Church must never be out to propagate her message, or to follow man-made policies; she must be out to follow the will of Christ. The Church fails whenever she tries to solve some problem in her own wisdom and strength, and leaves out of account the will and guidance of Jesus Christ.

The Holy Spirit

Readings: Acts 2:1-11; Gal 5:16-25; Jn 15:26-27, 16:12-15

The Holy Spirit is a spirit of power. We know him through the effects he accomplishes in our lives and in the world.

The language of faith for many young people is a foreign language. So, such words as redemption, grace, salvation, mortal and venial sin, and indeed the word 'spirit' as referring to the Holy Spirit, are incomprehensible to many, some of whom will be sitting in the pews this morning.

I have been asked on occasions, 'Do you believe in ghosts?' I went to a boarding school where, even in my adolescence, nearly fifty years ago, there was a strong belief that a former owner of the old castle still appeared yearly, mounted and in full armour. It was said that the horses' hooves could be heard quite clearly on the cobbled stable yard. I never met anyone who had seen this ghost. In the dictionary an alternative word for 'spirit' is 'ghost'.

This school was run by Jesuit priests. The school year was punctuated by longed-for feast days. For us youngsters this meant no class, a film in the evening, and a good meal. So St Francis Xavier, St Aloysius Gonzaga and St Ignatius of Loyola were names we remembered. They conjured up the spirit of the Jesuit Order. It was a spirit we imbibed unconsciously. It was a spirit that led men into arid deserts, lush rainforests, noisy cities, because they believed that they had 'news too good to keep', news about Jesus. A spirit in this sense is intangible, unseen but absolutely real.

This school has had many successes on the football field in recent years. At a cup match I overheard a spectator saying 'that team has great spirit'. And indeed it had. Every round of the cup they grabbed victory from what looked like inevitable defeat. Again this team spirit is unclassifiable but it is real. It is seen only in its effects. What I am trying to say is that we cannot see, touch or feel this thing called 'spirit' but we can know about it through its effects. Jesus had promised to send 'the Spirit' and he called it a 'spirit of power'. And that is what we see. A transformed group, once clinging together, fearful and timid, now courageous, articulate, strong, people of action. Something extraordinary had happened. What was it?

The Holy Spirit is more than a spirit, he is a Person. The Third Person of the Trinity who enables people to reach out beyond themselves. The Spirit is that power that cures the inner soul of sickness, that motivates the weak to sainthood, that empowers parents in their stewardship of their children, and helps us to reach out to achieve greatness in our service of God and human beings. Even Jesus spoke of the Spirit as the source of what he said and did: 'The Spirit of the Lord has been given to me, for he has anointed me. He has sent me to bring the good news to the poor. . . .'(Luke 14:18) Besides being a spirit of power, the Holy Spirit is also the spirit of love. The Trinity is a community of love. We pray today:

> Heal our wounds,
> our strength renew,
> on our dryness pour thy dew,
> wash the stains of guilt away.
>
> Bend the stubborn heart and will,
> melt the frozen, warm the chill.
> Guide the steps that go astray.

The acts we implore the Spirit to do for us are acts of love and compassion.

Hurricane Andrew

Readings: Acts 2:1-11; Rom 8:8-17; Jn 14:15-16, 23-26

How is it that the Holy Spirit worked so powerfully in the early Church? Do we have any expectation or faith that the Spirit will pour out his gifts in the Christian community?

Andrew, a simple name for people to curse, fear, blame and remember. Andrew proved a most powerful, if petulant, child. The hurricane rampaged across the Bahamas and the populous tip of southern Florida and into Louisiana's Cajun country. It had enough strength and power to throw trucks on to the top of buildings, destroy houses and vaporise mobile homes. It impaled yachts on pier palings and even stripped paint off walls! With winds of up to 164 m.p.h., in 1992 Andrew proved to be one of the costliest natural disasters in American history. There was another wind that hasn't abated in over 2,000 years. 'And suddenly there came from the sky a noise like a strong driving wind, and it filled the entire house.' What sort of wind was this?

Dorothy Ranaghan, in the book *As the Spirit Leads Us*, speaks of the powers of the Spirit unleashed in the charismatic renewal sweeping through the Catholic Church: 'I think the Spirit of the New Testament is like a spirit of enthusiasm, the spirit we get to accomplish any kind of task or project. It's like when we speak of "spirit" in a pep talk for a football game, that's the kind of spirit that accompanies us as Christians. We find joy in and through each other and that spills over into what we do'. This vision of the Spirit is psychological rather than a theological or spiritual reality.

The powers of the living God, the breath of the divine union of the three Persons who form the Godhead, possess us: we do not possess them. On this day we have to ask ourselves: Is the Holy Spirit the moving force behind our Christian lives? Is the Holy Spirit the only source of life and power on our Christian journey? Is the Holy Spirit a person who lives, acts and has characteristics that are recognisable?

In one of his post-resurrection appearances Jesus asked his disciples not to depart from Jerusalem, but to wait for the promise of the Father which, he said, 'you have heard from me, for John baptised with water, but before many days you shall be baptised with the Holy Spirit'. On another occasion he said, 'I will ask the Father, and he will give you another Counsellor, to be with you forever, even the Spirit of truth'. Finally he told them to go into Jerusalem and wait for the promise of the Father and 'you shall receive power from on high'.

How is it that so few Christians seem to experience the power of the Holy Spirit in their lives? I have met many people who are struggling joylessly on the Christian journey. There is staleness in their relationship with God. Where are the signs and wonders that characterised the early Christian community? Can the Acts of the Apostles come alive again?

The words that come to me as I write this are – hunger and expectation. Have we a hunger for God in our hearts? God is the only one who will fill my deepest longing. We cannot manipulate the Spirit into our lives like a puppeteer. The Spirit comes to an emptying heart being readied to receive him. The second thing is expectation, that is, expectant faith. God will and can act. I can recall on a number of occasions in the sacrament of Reconciliation giving personal advice to people. I had a sort of out-of-body experience and found myself saying, 'This isn't you, Martin Tierney, you are speaking a truth way beyond your competence or knowledge.' I was. But I had a conviction that what was happening was that the Holy Spirit was anointing me, for that occasion, with the gift of wisdom. I had similar experiences when I received a charismatic insight into the life of the person whom I was helping. Again, I felt that the gift of knowledge was operating through the Spirit within me. There are times when we have to claim the promises of Christ. There are other times when the Holy Spirit will distribute his gifts for the up-building of the community.

Ordinary Time

Secularising The Sacred

Readings: Isa 49:3, 5-6; 1 Cor 1:1-3; Jn 1:29-34

Worldwide, different cultures and nationalities have rites of initiation. Through Baptism we become members of the family of God and share in God's life.

The Hopi indians live in the American southwest. Today, as in former times, a Hopi baby's grandmother on its father's side leads the preparations for the newborn child's 'naming'. Members of the tribe come from all over to participate in the ceremony. This is a very important event, which is held twenty days after the birth of the baby. Until then the baby has no name. Before dawn on the naming day, the baby receives its name in a ceremony at which the father sees his new child for the first time. Then, as the sun rises, the mother and the father's mother present the baby to the sun and repeat its new name. Among the Cherokee, the number seven is sacred. Therefore, on a Cherokee baby's seventh day of life, traditionalists in the tribe still take him or her to Long Man. There the medicine person prays for the baby while holding the newborn over the water. The baby is offered to the water seven times but does not touch it until the mother wets her fingers and gently places them on the baby. Such ceremonies are common to different cultures and tribes worldwide. Why is it then that Baptism, the sacrament of new life, is losing its meaning?

We are in a process where the sacred is being secularised. What were formerly rites of passage, with a deeply religious significance, are becoming occasions for purely secular celebrations prefaced by a religious ceremony, clearly of less significance. As the spiritual dimension and meaning become clouded the profane takes over. As the extravagance of First Communion and Confirmation celebrations increases, the spiritual meaning of these important rites of initiation decreases. Last week we had John the Baptist; today might be an opportunity for a fuller explanation of the sacrament of Baptism.

Baptism is a rebirth; a being born again. Through my birth to Joan and Martin Tierney I became a Tierney and will always remain one! Shortly after that happened I was brought to University Church in St Stephen's Green, Dublin and I was born into another family – the family of God, the community that is the Church. I remain a member of both families until death. In Baptism I was marked with the sign of Christ. That mark remains with me until the end. In this new family I have brothers and sisters to help me along the way. We acknowledge a common father when we say together 'Our Father...' Just as my mother and father helped me to grow physically and emotionally, my new family will help me to grow throughout my life by other milestones where Christ will touch me – Holy Communion, reconciliation, marriage, etc.

The priest baptises 'in the name of the Father and of the Son and of the Holy Spirit'. In the same way he absolves 'in the name of the Father and of the Son and of the Holy Spirit'. He is not forgiving in his own personal name no more than he is baptising in his own personal name. It is in the power of the Trinity that he acts. Indeed, every sacrament is an act of Christ. Just as a criminal is arrested 'in the name of the law' or one is decorated 'in the name of Her Majesty's Government', so in the case of Baptism 'in the name of...' has a special significance. One is introduced into the life of the Trinity, sharing the life of God, through Baptism. Grace is God's life in us.

How many parents, themselves baptised, ask Baptism for their child because it is the custom; because at any rate it will not do any harm; because it may even bring good luck; because if he or she were not baptised it might complicate things when the child came to be married; because it would please the grandparents; because it is a nice opportunity for a family celebration? Baptism is not a gesture, it is the beginning of a faith journey.

The First Disciples

Second Sunday in Ordinary Time

Readings: Sam 3:3-10; 1 Cor 6:13-15, 17-20; Jn 1:35-42

Many people today are seeking a meaning to life. This was the position of the people in today's Gospel. 'To seek truth with a sincere heart' is a lifelong pilgrimage.

There is a frantic search for meaning in the world today. The fastest-growing section in most bookstores is the New Age or Mind, Body, Spirit section. Our retreat houses are filled with groups searching for a philosophy of life, usually one not based on the Christian tradition. To have come from the 'wisdom of the East' appears to be a guarantee of a gilt-edged product! The pace of change and the cultural shift in ways of behaving and acting has, understandably, created a climate of confusion. This Gospel story illustrates the theme of seeking.

Jesus began by asking these two men the most fundamental question in life: 'What are you looking for?' It was very relevant to ask that question in Palestine in the time of Jesus. Were they legalists, looking only for subtle and recondite conversations about the little details of the Law, like the scribes and Pharisees? Were they ambitious time-servers looking for position and power like the Sadducees? Were they nationalists looking for a political demagogue and a military commander who would smash the occupying power of Rome like the Zealots? Were they humble men of prayer looking for God and for his will, like the Quiet in the Land? Or were they simply puzzled, bewildered, sinful men looking for light on the road of life and forgiveness from God?

My experience has been that people who join cults or new religious groups are essentially 'seekers', good people searching for meaning and direction in their lives. They find the traditional mainline Christian denominations unconvincing. Despite this, the person who is 'seeking the truth with a sincere heart' must be pleasing to God. God does not leave a person to search and search until that person finds God; God goes out to meet the person. As Augustine said, we could not even have begun to seek for God unless God had already found us. It is always God who takes the first step.

Every now and again we should ask ourselves: 'What am I looking for? What are my aims and goals? What am I really trying to get out of life?' Some are searching for security – a position that is safe, money enough to meet the needs of life and to put some aside for the time when work is done. This is not a wrong aim, but it is a low aim, and an inadequate thing to which to direct all life; for, in the last analysis, there is no safe security in the chances and the changes of this life.

Some are searching for what they would call a career, for power, prominence, prestige, for a place to fit the talents and the abilities they believe themselves to have. If this be directed by motives of personal ambition it could be a less than noble aim. If it be directed by motives of the service of our fellow human beings it can be a high aim. But it is not enough, for its horizon is limited by time and by the world.

Others are searching for some kind of peace, for something to enable them to live at peace with themselves, with God, and with other people. The answer of John's disciples was that they wished to know where Jesus stayed. They called him 'Rabbi'; that is a Hebrew word that literally means 'My great one'. They wished to linger longer with him and talk out their problems and their troubles. The person who would be Jesus' disciple can never be satisfied with a passing word. This person wants to meet Jesus, not as an acquaintance but as a friend in his own house. Many people who are on a seeking pilgrimage haven't ever entered into a personal relationship with Jesus Christ. They may be abandoning an institution but in doing so they are also abandoning the Person of Jesus. It may be that the Church has been more of an obstacle than a help, particularly to those who don't understand it fully. But religion is primarily a relationship; it is a relationship with Jesus, the compassionate one.

Second Sunday in Ordinary Time

Can This Marriage Be Saved?

Readings: Isa 62:1-5; 1 Cor 12:4-11; Jn 2:1-11

Many people have lost confidence in the possibility of a person remaining faithful for life in marriage and to life-long commitments. The Church teaches that Cana is for ever.

In the 1950s a popular women's magazine ran articles that asked the question, 'Can this marriage be saved?' The answer was usually yes. In those days divorce was looked upon as an undesirable social problem. Now the magazine articles ask, 'Should this marriage be saved?' They incline towards the answer no. People have lost confidence even in the possibility of a man being faithful to a woman for life, and vice versa. This lack of confidence in life-long commitments is not unique to marriage. Since the Second Vatican Council well over 100,000 priests have left the active ministry. Even allowing for the fact that mistakes and wrong decisions are made, the collapse in life-long committed relationships is alarming. The Church teaches that Cana is for ever; that the promises made at marriage are meant to be kept. By and large the world used to agree that this is how it should be.

Marriage is collapsing under the unrealistic expectation that it will always deliver life-long fulfilment to each of the partners. No one person can fulfil all my needs. People today are more tuned in to their own personal needs, sometimes to the exclusion of the needs of 'the other'. The pace of life has meant that there is less time for working couples to give each other the space they need to work on their own relationship. Because of changing gender roles, particularly in the working environment, there is more danger of couples slipping into the 'married single' category, and starting on the slippery slope that leads to division and separation. The decline in religious practice has meant that the motivation provided by faith, and supernatural values, is no longer present. The close-knit family supports that were present in the past are not as strong today.

Broken promises lead to broken hearts, tearing apart husband and wife. The film *Kramer Vs Kramer* illustrated this in one memorable scene. Ted's weeping son admits he feels guilty for having driven his mother away. This unanticipated shock sobers Ted even more, as he consoles his son with an honest confession: 'Mommy left because I tried to make her a certain kind of wife. For so long she tried to make me happy. When she couldn't and tried to talk to me, I was too wrapped up to listen'.

What is missing today is authentic marriage spirituality. Couples of faith will realise that God dwells within the marital union in a unique way. Jesus said that God is love and those who live in love live in God and God lives in them. If God is love, then every act of love, sensitivity, kindness between couples is charged with the goodness of God. Every sacrament is an act of Christ. Where love is present Christ is present. It makes sense then, that those who publicly affirm their exclusive and committed love for one another take this fact seriously. In marriage Christ enters into the human condition and is powerfully present 'in good times and in bad' to both partners. The giving and receiving of love is a sacramental action that happens not once on the day of the marriage but every day as the couple grow together.

Finally, many couples falsely believe that love is a feeling, a warm glow inside that makes them feel good. Feelings are fickle. One day all is right with the world, another day we feel different. An argument, loss of a job, a sick child, difficulty with an in-law drags us down. Feelings are often like a roller-coaster – plenty of highs and lows. A relationship cannot be based on feelings alone although these will help. Something more is needed. Love is a decision. Every morning when I wake up I decide to love my husband/wife although it may cost me a lot. A decision is an act of will and not an emotion. It is more likely to sustain a life-long relationship and really it is simply a daily confirmation of the promises made at the altar on the day of the marriage.

Saints Alive

Readings: Isa 8:23-9:3; 1 Cor 1:10-13,17; Mt 4:12-23

Dorothy Day heard a voice saying 'come follow me'. She gave up everything. She worked tirelessly for the poor and destitute and died without leaving enough money for her burial.

Dorothy Day began her adult life as a communist and ended it as a Catholic influenced by communist ideals. She was born in Brooklyn in 1897, and raised mostly in Chicago. 'I really led a very shiftless life, doing for the first time exactly what I wanted to do.' In 1916 her family moved to New York and she became a regular correspondent for left-wing publications. She got involved in the hot issues of the day: women's rights, free love and birth control. In 1917 she joined pickets in front of the White House in protest against the brutal treatment of women suffragists in jail, and wound up serving thirty days in the workhouse at Occoquan. She had a series of lovers, got pregnant by one, and had an illegal abortion. On the rebound from that affair, she got married; but the marriage lasted only a year. In 1926 Day found herself pregnant again. This time she was determined to have the baby. 'My joy was so great that I sat up in bed in the hospital and wrote an article about my child, wanting to share my joy with the world.' The child's father was a committed atheist, but Day was determined to have her baptised as a Catholic and to become a Catholic herself. It was impossible to do this and have her lover too, so after much heartache she broke up with him one day and was baptised in the Catholic Church the next.

Day opened 'Houses of Hospitality' in the slums of New York and elsewhere, their purpose to house the homeless and feed the hungry. She fought unceasingly for the rights of workers, of the poor, of the destitute, 'the rights of the worthy and the unworthy poor'. As she herself put it 'We can to a certain extent change the world; we can work for the oasis, the little cell of joy and peace in a harried world.'

By the 1960s Day was acclaimed as the 'grand old lady of pacifism' and left-wing Catholics such as Thomas Merton and the brothers Berrigan, as well as scores of young draft-dodgers, sought her out. Dorothy Day died in 1980. After a lifetime of voluntary poverty she left no money for her funeral. It was paid for by the archdiocese of New York.

So it is possible to hear the call of Jesus and respond in the modern world. Dorothy Day is one such wonderful example. God calls everyone to a specific mission. The apostolate may be different for each. But do we hear the call?

There is a story of a child who went up to his rabbi one day and asked, 'Rabbi, how come God doesn't speak to us any more? I mean he spoke through Moses and the prophets. Now he says nothing.' The rabbi took the little boy on his knee and replied, 'My son, today we do not bend down low enough to listen.'

God does speak to us, even through the circumstances of our daily lives. In our pell-mell scramble through life we cannot hear his voice. He is still saying 'Come follow me'.

Third Sunday in Ordinary Time

The Gospel Of Mark

Readings: Jon 3:1-5; 1 Cor 7:29-32; Mk 1:14-20

For most of this year we will be reading the Gospel of Mark, so a few words of introduction might be helpful.

It is generally agreed that Mark's Gospel was the earliest. A close examination of the Gospels of Matthew, Mark and Luke makes it clear that Matthew and Luke had Mark before them as they wrote; and they used his Gospel as the basis into which they fitted the extra material they wished to include. The Gospels of Matthew, Mark and Luke are known as the synoptic Gospels. The word 'synoptic' comes from two Greek words meaning 'to see together'; and these three are so called because they can be set down in parallel columns and their common matter looked at. It would be possible to argue that, of them all, Mark is the most important. It would indeed be possible to go further and to argue that it is the most important book in the world, because it is agreed by nearly everyone that it is the first Life of Jesus that has come down to us. Mark may not have been the first person to write the Life of Jesus. Doubtless there were earlier simple attempts to set down the story of Jesus' life; but Mark's Gospel is certainly the earliest Life of Jesus that has survived. It is short and can easily be read in one sitting.

A continuous read of Mark's Gospel gives a fascinating panorama of the life of Jesus. In considering how the Gospels came to be written, we must try to think ourselves back to a time when there was no such thing as a printed book in all the world. The Gospels were written long before printing had been invented, compiled when every book had to be carefully and laboriously written out by hand. In such circumstances, only a few copies of any book could exist. It is thrilling to remember that when we read Mark's Gospel we are reading the first Life of Jesus, on which all succeeding Lives have necessarily been based.

Who then was this Mark who wrote the Gospel? He was the son of a well-to-do lady of Jerusalem whose name was Mary and whose house was a rallying point and meeting place of the early Church. (Acts 12:12) From the beginning Mark was brought up in the very centre of the Christian fellowship. He was also the nephew of Barnabas, and when Paul and Barnabas set out on their first missionary journey they took Mark with them to be their secretary and attendant. (Acts 12:25) This journey was a most unfortunate one for Mark. When they reached Perga, Paul proposed to strike inland up to the central plateau; and for some reason Mark left the expedition and went home. (Acts 13:13) For some years Mark vanishes from history. Tradition has it that he went down to Egypt and founded the Church of Alexandria there. Whether or not that is true we do not know, but we do know that when Mark re-emerges it is in the most surprising way. We learn that when Paul writes the letter to the Colossians from prison in Rome Mark is there with him (Colossians 4:10). In another prison letter, to Philemon, Paul numbers Mark among his fellow-labourers. (Philemon 24) And when Paul is waiting for death and very near the end, he writes to Timothy, his right-hand man, and says, 'Take Mark and bring him with you; for he is a most useful servant to me.' (2 Timothy 4:11) It is a far cry from the time when Paul contemptuously dismissed Mark as a quitter. Whatever had happened, Mark had redeemed himself. He was the one man Paul wanted at the end.

Poverty And Pain

Readings: Neh 8:2-6, 8-10; 1 Cor 12:12-30; Lk 1:1-4, 4:14-21

Jesus sets forth his priorities in his first public speech in the Temple. It is a big challenge to follow the 'liberation' movement inaugurated by Jesus.

In this century, there are a number of speeches that, because of their inspiring content, deserve to be remembered and passed on to future generations. Martin Luther King delivered such a speech in September 1963 at an enormous civil rights rally in Washington. In the course of this truly inspiring speech he said, 'I have a dream that my four little children will one day live in a nation where they will not be judged by the colour of their skin but by the content of their character. I have a dream today. And if America is to be a great nation, this must become true.' The Kennedy inauguration speech of January 1961 electrified the world. Words often quoted from this speech are: 'Ask not what your country can do for you, but what you can do for your country'. That great orator Winston Churchill gave many famous speeches. One delivered over radio at the height of the Battle of Britain in 1940 contained these memorable words: 'Never in the field of human conflict was so much owed by so many to so few'. The Gospel of today's Mass contain the charter for the public life of Jesus. Here is his inaugural speech, detailing his priorities in an unambiguous fashion. These are the words that should inspire all who follow Jesus.

> He has anointed me to bring the good news to the poor,
> To proclaim liberty to captives,
> Recovery of sight to the blind,

To set prisoners free,
To announce a year of favour from the Lord.

Why haven't these words, so full of promise and hope, been taken seriously in our own time? One schoolboy answered this question like this: 'If I did, most of my friends would reject me, just as many of Jesus' friends rejected him. And I just couldn't take that right now'. Freedom is in the heart. The greatest freedom is the freedom to choose good. Our world enslaves us with perceived needs. There are things we just 'cannot do without', the advertisers tell us. We buy into the myth that happiness lies in a new computer, washing machine, house, or washing powder. The world in which we live encourages insecurity. There is money in this! The future must be provided for. Leave nothing to chance. A creeping fear about the insufficiency of a pension or possible sickness depresses us. We accumulate goods and money with feverishness bordering on panic. Where is God in all this? This is what Jesus came to liberate us from. We are the prisoners that Jesus is speaking about. What has today's Gospel to say to me?

I can recall returning to Paris from India where I had spent some time in Calcutta and Bombay. It was Christmas time. In Paris the shops were bulging with every sort of luxury. The opulence confronted me and left me deeply depressed. I had left a world of nothing to go to a world of plenty, in nine or ten hours. The utter inequality of the global economic system is a scandal. Million die of AIDS in Africa while in the West the best medicines are available, often on a National Health System, free of charge. Why should people be penalised because an accident of birth placed them in Africa or India rather than America or Sweden?

In the face of globalisation a helplessness creeps into the psyche. How can I make a difference? I can only change myself. All change begins with the individual. I can read the charter for the ministry and ask how I can fit into the plan that Jesus inaugurated.

A Place For Everyone

Readings: Zeph 2:3, 3:12-13; 1 Cor 1:26-31; Mt 5:1-12

A beautiful book, The Scattering, *documented the trail of emigrants from Clare over many years, sparking the thought that God has a place for everyone.*

During the Millennium year, a Trust was established in Clare, to document the stories of Clare emigrants from Ireland who were scattered across the globe. It was the brainchild of Ennis businessman Dermot McMahon. One Sunday morning he was walking with his wife Mary on the beach at Fanore in North Clare. With the Atlantic on one side and the stony Burren hills on the other, he was struck by the beauty of it all. He wrote: 'How heartbreaking it must have been for people to have to leave all this behind, crossing the ocean to a strange country to make a new life. The pain of emigration must have been worse than a death in the family'. As I read *The Scattering – Images of Emigrants from an Irish County,* with tear-filled eyes, I thought, God has a place for everyone in this world. There is an old myth that God has cut out a hole in the sky to fit the contours of each person's body. That is our 'resurrection place'. Life is a search for that 'resurrection place'. When the time comes to die, we are meant to be directly under this aperture, specifically our own, that we may be drawn up into that Tír na nÓg, that Nirvana, prepared for us by God from the beginning of time. Many of the people I read about in *The Scattering* seem to have found their resurrection place, the place where God meant them to be.

The Beatitudes represented the promise of God's blessings on the 'poor in spirit', 'those who mourn', 'the meek', 'the hungry and thirsty', 'the merciful and those fighting for justice', 'the clean of heart', 'the persecuted and the insulted', and I saw them all in *The Scattering*.

When we are in that place where God wants us to be there is no such thing as failure. The beauty about *The Scattering* is that none of the people documented would ever have been known without this book. And yet each person, in the anonymity of their lives, is blessed and is blessing others. God takes care of those who encounter the divine and remain faithful to what he has called them to be. We rejoice and are glad in who we are – blessed. This is why the kingdom of heaven can be ours.

The good news is that in God's kingdom all needs are freely and graciously met – the sick are healed, the hungry are fed, the dead are raised.

> I know the plans I have for you – it is the Lord who speaks
> Plans for peace and not disaster.
> Reserving a future full of hope for you.
> When you call me, and come to me and pray to me
> I will listen to you.
> When you seek me you will find me. (Jeremiah 29:11-13)

Fourth Sunday in Ordinary Time

Leadership

Readings: Deut 18:15-20; 1 Cor 7:32-35; Mk 1:21-28

Jesus spoke with authority. Jesus constantly articulated the vision of the 'kingdom'. Many people today lament the lack of leadership in politics, business and especially in the Church.

It was immediately recognised that Jesus was a leader. 'His teaching made a deep impression on them because, unlike the scribes, he taught them with authority.' Many people today lament a lack of good leadership in politics, business and especially in the Church. What is the unique quality of leadership?

A few years ago, passing through a London airport, I bought a copy of the *Economist*. In it was a report of a conference of trustees and managers from more than five hundred of America's more elite institutions, the group of large philanthropic foundations whose purpose is to give away money. The theme of the conference was 'Exploring the many dimensions of leadership'. The conclusion of the conference was startling. There was, they agreed, nothing less than a crisis of leadership in American society; the nation was being guided, not by leaders but by managers, and its condition could be described as being over-managed and underled.

In 1997 the Priests' Council of the Diocese of Dublin, of which I was a member, came to a reasonably similar conclusion. The heart of the problem was leadership. The book *Reading the Signs of the Times* (Veritas) embodied the conclusions of a diocesan survey of the priests, in which it was claimed that 'concern at general Church leadership emerges as a significant source of stress'. And this is confirmed in questions relating to challenges for the future, which emphasise a less hierarchical approach, recommending developing a new system for selecting bishops, the appointment of younger parish priests and greater lay involvement, especially of women.

The first essential characteristic of leaders is that they are going somewhere, in other words, they are aiming at goals or objectives that lie in the future. Typically, a leader will ask 'Where do we see ourselves five/ten years from now?' The words of Jesus give us a pointer: 'He calls his own sheep by name and leads them out'. The leader is in front. Whether it is in a parish, a religious group, a diocese, one needs a vision that is constantly articulated in order to inspire. If leaders are merely reacting to the latest crisis or responding to the present need, they have virtually surrendered leadership.

Effective leadership demands quality communications. If the foot-soldiers have no idea of the plan, the vision or the proposed strategy by which the aims may be achieved, then they lose heart and become demoralised. One cannot be asked to imply or second guess what the leadership strategy is. In other words, one is not imparting the vision. Is it any wonder that insurrectionists first make for the local television or radio station on the occasion of a coup. They know that communication is power. Good communication is pivotal to attaining stated objectives. The words of Jeremiah give us a lead:

> His words in my heart like a fire,
> A fire shut up in my bones
> I am weary of holding it in;
> Indeed I cannot.

Most people are followers. They act most effectively when they are led by a vision. Think of Winston Churchill, elected to lead Britain's wartime government. He promised the people only 'blood, toil, sweat and tears'. The evidence suggests that theologians seldom make good leaders.

To Know God And To Make Him Known

Readings: Jer 1:4, 5, 17-19; 1 Cor 12:31-13:13; Lk 4:21-30

A prophet must swim against the tide, and will encounter opposition, perhaps even suffering. Preachers and prophets are needed so that, as one commentator put it, 'the rumour of God may be kept alive'.

Prophets seldom live in palaces. Few die in their own beds. Some of the prophets of the twentieth century have been people who were willing to bear great suffering to have their message heard. Solzhenitsyn, the great Russian prophet, was imprisoned from 1945 to 1953 for unfavourable comment on Stalin's conduct of the war. He was arrested and exiled in 1974 on the publication of *The Gulag Archipelago*, a factual account of the Stalinist terror. Dietrich Bonhoeffer, a Lutheran pastor and theologian, an opponent of Nazism, was hanged at Flossenburg concentration camp in 1945 on the personal orders of Hitler. Martin Luther King, civil rights campaigner, was assassinated in Memphis in 1968. Oscar Romero, an outspoken critic of the oppressive, American-backed government of El Salvador, was shot down during Mass in 1980, a year after he was nominated for the Nobel Peace Prize. Sheila Cassidy was arrested and tortured in Chile for treating a revolutionary at the time of the Pinochet coup. Hans Küng's questioning of received interpretations of Catholic doctrine led to the removal of his licence to teach as a Catholic theologian in 1987.

Prophets swim against the tide. They engender great passions both for and against. Many are not recognised during their own lifetime. They generally have to accept personal suffering for their beliefs and opinions. They have an interior strength and self-belief that enables them to withstand opposition. Is it any wonder then that Jesus received similar treatment in the synagogue? His words have echoed down the centuries: 'No prophet is accepted in his own native place'.

The job of prophet and preacher is the task of the whole Church. The New Testament declares that we Christians are a chosen race, a royal priesthood . . . a people set apart to sing the praises of God. Each one of us can fulfil this mission according to our own circumstances and ability, but no one is exempt from the call. It derives from our Baptism and is made, as it were, official at our Confirmation. This mission is fulfilled primarily through the witness of Christian living – allowing the influence of the Christian teaching to be seen in our lives and work and attitudes. These words are easy to write, but in the affluent climate in which we live this will demand courage. Proclaiming Jesus will incur the wrath of pundits and commentators. One will be isolated and abandoned. But this is the essential task of the Church. The Church exists in order to evangelise – to know God and to make God known. To be a prophet for the Gospel will appear to be a thankless job. Today's Gospel will be a consolation. Jesus has been there before us. He experienced opposition – 'the people were filled with fury'.

The word 'evangelisation' comes to us from ancient history, when a slave was chosen to bring back to the ruler the good news of victory in battle. The bearer of this good news was always granted his freedom and so he would come running, nearly dancing for joy, as he bore the news that would gain his freedom for him. We will only be prophets and proclaimers of the Gospel if we really believe it is 'good news', news that will set us free.

The Salt Of The Earth

Readings: Isa 58:7-10; 1 Cor 2:1-5; Mt 5:13-16

The Enniskillen bombing was a savage deed that revealed what it really means to be the 'salt of the earth'.

It was 8 November 1987 at 10.43 a.m. A massive bomb exploded in the quiet market town of Enniskillen in County Fermanagh. This was Remembrance Day. A large crowd, including Gordon Wilson, his daughter Marie, and Ronnie Hill, a local schoolmaster, had gone to the town's cenotaph, where there was to be a wreath-laying ceremony. They were remembering the dead of two world wars. They were instantly to become victims of what are euphemistically called in Ireland 'the Troubles'. Gordon Wilson comforted his daughter Marie, a nurse, as she lay dying beneath the rubble. 'I love you very much, Marie' were his last words to her. Ronnie Hill lay beneath the rubble. He would never regain consciousness. For over ten years he lay in a coma, nursed by his beloved wife Noreen, until he breathed his last breath. Gordon Wilson, a local merchant and a Methodist, offered forgiveness to the IRA killers and prayed for them, without bitterness. Noreen Hill, a Protestant, said, 'When people ask me am I full of bitterness and hatred I tell them I never felt those emotions. They were never part of me.' She described how she rushed to the Erne Hospital and the first person she met was Monsignor Seán Cahill. She said, 'I didn't see a cleric or a Catholic, I saw a friend.' Over the succeeding sad years Noreen gave a tremendous witness to Christian fortitude. Gordon spent the rest of his life preaching reconciliation. I listened to his story on tape and the tears welled up in my eyes. The miracle that

God worked in those people was truly remarkable. Quite ordinary people being the 'salt of the earth'.

To be the salt of the earth is to be a life-giving person. 'I came so that you might have life,' said Jesus. That life that Jesus came to give is to be lived and transmitted through those who believe in Jesus. Am I a life-giving person? Are people the better for having met me? How can I be the salt of the earth if I am a garrulous, quarrelsome person? As a Christian I need to choose 'life' every day. If I spread negativity and death rather than life then there are questions I need to ask myself.

When you are next in London, please go to St Paul's Cathedral to gaze on that wonderful painting by William Holman Hunt, entitled *I am the light of the world*. A man stands knocking at an ivy-encrusted door, a lantern in his hand. The lantern is meant to stand for Christ as the source of illumination, according to the biblical metaphor, 'your word is a lamp for my feet, and a light for my path'. Hunt set the scene at night. He explained to a friend that he wanted 'to accentuate the point of its meaning by making it the time of darkness, that brings us to the need of this lantern in Christ's hand. He being the bearer of light to the sinner within, if he will awaken'. The last word alludes to the fact that the door has no handle and therefore can only be opened from the inside. This represents, said Hunt, 'the door of the human heart'. If we are to be the salt of the earth and the light of the world then the door of our heart has to be open to Christ and his healing power. Our hearts can only be opened from the inside!

Fifth Sunday in Ordinary Time

The Healing Power Of Jesus Christ

Readings: Job 7:1-4, 6-7; 1 Cor 9:16-19; Mk 1:29-39

Jesus desires our healing. The healing of sinfulness can lead to healing in other areas of our lives.

Organise a conference, write a book, insert the word 'healing' in the title and you are assured of success! The search for personal healing is global. It crosses religious, political and gender divides. The New Age movement has tapped into an awareness that we are all broken people and to a greater or lesser degree in need of healing. Some blame their mothers, fathers, school teachers, unsatisfactory relationships or traumatic experiences of the past as the cause of their brokenness. The struggle with failing health naturally prompts a search for healing. Counselling is a major growth industry. The 'inner journey' or the quest for self-knowledge is part of the search for healing.

Jesus claimed he came into the world to teach and to heal. 'He healed many who were sick with various diseases, and cast out many demons.' (Mark 1:34) If Jesus is the same yesterday, today and forever, does he still heal? How is it that so many people who look to him for relief, whether physical or mental, do not find it? Or do they? Jesus wasn't a magician. He did not look for any adulation as a consequence of healing people. But he did look for one thing – faith! Over and over again we are told that Jesus said to the person who had been cured, 'Your faith has made you well.' In the case of the paralysed man it was the faith of the community – 'seeing their faith'.

This faith is not the same as subscribing to a creed or a set of doctrines. The sick person has faith when he or she becomes convinced that they can and will be cured. This faith means a conviction that God is good to people and that he can and will triumph over evil. The power of faith is the power of goodness and truth, which is the power of God. It is the opposite of fatalism. Fatalism says 'nothing can be done about it' or 'there is no hope' or 'you must accept reality'. Faith says that Jesus can and will act. The only desire of the heart of Jesus was to liberate people. His motive was compassion. There are basic prayer-ways for healing: prayer for repentance (for personal sin); prayer for inner healing (healing of memories or emotional problems); prayer for physical healing (physical sickness); prayer for deliverance (for demonic oppression).

In the Church every sacrament is an 'act of Christ'. Today we touch the hem of his garment, primarily through the sacraments of healing. The first and deepest kind of healing that Jesus brings is the forgiveness of our sins. Our repentance and God's forgiveness are actively engaged in the sacrament of Reconciliation. I think I am right in saying that the dis-ease caused by our own sinfulness can manifest itself in many ways, including, on occasions, physical symptoms. A healing of sinfulness may lead to healings in other areas of our lives. All the sacraments transmit the life of Jesus to us – we touch him and are changed by the encounter. When we meet Jesus with an open heart we will be healed.

Fifth Sunday in Ordinary Time

They Left Everything

Readings: Isa 6:1-2, 3-8; 1 Cor 15:1-11; Lk 5:1-11

Something deep happened in the heart of Peter in this encounter with Christ. A conversion experience perhaps? The ministry of all Christians is to lead people to Christ – the one who saves.

When I read today's Gospel my thoughts immediately went to that classic of French literature by George Bernanos, *The Diary of a Country Priest*. Although it is at least thirty years since I read the book, one passage has stuck in my memory, perhaps because what I remember is so reminiscent of Ireland today. Bernanos puts these words on the lips of M. le Curé, 'My parish is bored stiff; no other word for it. Like so many others! We can see them being eaten up by boredom, and we can't do anything about it. Perhaps some day we will catch it ourselves – become aware of the cancerous growth within us. You can keep going for a long time with that in you.' These words seemed to be the very antithesis of the response of the disciples to the miraculous draft of fishes and the words of Jesus – 'they left everything and followed him'. This spontaneous reaction of the disciples seems so full of enthusiasm, zeal, courage. How would I have to change to make this happen in my life? In the life of the parish?

There is a movement in the Gospel from the scepticism of Peter, 'Master, we have worked hard all night and have caught nothing. . .', to the enthusiastic initiative of leaving everything and following Jesus. There is also the prayerful confession of Peter, 'Depart from me, Lord, for I am a sinful man'. Are we talking about a deep conversion experience here? Today people do not experience a need to be saved.

Nor do many people admit to or recognise their own sinfulness. If that is true, how can conversion happen? Peter's admission, 'I am a sinful man' and, by implication, his acknowledgement of the need for 'salvation', is the beginning of what it means to be converted anew. I am tired of hearing that people have been sacramentalised but not evangelised. How do we share the faith with others? Here are some structured steps that may be helpful.

1   We have to be willing to meet people and to befriend them. A smile or a simple 'hello' is where it begins. Being friendly and pleasant with people is more important than we may believe.
2   Learning to relate to people means that a confidence can be established that can lead to sharing faith. Take a genuine interest in their lives and their activities.
3   Giving your own personal testimony, or simply saying what faith in Jesus means to you, can be a powerful witness.
4   The core message of Jesus is in the Gospels. Why not either share the Gospel or even buy a copy of a Gospel and give it away?
5   The time may come when a person can be invited to take a step or make a commitment towards accepting Christ in a full and complete way. This involves repentance and prayer.
6   If a person accepts Christ, how is their faith to grow? They need your ongoing support. This could take place within a prayer group.
7   The local Church must accept responsibility for the continuing growth of the new Christian. In the Catholic tradition the sacramental life of the Church will foster growth in holiness.

Just as in today's Gospel, God meets people where they are. Sinfulness isn't a stumbling block to following God's call. If we pay attention to details in this Gospel, we might be caught by surprise. Peter is a simple fisherman. The call comes while he is at work near his boat. This is no holy person in a holy place. This is an ordinary person like us going about his daily business.

The Masks We Wear

Speaks of the law not as an end in itself, but as a way to channel the virtue behind it.

Readings: Eccl 125:15-20; 1 Cor 2:6-10; Mt 5:17-37

but conversion ... love not of conformity in outward way

We relate to the world through our masks. The mask is worn to win acceptance and approval. However, it is the heart that counts. The heart of the problem is the human heart.

We all wear masks to win the approval of others. Early in life we learn that certain kinds of behaviour win the affection and respect of others. We discover, for example, that being angry or sulky wins disapproval. So we tuck the bad stuff away in the subconscious and develop the masks of approval. And hence the mask of the clown, the Mother Superior, the Mr or Mrs Clean, or the 'hale fellow well met' person, are paraded before the world. Our behaviour is often dictated by the masks we wear. Who can expect the car salesperson to drop their mask the minute they leave the salesroom? There are times when we believe and live only through our masks. In recent times we have seen the masks peeled away from public figures like Jeffrey Archer and Jonathan Aitken.

Beneath the mask there is a heart. Someone once said 'the heart of the problem is the human heart'. It is from the heart that all good and evil come. In the Gospel today Jesus tackles this problem by framing the commandments in the context of a new covenant or law inaugurated by himself. This is the law of love. What he reveals in the Gospel today is a 'new way of living, a way of living that comes from the heart.

The first correction to the law concerns love, and in this case Jesus rules out negative expressions of love. The commandments as a rule of

in the. judged not on evil avoided, but on good done.

life demand a high regard for the dignity and value of other people. Murder disregards this but so do all sorts of other actions like losing one's temper, name calling, and a refusal to extend the hand of forgiveness. The importance of forgiveness is shown by the fact that it in a way takes precedence even over strictly religious duties. So in this case the correction that Jesus makes is that one must respect not simply the legal right to live but also those things that help someone to live a full life and one of self-respect.

It is only in recent times that popular magazines have written about recreational sex. With the discovery of new and efficient ways of contraception, sex became disengaged from the procreative act. After the urge for self-preservation, the second strongest instinct in the human person is that of sex. Our sexual instincts have the capacity to run riot. Because the sexual instinct is essentially relational, disordered, it can damage and hurt other people. Jesus knows that and talks about 'adultery of the heart'. He says that the person 'who looks lustfully at a woman has already committed adultery with her in his heart'. As I said above, the heart of the problem is the human heart.

The Church has never accepted self-mutilation as a remedy for sin, particularly not in the case of Origen's self-castration to avoid sexual sins. The third correction simply disallows an abuse that was tolerated by the law, that of remarriage after divorce. Some scripture scholars interpret the phrase of Jesus prohibiting divorce 'except on the grounds of fornication', as in fact meaning 'a marriage prohibited by Jewish laws'. The only divorce permitted is one where there is no real marriage.

Finally, Jesus implies that there should be no real need for oath-taking. A level of trust ought to exist in an environment of openness and mutual confidence. Unfortunately, even the oaths taken in court today mean very little in so far as perjury is not considered with the gravity it deserves. In short, what Jesus teaches by his corrections of the law is merely a matter of honouring to the full the human values that we find it so difficult to honour.

The Extraordinary Compassion of Jesus

Readings: Lev 13:1-2, 44-46; 1 Cor 10:31-11:1; Mk 1:40-45

By his own compassion Jesus willingly put himself outside the pale of the politically correct. The law of love, in the life of Jesus, superseded every other law. Would that it could be the same today.

During our own famine, 'famine fever' was dreaded as much as the hunger itself; it was highly contagious. Fr Peter O'Leary in his book, *Mo Scéal Féin*, describes how even close neighbours wouldn't enter the homes of those suspected of having famine fever. In Carrigaholt parish in County Clare a number of priests died in succession of 'famine fever'. Having the fever meant exclusion and usually death.

In the New Testament there is no disease regarded with more terror and pity than leprosy. When Jesus sent out the Twelve he commanded them, 'Heal the sick, cleanse lepers.' (Matthew 18:8) The fate of the leper was truly hard. There are three kinds of leprosy. There is nodular or tubercular leprosy. It begins with an unaccountable lethargy and pains in the joints. Then there appear on the body, especially on the back, symmetrical discoloured patches. On them little nodules form, at first pink, then turning brown. The skin is thickened. The whole appearance of the face is changed till the person loses their human appearance. The nodules grow larger and larger; they ulcerate and from them comes a foul discharge. The eyebrows fall out; the eyes become staring; the voice becomes hoarse and the breath wheezes because of the ulceration of the vocal cords. The hands and the feet also ulcerate. The average course of the disease is nine years, and it ends in mental decay, coma and ultimately death. Then there is anaesthetic leprosy. The initial stages are the same; but the nerve trunks are also affected. The infected area loses all sensation. As the disease develops, the injury to the nerves causes discoloured patches and blisters. The muscles waste away; the tendons contract until the hands become like claws. There is always disfigurement of the finger nails. There ensues chronic ulceration of the feet and of the hands and then the progressive loss of fingers and of toes, until in the end a whole hand or a whole foot may drop off. The duration of the disease is anywhere from twenty to thirty years. The third and commonest kind of leprosy is a type where nodular and anaesthetic leprosy are mixed. That is leprosy proper, and there is no doubt that there were many lepers of this type in Palestine in the time of Jesus. The term leprosy seems to have been used to include psoriasis, a disease that covers the body with white scales, and which would give rise to the phrase 'a leper as white as snow'.

Any such skin disease rendered the sufferer unclean, and he or she was banished from the village or town or community of people, and obliged to dwell alone outside the camp, go with rent clothes, bared head, a covering upon the upper lip, giving a warning of his or her polluted presence with the cry, 'Unclean, unclean!' We see the same thing in the Middle Ages, which merely applied the Mosaic law.

If ever a leper was cured – and real leprosy was incurable – he or she had to undergo a complicated ceremony of restoration, which is described in Leviticus 14. The person was examined by the priest. Today we have one of the most revealing pictures of Jesus. He did not drive away a man who had broken the law. The leper had no right to speak to him at all, but Jesus met the desperation of human need with an understanding compassion. Jesus stretched out his hand and touched the man who was unclean. To Jesus he was not unclean; he was simply a human soul in desperate need. Having cleansed him, Jesus sent him to fulfil the prescribed ritual. He fulfilled the human law and human righteousness. He did not recklessly defy the conventions, but, when required, submitted to them. Here we see compassion, power and wisdom all conjoined.

A Charter for Healing

Readings: Jer 17:5-8; 1 Cor 15:12, 16-20; Lk 6:17, 20-26

People want to participate in their own healing and well-being. At times, the sacraments may appear like a form of magic – a healing without consent.

How is it that so much of what the Roman Catholic Church teaches is ignored, even by its own members? Doctrinally, the Church is the Body of Christ and the Pope is Christ's Vicar on earth. The Holy Spirit has promised to be 'with it until the end of time'. With credentials like that it is spiritual suicide to ignore what it teaches! Reflecting on the Beatitudes (Be-attitudes) in today's Gospel, I believe there are deeper lessons to learn. Patients, and we are all patients, need to participate in their own healing process. Many people turn to alternative remedial therapies because they no longer want to be 'the heart case in bed fourteen' or 'the patient with the interesting colon in bed ten'. Patients feel uncomfortable when people in white coats, with stethoscopes around their necks, dictate the course of their treatment, frequently without reference to them. Could it be that many sacraments are seen in the same way? Somebody, this time with a Roman collar, doing things to them. Like with the doctor, they are assured that the things being done are good for them and will make them better.

Patients don't want to be cases – they want to be healed. They want to participate in their own well-being or their own death. As much as they want to be well they want peace and understanding. In 1993 I spent three months in Santa Fe, New Mexico, where the Pueblo Indians have their reservations. During the period of Lent they hold special rituals that combine elements of their Native American spirituality and that of the Roman Catholicism brought by the missionaries. Three days are set aside to deal with sin. The elders and the people discern and identify what the sin of the tribe has been over the past year. This is then ritualised. This was the ceremony I was lucky enough to attend. In the village square, surrounded by their adobe houses, everyone assembled – from the youngest child to old grandparents. To the tune of just a single drum they began to dance. Around and around they went. Some took a break and others replaced them. At times the rhythm and tempo of the drumming changed. This ceremony took place over three days. On the final day, at one point the drumming intensified and reached a high-pitched crescendo. Suddenly from the side alleys of the village square, people dressed in evil-looking masks and dark clothing rushed into the centre of the dancing villagers, gesticulating and shouting in high-pitched voices. Some of them had long poles upon which were hunks of raw meat. They ran hither and thither shouting loudly. The villagers joined in. I didn't know what they were saying as everything was in their native language. They had identified gluttony as the sin of the tribe for that year. This was a ceremony of acknowledgement and of purging. All were alive to what was happening. The point I am making is that the whole tribe were participating in the healing process. There was a huge involvement.

I believe that the pastoral strategy of Jesus was to get people to involve themselves in their own spiritual healing process. The Beatitudes are 'be-attitudes' or a way of 'becoming' what God wants people to be. Jesus was setting goals in the blessings and the woes of the Beatitudes of the Gospel. Change may not happen by turning the world upside-down but by knowing that 'blessings' are available. All healing involves a degree of choice. This is what Jesus puts before people today.

Sixth Sunday in Ordinary Time

Exploring The Topic Of Forgiveness

Readings: Isa 43:18-19, 21-22, 24-25; 2 Cor 1:18-22; Mk 2:1-12

In the book, *The Spirituality of Imperfection – Storytelling and the Journey to Wholeness,* the authors Kurtz and Ketcham tell the following story:

'When we spoke a year ago' the interviewer started off, 'you said that you "just couldn't forgive" and you said the same thing just six months ago, when we last spoke. So tell me, what else happened to you during the period of time when somehow you forgave?' Almost inevitably, the response began: 'Oh, nothing special – just the usual,' and then the conversation would run: 'well, yes, but wait a minute – it's not really connected, but I guess I should mention it, especially as it does have to do with forgiving. . . . I got involved in this thing at work, an affair with a guy in the office. I love my husband, this was really just playing around, it wasn't serious and I didn't intend it to last, but well, my husband found out about it, and he was really hurt and really angry. I thought, "there it all goes, I've really blown it". . . . and you know what? I mean, you probably won't believe this, but he forgave me. We were sitting there one night, after the kids were in bed, and I saw this determination on his face, and I figured, "Here it comes – now I hear about divorce lawyer." But instead he came over and put his arms around me and started crying and saying he hurt, but he didn't want to lose me forever, and could we just close the door on that thing at work and try to be lovers ourselves again! Well, I could hardly believe it. But somehow, that how it's been working out. Oh, we still have our ups and

downs and our spats about the kids and all, but hey, we're
making it! and it's so good to know that he loves me even though
I did that, to know that he's forgiven me.'

A former inmate of a Nazi concentration camp was visiting a friend
who had shared the ordeal with him. 'Have you forgiven the Nazis?' he
asked his friend. 'Yes.' 'Well, I haven't. I'm still consumed with hatred
for them.' 'In that case,' said his friend gently, 'they still have you in
prison.'

The human experience of forgiveness is so liberating. But what does
it mean? How is it done? I believe forgiveness and reconciliation are
rooted in relationships of love. In the story above the woman says 'I
love my husband'. The wounded husband says 'Can we try to be lovers
again?' The reconciliation is joyful, healing and complete because
neither husband nor wife want to lose the great love they have for one
another. If we could fathom the depth of the love of God for us we
would never want to lose it. Sin, forgiveness and reconciliation need to
be preceded by some appreciation of love – the love of God.

When you hurt someone you love, the pain can spiral out of
control. The story of the hurt is played and replayed in the mind.
Forgiveness and reconciliation are longed for. Perhaps people no longer
go to the sacrament of Reconciliation because they haven't appreciated
the love of the infinite God. They haven't experienced the pain of a
broken relationship with the One who always loves, no matter what.
Because the relationship isn't real in the person's life, the pain of sin is
not felt deeply enough to seek forgiveness and reconciliation.

Many people are talking about the Church saying 'sorry' for its past
sinfulness. Sorry isn't enough. Without love, sorry is only a word. How
can we say 'sorry' without passionately loving those whom we have
hurt. Can we tell them we love them? Even if they are demanding
compensation and redress? Can we say 'sorry' against all the advice of
lawyers and other legal eagles? Can we say sorry because it is only in
reconciliation that freedom can be found?

Sickness

Readings: Isa 43:18-19, 21-22, 24-25; 2 Cor 1:18-22; Mk 2:1-12

To be sick is to be debilitated. It stifles creativity and initiative. Jesus loved the sick. They were special to him. Sickness will always be with us as it was in the time of Jesus.

Health can be so central to happiness. I have seen many forms of sickness over the years. I can recall praying with a man, for a number of years, who was suffering terribly from depression. His suffering was deep and persistent. On one occasion I visited a convent in Indonesia and was asked to pray for a former Superior who was tortured with scruples. By all accounts she had been a remarkable woman. She had initiated a whole variety of works for the poor among whom she lived. Now she was bedridden and hadn't a moment's peace in her life. She was the cause of me giving up smoking! Finding a covered blanket at my feet in the middle of a swarming crowd near Dalhousie Square in Calcutta was unremarkable. When I lifted the blanket there was a little old lady, obviously very close to death, and that was shocking. She belonged to no one. Every age has its own suffering. In 1847 the parish priest of Liscannor in County Clare wrote to the London *Times* begging help for famine victims. He detailed how he had found four bodies in a local quarry, one of whom had been eaten by dogs! Drug abuse is the scourge of today. In late August 1998 I came across a surreal scene. In the church porch three young men, each with one of their shoes off, were injecting heroin into their big toes! There wasn't another suitable vein in their bodies. Then there are heart attacks, double and triple by-passes and cancer. It is the exceptional person who sails through life without being touched by suffering.

Above everything else the ministry of Jesus was drawn like a magnet to those who were suffering. He quite obviously felt most at home with misfits, the sick and the outcast. Because we wear masks, which we begin to believe in ourselves, we can convince ourselves that we don't belong in the category of a misfit. I know I do. What person has his or her life so much in order that they don't need the ministry of healing? The jocularity of the alcohol-filled youngster in Temple Bar on a Saturday night doesn't deceive me. More is needed than this world can give. The shattered and dead bodies of young drunk-drivers, and the number who simply have had enough and killed themselves, convinces me that the healing ministry of Jesus is needed now more than ever.

There are times when we need friends to help us. A friend is an anchor, a lifeline, a security net, that can help us from falling deeper and deeper. That's what the man in the Gospel had – friends. They were real friends who were willing to open up the roof of the house in order to lower their mate into the healing gaze of Jesus. Jesus complimented them by saying 'seeing their faith' and he rewarded them for their faith by saying to the paralysed man, 'Get up, pick up your stretcher, and go off home'. He was rewarding them as well as having compassion on the sick man. Those who are sick have a right to know of the love that Jesus has for them. He is their special friend every day.

His Life Said All There Was To Say

Readings: 1 Sam 26:2, 7-9, 12-13, 22-23; 1 Cor 15:45-49; Lk 6:27-38

The best sermon on love is the one that is lived.

I am frightened by the word love. Firstly, because I am acutely conscious of how I fail to measure up to the demands of love. Secondly, it has become the coinage of the market place and of the advertiser, who have debased its nobility. Preaching about love appears to me to have a futility about it. Love can't be preached about, it can only be lived. Would a textbook on love make me a different person? I doubt it! Love begins deep inside, by deciding to love. I have met people who loved. When I was a student I helped in the Morning Star hostel run by the Legion of Mary for destitute men, in Brunswick Street, Dublin. A permanent worker there, Tom Doyle, made a deep impression on me. He was a simple man in shabby clothes, quiet spoken, and utterly dedicated to the poor men. He radiated what to me was love. Abuse regularly came his way but it was met with understanding and gentleness. He never seemed to be in a leadership role, or vested with authority, and yet he commanded such respect that without him the Morning Star would have been a mere building, not a home. He was unobtrusive, a person who never sought the limelight. I am certain that his life was always focused on the Lord and on ultimate union with God. Tom Doyle, now with God, preached a sermon on love every day he lived. I only know about love through people like Tom Doyle.

The love that Tom Doyle had wasn't a matter of will-power alone. If Christ is love, and if we believe he dwells within us, then isn't it logical that the Christ in us will want to reach out to the other – the confused, destitute, isolated and wounded? And so, in some funny, peculiar way, to love means getting out of the way and allowing Christ to reach out through us. Am I right? It is the 'ego', the self and the selfishness, that blocks the possibility of Christ reaching out through us. We put our own obstacles in the way of love.

One of the spiritual classics of all time is *Abandonment to Divine Providence* by Jean-Pierre de Caussade. He was ordained three hundred years ago this year. Jean-Pierre taught that we have to accept that God is in control of our lives, and hence allow the Holy Spirit to work within us by abandoning our selves to the will of God. He taught, as St Teresa did, the Sacrament of the Present Moment. God is not looking for big flamboyant gestures, but only for the effort to carry out his will; not only for this day, or this hour, but for this very moment.

We live in a culture of blame. Our tabloid press circles like vultures above the corpses of the fallen – the Jeffrey Archers, John Gilligans, Catherine Nevins and others. Our tribunals provide the voyeuristic delight that was provided by the 'bread and circuses' of ancient Rome. Someone once said to me, 'Neither praise, nor blame, but only seek to understand.' Who knows the inner workings of another human being? 'Father, forgive them, for they know not what they do.' Somehow forgiveness is at the heart of love. Lack of forgiveness is such an obstacle to love that the two cannot co-exist in the same person.

One of our diocesan priests, Fr Paddy Kelly, died earlier this year. Although confined to a wheelchair for a long time, Paddy struggled, day after day, to fulfil his duties. He never complained. Being dependent on others all the time must have been a real burden to him. Nevertheless, there was always a smile on his face and a gentle word on his lips. He too, like Tom Doyle, was 'a man without guile'. He wasn't a great preacher in words; his life said all there was to say.

New Wine,
Old Wineskins

Readings: Hos 2:16-17, 21-22; 2 Cor 3:1-6; Mk 12:18-22

The Gospel presents a serious challenge to us to reflect on our willingness to change as a Christian people.

Is the Roman Catholic Church today lacking in courage? Jesus came from a reasonably comfortable background, as did most of the disciples. Carpenters, fishermen, tax-collectors and such like were 'respectable'. The remarkable thing about Jesus was that, although he came from the middle class, and had no appreciable disadvantages himself, he mixed socially with the lowest of the low and identified himself with them by choice. Sinners, those with whom Jesus consorted, were excluded from the synagogue. To mix with such people was a radical departure for the disciples. It is difficult to underestimate the later move of the early Church from the synagogue and its rituals. It demanded enormous courage to take this step into the unknown.

In the Gospel Jesus speaks of sewing a new patch on an old garment. The word used means that the new cloth was still undressed; it had never been shrunk; so when the garment got wet in the rain the new patch shrunk, and being much stronger than the old, it tore the old apart. There comes a time when the day of patching is over, and re-creating must begin. Luther, initially, thought that it was not possible to patch up the abuses of the Roman Catholic Church; the time for reformation had come. In the time of John Wesley, for Wesley at least, the time for patching the Church of England was done. He did not want to leave it, but in the end he had to, for only a new fellowship

Eighth Sunday in Ordinary Time

would suffice. It may well be that there are times when we try to patch, when what is wanted is the abandonment of the old and the acceptance of something new.

It is interesting to note the tone of those who long for the certainties of the past. The linear, Western way of thinking, which categorises everything into good or bad, black or white, right or wrong, is so appealing to them. Not for them the uncertainty of Isaiah: 'Truly you are a hidden God'.

If new wine was poured into old hardened skins, the still-fermenting wine gave off gasses that caused pressure on the skins. The old hardened skin lacked elasticity and burst, and the wine and the skin were lost. When our minds become so settled and fixed in their ways that we are unable to accept new truths and to contemplate new ways, we no longer have much to contribute.

In the middle of the nineteenth century, the great Cardinal Newman suffered because of his openness to change. The idea of development of doctrine within the Roman Catholic Church (which is now largely accepted) received a frosty reception. When he wrote an article entitled 'Consulting the Faithful in matter of Doctrine' he walked on the edge of the precipice. Newman believed that it was appropriate for the bishops, before making up their minds about a matter of teaching, to consult the living faith of the laity. This has yet to be universally accepted. In matters of conscience he was unwilling to pour new wine into old skins. He wrote: 'If I am obliged to bring religion in to after-dinner speeches (which indeed does not seem quite the thing) I shall drink – to the Pope, if you please, – still, to Conscience first, and to the Pope afterwards'. A willingness to change, to experiment, to do things differently in the pastoral life of the Church, may be what the times we live in are calling out for! But the courage, faith or trust, whatever you like, are lacking. What would have happened if the early Church felt the same way? There would be no Church.

Change

Readings: Hos 2:16-17; 2 Cor 3:1-6; Mk 2:18-22

Could it be that in the beginning of the twenty-first century we are witnessing the emergence of a new form of Catholicism – less structured, less hierarchical? Young Catholics and many older ones pay little attention to papal statements and interventions. The parable of the 'new wine, old wineskins' may have a message for us.

In some Pentecostal circles there is a belief that it is not possible for Catholics to 'be saved'. In the many conversations I have had with them over the years, today's Gospel is quoted, 'Nobody puts new wine into old wineskins', meaning that even if you have had a conversion experience you cannot consider yourselves really saved if you remain in the Roman Catholic Church. In fact, the test of the genuineness of your conversion is to leave the Church. Among Pentecostal Churches the topic 'Can Catholics be saved?' is frequently discussed. How could you have a conversion and remain in an unreformed Church?

There are two sayings in the Gospel which illustrate the fact that the new way of life revealed by Jesus cannot be limited by ancient observance. First, a new patch must be treated with water to ensure that it has already shrunk before it is used; if this precaution is not taken, when the rains come the new patch shrinks in the old garment, which then begins to tear apart. Second, new wine ferments. An old wineskin cannot withstand the gases of this new liquid, and so it explodes.

Jesus appeals to his hearers to be open to the changes that his new dispensation will bring. Those of us who are older talk about the

Second Vatican Council as if it was yesterday. Young people today are as far from the Vatican Council as I was from the Boer War when I was born. For them it really is history. Even to speak of 'the Council' must sound anachronistic in the ears of young people. Anyone who is thirty or younger was born into a world of change. The question is – what is the relevance of the Gospel of Jesus in this age? Where does it fit into the change we observe all around us?

Young Catholics in the New Millennium (University College Press, Dublin) poses a number of interesting questions? 'With the changes in Catholicism that appear in the lives of young adults, are we seeing the end of Catholicism in the West? Or can it survive and even expand in the future? Has the Catholic Church as an organisation promoted its own downfall? Young Catholics and many older ones pay little attention to papal statements and interventions. The Catholic culture of the West is one that implies semi-autonomous intellectual autonomy as essential for survival in late modernity.'

The core of Catholicism cannot be in the structures or the institution alone. The organisation is there only to promote the growth of faith in Jesus and to make his name known. Its slogan might well be 'to know God and to make him known'. The Gospel today may well be saying to us that we should look to Jesus first, and to the Church only as the instrument or guide that helps us know him better.

It could be that there is a greater change happening than anyone can anticipate. For the early Church the struggle to sever the ties with Judaism wasn't easy. They established themselves as an active 'sect' among fellow Jews. Only gradually did the claims of the law cease to bind their behaviour. They continued 'with one accord daily in the Temple'. Could it be that we are witnessing the painful emergence of a new, less structured, less hierarchical, form of Christianity?

The Mask I Wear

Readings: Sir 27:4-7; 1 Cor 15:54-58; Lk 6:39-45

Many people relate to the world outside themselves through the mask they wear. 'Take off your masks' says Jesus. 'Acknowledge who you are before me and others' – only then can you afford to correct others.

Brendan Bracken is remembered by history as Winston Churchill's closest friend. Some thought, wrongly, that he might have been his illegitimate son. He became Minister of Information in Churchill's wartime government. Bracken became a powerful person of influence, particularly within the media, and on the right wing of the Conservative Party. Bracken, a man of no religion, was described by Randolph Churchill as 'a man of mystery, a secretive eccentric, a wonderful friend, a freak, perhaps a genius, certainly an expert in the art of make-believe and fantasy'. In fact, Brendan Bracken was a 'Christian Brothers' boy', schooled at O'Connell School in North Richmond Street in Dublin. His father, a sincere nationalist, was one of the seven men who founded the Gaelic Athletic Association in Hayes' Hotel in Thurles in November 1884. The biography of Bracken has been quite excellently written by Charles Lysagh. Bracken never let his mask slip throughout his life. Few knew who he was.

I use the example of Bracken, whose life epitomised what it means to wear a mask, to illustrate one of the issues of today's Gospel. The first three vignettes in the Gospel address people who wear masks. When Jesus says 'you hypocrite!' the word refers to Greek actors who wore masks to look like the characters they were playing. The blind person who lets on to be sighted; the student who assumes the role of the teacher; someone who gets worked up over the misbehaviour of another but ignores their own misbehaviour – are all wearing masks. The masks we wear give us a feeling of superiority. They make us feel better, accepted, loved. For instance, if I wear the mask of the Mother Superior I project the image of a well-organised, efficient, on-top-of-things person, knowing what is right for me and for others. I am afraid to show my imperfections or limitations and take the chance of being thought of as a failure. It is through my mask that I win the approval of others.

My mask is the way I act in order to look good and create a positive image about myself. The mask can hide a poor self-image and help one to cope with unmet needs. Early in life we learn to present to the world those qualities that we perceive the world most likes to see in us. We begin the mask from our mother's knees. For instance, if we observe that qualities of submissiveness, obedience and docility are to our advantage, the opposite ones of rebelliousness, stubbornness and independence will be tucked away in an inner world. We learn very early in life that certain types of behaviour earn rewards and win the affection of others. We also learn that other types of behaviour win disapproval. The Gospel is urging us 'to thy own self be true'. Own who you are – warts and all. God wants all of who you are. We don't need to, nor can we, wear masks before God.

The Gospel applies itself to those who display moral superiority. These people are willing to guide and correct others but are totally unaware of their own moral lapses or 'blindness'. The fall from grace of so many people from all walks of life ought to have warned us that 'the high moral ground' is a lonely place to be. The Bible tells us: 'He who thinks himself to stand let him take heed lest he fall'. Would-be critics of others must look to themselves before presuming to look to the faults of others.

The Fall Of The Mighty

Readings: Deut 11:18, 26-28, 32; Rom 3:21-25, 28; Mt 7:21-27

In recent years well-known preachers and teachers have fallen from grace. It is the message, not the person who preaches it, that we should focus on.

The pulpit is one of the most dangerous and lonely places in the world. To fall from the pulpit is to fall from grace. Over the past decade or two, particularly in the 'electronic Church' in the US, the mighty have fallen. Jimmy Swaggart, a televangelist once named in a *Good Housekeeping* poll as the second most influential man in the United States, fell horribly from grace when his sinfulness was exposed. The same happened to Jim and Tammy Bakker, founders and presenters of the hugely popular PTL (Praise the Lord) network, which was screened across continents at one time. Afterwards, Jim claimed: 'The deceitfulness of riches and the lust for other things had choked out the Word of God in my life and in the lives of my family members and co-workers. God does not promise riches or prosperity, but he promises to never leave or forsake us, no matter what pain or trial we're going through'.

Other prominent Christian leaders, from different denominations, have also fallen from grace. The names of Milingo, Casey, Wright, Robertson created a media frenzy when they tripped and fell. The Lord's warning in today's Gospel is timely: 'It is not those who say to me, "Lord, Lord, who will enter the kingdom of heaven?", but the person who does the will of my Father in heaven'. The responsibility on the preacher to bring his life into conformity with the words he preaches is very great indeed.

Over the years many good and not so good people have captured huge audiences as preachers. One thinks of great men like Fr Patrick Peyton, or Archbishop Fulton Sheen. Billy Graham and Martin Luther King are others who captivated audiences by their preaching. Many of them did enormous good. However, it is not the person but the message that matters. It is not even the message in itself, but translating the hearing into 'doing', that is the final test. The Gospel today is saying, 'Listen to the preacher, but the Word and the doing of the Word is what will lead you to heaven'.

Because of our brokenness, spiritually and psychologically, we are all in need of healing. But the healer is Christ. Christ is present within: 'If any one loves me my father will love him and we will come and take up our abode within him'. The kingdom of God is within you. Listen to the voice within.

Today many people say 'Nobody is going to tell me what to do, I can make up my own mind'. But doing God's will entails a search for truth. How do we find out what God's will is for us? We find out God's will through prayer, seeking enlightenment, the wisdom of the Church, and ultimately our conscience. We pray at every Mass for 'all those who seek you with a sincere heart'. There is a seeking involved.

When we have determined what we think to be God's will for us we will normally experience an accompanying peace. Our heart will be at rest.

> To you alone, O Jesus, I must cling;
> And running to Your arms, dear Lord,
> There let me hide;
> Loving with childlike tenderness.

Ninth Sunday in Ordinary Time

Keeping The Sabbath

Readings: Deut 5:12-15; 2 Cor 4:6-11; Mk 2:23-36

Keeping the Sabbath is a thing of the heart rather than the rulebook.

Nowadays many people make the distinction between religion and spirituality. Spirituality is a lot like health. We all have health; we may have good health or poor health, but it's something we can't avoid having. The same is true of spirituality: every human being is a spiritual being. The question is not whether we 'have spirituality' but whether the spirituality we have is a negative one that leads to isolation and self-destruction or one that is more positive and life-giving. People today say something like, 'I am not a very religious person but I have a spirituality of my own.' I am not sure if the distinction is completely valid. Religion is primarily a 'relationship'. It is a relationship with the God who loves us. That is essentially a spiritual relationship. Everything that religious institutions and Churches do, ought to be ordered towards our holiness, that is, our growth in relationship with God.

The Churches are, or ought to be, ordered towards a growth in spirituality. Unfortunately religion has been identified with rules and regulations that have at times obscured the spiritual. In the past many of these rules were petty in the extreme. This is what Jesus is hitting out at in the Gospel. Sunday is an important day to be kept holy, but there is a great deal more to religion than Sunday observance. Christianity has at all times consisted far more in doing things than in refraining from doing things. What we do on Sunday is to externalise our inward dispositions and desires in our relationship with God. It is normal that we express in an external way the inward dispositions of the heart. Flowers can say: thank you; I love you; I hope you get better soon. The advertising slogan of Interflora is 'Say it with flowers'. In the Mass we praise God, we ask God, we thank God, we worship God, we listen to God, and we build community. For Roman Catholics, the Mass is the pre-eminent way in which we do this as part of a believing community. It is not so much the 'going to Mass' or indeed 'getting Mass in'; it is the heart that matters, rather than the doing.

People matter far more than systems. Persons are far more important than rituals. People have a claim on our compassion and care. The 'law of love' supersedes all other claims. Perhaps making the missing of Mass a 'mortal sin' did a serious disservice to what our true relationship with God ought to be.

While 'going to Mass' is not the beginning or end of our religious expression, nevertheless, the keeping holy of the Sabbath demands some response from us. When we cease to attend Mass we deny ourselves the possibility of being moulded or shaped by the Gospel. Where will we receive the nourishment of God's Word if we cease to practise our religion? We also deprive ourselves of meeting Christ in the sacrament of his love – the Eucharist. To miss Mass without some reasonably compelling reason, it seems to me, is to put in jeopardy the possibility of deepening our relationship with Jesus.

Cancer

Readings: 1 Kings 8:41-43; Gal 1:1-2, 6-10; Lk 7:1-10

Bible stories sometimes hide the pain and the pathos of daily living. Someone is very ill. Jesus does something about it.

On the day before her wedding Treya Wilber discovered a lump on her breast. Immediate surgery was advised. Here is her account of the awful truth dawning on her: 'Suddenly I am awake. Uneasy, disorientated. It must be three or four in the morning. Something is terribly, terribly wrong. The night is dark and still; I see the stars through the skylight. A terrible ache rushes into my heart, tightens my throat. Fear. Of what? I notice my hand, resting on my right breast, sensing the stitches beneath. I remember. Oh no, no. My eyes squeeze shut, my face contorts, my throat closes in fear. Yes I remember. I don't want to remember. I don't want to know. But it is here. Cancer. I have cancer'.

Faenius Rufus was a centurion. He was in a posting not of his own choosing, on the outskirts of the Empire, far from his wife Paulina and his two sons, Milichus and Flavius, in Rome. He was a conscientious man who had risen to the position of centurion. He was in command of an outpost without a lot of support. He tried to be as friendly to the native Jewish people as they would allow. There wasn't much trouble where he was, and he was delighted to be able to give a hand to repair their synagogue. He had a great servant, Silvanus, whom he had brought from Rome. He could rely on him to be his eyes and ears in the community. Silvanus was intensely loyal, and they had grown very fond of each other. Silvanus developed some worrying symptoms. He began to lose weight and he was passing blood. Rufus knew there was very little he could do. They didn't have a doctor on the outpost. The journey to Jerusalem would be too much for him. Rufus saw him wasting away with great sadness. In addition, Silvanus was in a lot of pain. Rufus had heard of Jesus. Who hadn't? He thought, 'This man is reputed to be a healer. I am not sure what God he calls upon. But God does care for each of us. Maybe I will take a chance that the God of Jesus can cure Silvanus.' He knew this wasn't an easy decision because being a Gentile meant that his relationship with the Jews was invariably brittle. 'I will put my trust in God and ask some of my Jewish friends to approach Jesus for me,' he said to himself. 'I am sure Jonathan and Levi will do it for me.' Then he thought, 'Surely one word from Jesus would be enough, he needn't come in person.' He was confident that Jesus would heal poor Silvanus, who was now in agony. Anyway Jonathan and Levi spoke to Jesus about Rufus and his servant. Jesus was really amazed. A lot of people thought he was a fake, a charlatan. Here was a Roman, a non-Jew, who had enough faith to come and ask for a healing. He told the bystanders how important faith in God was and how wonderful the faith of Rufus, the Gentile centurion, was. In silent prayer Jesus called on his Father to heal Silvanus. He raised his head and smiled to Jonathan and Levi. 'Off you go,' he said. 'There is a surprise waiting for you when you get back.'

Ninth Sunday in Ordinary Time

The Call Of Matthew

Readings: Hos 6:3-6; Rom 4:18-25; Mt 9:9-13

The choice of Matthew to be a disciple was a strange one. A tax-collector, acting on behalf of the Roman authorities, was a pariah in society.

Tax-collecting was franchised out to the highest bidder. Anything over and above the set amount to be collected could be pocketed by the franchisee. The temptation was to press heavily on the people to extract as much money out of them as possible. This is the first reason why tax-collectors were not very popular at the time of Jesus. The second is that the Romans were seen as occupiers – a hostile, alien power, on soil that was not their own. The tax-collector then was a sort of quisling, a fifth columnist, a traitor to the cause of the Jews. And yet Jesus picked Matthew. He said to him, 'Follow me.' And Matthew got up and followed him. Matthew seems like a strange choice on the part of Jesus!

There was once a sculptor who worked hard with his hammer and chisel on a large block of marble. A little boy who was watching him saw nothing more than large and small pieces of stone falling away left and right. He had no idea what was happening. But when the boy returned to the studio a few weeks later, he saw to his great surprise a large, powerful lion sitting in the place where the marble had once stood. With great excitement the boy ran to the sculptor and said, 'Sir, tell me, how did you know there was a lion in the marble?' (H. Nouwen, *Clowning in Rome*)

The mystery of a vocation arises from the fact that God cannot directly intervene in the history of the world. He needs people who are willing to give him their 'flesh and bones', their bodies, their talents and gifts, through which he then will make himself present in the human situation in order to do what he wants for the people and the world. He chooses the inadequate, the fearful, because Jesus saw the potential of each and every human being. 'If Yahweh set his heart on you and chose you, it was not because you outnumber other peoples… it was for love of you.'

When our Lord went up to heaven after his resurrection one of the accompanying angels asked him: 'Lord, who will carry on your work on earth?' Jesus pointed to his disciples who were still standing down on the mountain from where he had departed and said: 'These men down below, my disciples, they will carry on my work.' But the angels, seemingly not too impressed with this band Jesus had chosen as his messengers, asked, 'Just suppose they fail in their task, do you have another plan?' Jesus paused for a long time and replied, 'No, there is no other plan. They are all that I have to carry on my work.'

Jesus called to him 'those whom he desired'. The will of God is at the heart of what a vocation is. He called them first of all 'to be with him'. A vocation is a way of being rather than a way of doing. Being with Jesus, as a companion, is where the strength to continue the journey of serving the Lord in good work comes from. Every person is called separately and must follow alone.

As today, not all responded as spontaneously and generously to the call of Jesus as Matthew did. In Luke 9:59 we read of one who wanted to follow Jesus on his own terms. But the road to faith passes through obedience to the call of Jesus. Responding to the call will inevitably lead to a life of sacrifice. Matthew must leave his tax-collecting table and Peter his nets. They must 'burn their boats' and plunge into absolute insecurity in order to learn the demand and the gift of Christ. I appreciate that to the non-believer this is strange, virtually incomprehensible. It will always be thus!

Tenth Sunday in Ordinary Time

Sin And Satan

Readings: Gen 3:9-15; 2 Cor 4:13-5:1; Mk 3:20-35

In the past thirty years attitudes to sin and Satan have altered radically. The fissure between what the Church teaches and what Catholics believe and practise has grown deep and wide.

I grew up at a time when the 'sin cycle' was the ritualised form of religion. Mortal sin was an ever-present reality. It was something that could occur all too frequently, given the prevailing views on sexual morality and church attendance. 'Impurity', ranging from entertaining impure thoughts and masturbation to dancing as a 'proximate occasion of sin' and then to petting and sexual intercourse outside marriage, was the cause of mortal sin among most young people. Any of these were considered grievous, containing 'no parvity of matter' as the moral theologians of the day put it. If one died without confessing or making an act of perfect contrition, the consequence was hell for all eternity! Sorrow for one's sins and a resolve never to do the same again and going to confession was the only remedy that could complete the cycle. Most people, I think, spent a lot of time sinning and rising again. Some eventually saw this as an impossible exercise and ceased trying.

The 'sin cycle' religion has virtually disappeared. In *Young Catholics in the New Millennium* (University College Press, Dublin) the following best illustrates the prevailing attitude: 'Catholics tend to judge moral issues on grounds of human and individual rights. There is no absolute code of behaviour that is right for everyone. Morality is a matter of making choices in a given set of circumstances. The only limiting condition is that decisions should not harm others or violate their rights'. So how does today's Gospel with its emphasis on sin and Satan speak to the Catholic of today?

The *Catechism of the Catholic Church* retains its rigid teaching on sin: 'Sins are rightly evaluated according to their gravity. The distinction between mortal and venial sin, already evident in Scripture, became part of the tradition of the Church. Mortal sin attacks the vital principle within us – that is, charity....'

The spirituality underpinning the 'sin cycle' was the perfection model of spirituality. 'Be perfect as your heavenly Father is perfect.' The aim was for perfection – a sinless way of life. This type of spirituality was based on obedience; in particular obedience to the Church. The Church regulated or dictated 'good' and 'bad behaviour'. Much of its teaching was delivered at the annual mission. The Western, linear type of thinking was the foundation of the perfection model of spirituality – things were right or wrong, good or bad, black or white. There was little room for shades of grey in this spirituality.

Gradually this model of spirituality gave way to a 'developmental model of spirituality'. This took one's actions within the overall context or direction of one's life. It was life as a pilgrimage. It depended less on the dictates of the Church and more on the individual conscience to dictate the rightness or wrongness of one's actions. It tended to be more scripturally based. The individual action in isolation from the rest of one's life is seldom judged. It is rather the direction, or fundamental option, of the individual that counts.

The vast majority of Catholics no longer frequent the sacrament of Reconciliation. They feel no need of an intermediary between the person and God.

Tenth Sunday in Ordinary Time

The Widow's Son

Readings: 1 Kings 17:17-24; Gal 1:11-19; Lk 7:11-17

In our distress in the face of suffering we often forget that 'the Lord is close to the brokenhearted, and those whose spirit is crushed he will save'.

During the 'intifada', Palestinian funerals flicker daily on our television screens. In Palestine grief is public, raucous and overwhelming. Women throw themselves on the coffins of their loved ones. They wail with anguish and distress. Luke the doctor would have had a particular interest here. Jesus was drawing near the gate on the small village of Nain in Lower Galilee. Shrill cries, more like shrieks than sobs, came to his ears. It was a funeral procession on its way to the cemetery. First came the distressed mourners and flute players, then four men carrying a stretcher or an open coffin with a corpse wrapped in a shroud; finally almost the whole village. Rabbis assisted at funerals, for accompanying a dead man to his last resting place even took precedence over the study of the law. The bearers relieved one another at intervals, and each pause was a signal for fresh laments. A poor woman was mourning her only son.

It is impossible to attend Oriental funerals without an emotion which custom itself does not entirely dull, even if there be a suspicion that the grief is a little artificial. But the sorrow of the widow, who in losing her son had lost everything, was so harrowing that the heart of Jesus was stirred. In the nature of things we live in a world of broken hearts. His first words were 'Weep not'.

To the compassion of Jesus, Luke adds the power of Jesus. Some commentators suggest that the man wasn't dead but was in some sort of a trance and was saved from being buried alive. The fact is that Jesus claimed for life a boy who had been marked for death. Jesus is Lord of life and death. Jesus silenced the mourners and turned to the youth stretched out on the bier, his body tightly bound with bandages and his face covered with a winding sheet. 'Young man,' he said to him, 'I say to you arise.' The dead man sat up and began to speak. Put yourself in the place of the bereaved. This son was her only support, her insurance in her old age, her comfort in the absence of her dear husband. He was all she had. He was speaking! This miracle was so public. It was unequalled for evidence and publicity. It is self-evident that the whole village realised that this was extraordinary, beyond the capacity of them to understand in human terms. 'A great prophet has risen in our midst' was the understandable reaction.

The words that always come to me in the face of death and mourning are those of Psalm 33: 'The Lord is close to the brokenhearted, and those whose spirit is crushed he will save'. When we are in trouble Jesus is close to us. He understands suffering and pain. One fifth of the Gospels is taken up with the healing miracles of Jesus. He knows suffering to its core.

The Courage Of Terry Fox

Readings: Ezek 17:22-24; 2 Cor 5:6-10; Mk 4:26-34

'The Kingdom of God is like a mustard seed....' That seed snuggles inside the breast of everyone. Hope, faith and the grace of God can produce something wonderful, something we never imagined.

Terry Fox lost his leg to cancer when he was a teenager. While in the hospital, going through chemo, he was affected by the amount of suffering in the cancer ward and decided that, in his words, 'somewhere the hurting must stop'. He decided to run across Canada to raise funds for Cancer research in that country. During his 'Marathon of Hope', Fox ran twenty-eight to thirty miles per day on one real leg and one artifical leg. Halfway across, outside Thunder Bay in Ontario, the cancer spread to his lungs. A few months later he died. He lifted a nation through his courage and tenacity. To this day every first weekend in September there is a Terry Fox Run. There is also a mountain named after him in the Canadian Rockies and a huge memorial to him outside Thunder Bay.

The Kingdom of God is within. The beautiful story of Terry Fox illustrates the potential for growth of the 'Kingdom' within. The Kingdom of God is like a mustard seed, the smallest of seeds on earth, yet what wonderful things can happen in the lives of quite ordinary individuals when this seed is nourished by God's grace.

Negative people are toxic! In one of my assignments I came across a person who, when any new project was mooted, launched into a list of the obstacles that would have to be overcome and the reasons why it couldn't be attempted. I had to avoid her. Toxicity is contagious.

Today's parable is about the possible. The mustard seed can and will grow into the largest of trees if it is God's will, and we rely on God's power. There are times when I am amazed at the fidelity and perseverance of many people in the Christian life. In the parish there are wonderful people, many of them drawing the old-age pension, who still believe in miracles.

The following anonymous contribution illustrates what I mean:

> Youth is not a time of life... it is a state of mind.
> Nobody grows old by merely living a number of years;
> people grow old only by deserting their ideals.
> Years wrinkle the skin, but to give up enthusiasm wrinkles
> the soul.
> Worry, doubt, self-distrust, fear and despair...
> these are the long, long years that bow the head and turn
> the growing spirit back to dust.
>
> Whether seventy or sixteen, there is in every being's heart
> the love of wonder, the sweet amazement at the stars
> and the starlike things and thoughts,
> the undaunted challenge of events,
> the unfailing childlike appetite for what next,
> and the joy of the game of life.
> You are as young as your faith, as old as your doubt;
> as young as your self-confidence, as old as your fear;
> as young as your hope, as old as your despair.

The Priest
– Another Simon Of Cyrene

Readings: Ex 19:2-6; Rom 5:6-11; Mt 9:36-10:8

The priest is in the privileged position of being asked to carry the cross behind Our Lord. To walk alongside the bruised and the battered and to point to ultimate realities – that is the mission of the priest.

Coming into the presbytery one evening I noticed a package on the hall table waiting for me. My name was misspelled; the packaging was torn. A Thank You card accompanied it. The card said, 'To Father Tearily (!) tahk you for all and everything. Thanks you Jane and Patrick' (not the real names). I was thrilled to get this card.

Jane and Patrick were at the bottom of the heap. Jane was an alcoholic; a two-bottle-a-day Vodka drinker. She was also a drug addict. Her boyfriend Patrick was slightly retarded. He clung to Jane, despite her tantrums and drunkenness, as his only living support. Jane got pregnant but because of her alcoholism she wouldn't go to the hospital. The queues were so long she just couldn't endure the wait without a drink. Sometimes the wait as a public patient could be five or six hours. One day they left their pathetic little bundle of belongings in the presbytery and disappeared. A week later I got a phone call, 'Father would you bring our stuff! We have got a room. It's a palace!' The palace was a dingy small room in a grotty part of the city. A palace it was not!

Why am I telling you this story? My image of the priesthood has always been that of Simon of Cyrene. He was dragged reluctantly from the curious mob to carry the cross behind our Lord. He wasn't a volunteer. He displayed little enthusiasm for what he was being asked to do. His mates would probably slag him. He was cute enough to know that he too would be the subject of the jeers and insults of the mob. He wasn't relishing the task. But he did it. He carried the cross, helping Jesus to struggle on; falling and rising again, to Calvary, and ultimately resurrection. For me the priest is another Simon. He is one who tries to dedicate his life to lifting the cross a little, so that the sufferer can struggle on to the final victory.

Jane and Patrick in the eyes of our world are nothing more than human debris. I saw in the 'Thank You' card the beauty within. Think of the ten lepers. Jane and Patrick were the ones who came back to give thanks. To be a priest is to be in a position to struggle along with the Janes and Patricks of this world. Like Simon of Cyrene, that's a privilege.

In Mark's Gospel we are told that 'Jesus called to him those whom he desired'. His will is at the very centre of what it means to be a priest. He called them to be companions with him. To be called to be a 'companion' of Jesus is special. A priest is one who tries to be 'with Jesus as a companion', in order that he may go out and tell people what he has experienced. To know God and to make God known. A priest is anointed at his ordination. He is consecrated, set aside, to 'bring people to God and God to people'. He will often be there when 'the rubber hits the road'. He will be there in times of death, tragedy, pain, loss, and also at weddings, anniversaries and celebrations. He is there as a support, a comforter. But he is there, too, to point to the deeper meaning of life. People's search for meaning is reaching a point of desperation in our world. We have a crisis of meaning. The priest is saying in the words of the psalmist, 'The Lord is close to the brokenhearted; those whose spirit is crushed he will save'. In other words, his presence is pointing, not to himself but to Jesus – the way, the truth and the life. The priest by his life is trying to point to the ultimate realities of life (and death).

The Pharisee And The Prostitute

Readings: 2 Sam 12:7-10, 13; Gal 2:15-16, 19-21; Lk 7:36-8:3

No one is outside the scope of God's forgiveness. The woman in today's Gospel wanted to lay down her burden of guilt at the feet of Jesus. He accepted her with love, compassion and forgiveness.

In the secular press there are often references to 'Catholic guilt'; behind this, I believe, is an attempt to anaesthetise the conscience to the reality of guilt. There is a healthy guilt! There are times when it is good to feel guilty! A guilt arising out of sinfulness and wrongdoing is a sign of health and wholeness. The woman in today's Gospel, who is often identified as having been a prostitute, knew and recognised her guilt. She obviously experienced a need to be liberated from the burden she was carrying. To dull and harden the conscience, so that it never experiences guilt, is not something that anyone can do for a lifetime and feel happy about.

When a guest entered a house three things were always done. The host placed their hand on the guest's shoulder and gave the kiss of peace. Cool water was poured over the guest's feet to clean and comfort them. Either a pinch of sweet-smelling incense or a drop of attar of roses was placed on the guest's head. Good manners demanded that these things were done. In this story all three were omitted. This was an act of significant discourtesy.

Jesus was often critical of the Pharisees. There is no explanation as to why he was dining in this house. It was natural that the guests reclined at table. They lay on low couches, resting on the left elbow, leaving the right arm free. During the meals sandals were taken off.

The dialogue has been constructed in order to point out that it was the woman's faith that enabled God's forgiveness to become effective in her. Jesus had convinced her that all her debts had been cancelled. Forgiveness meant the cancellation or remission of one's debts to God. To forgive in Greek means to remit, to release or liberate. To forgive someone was to liberate them of their past history. When God forgives he overlooks one's past and takes away the present or future consequences of past transgressions.

It was her faith in the power of forgiveness that healed this woman of past sinfulness. The moment she believed she was forgiven, her life was utterly transformed. She was a new person. Jesus' faith in God's unconditional forgiveness had awakened the same faith in her. How exactly he did it we do not know. It might have been by a simple gesture of friendship and acceptance. Perhaps nothing more than allowing her to wash his feet. He had not rejected her as prophets were expected to do. The result was a kind of healing or salvation, which she experienced as relief, gratitude, joy and love. 'Her sins, her many sins, must have been forgiven her, or she would not have shown such great love.' Her grateful and unconditional love and uncontrollable joy were a sure sign of her liberation from sin. Joy was, in fact, the most characteristic result of all Jesus' activities amongst the poor and the oppressed.

The new confessor is the chat-show host. Yet there is little he or she can do but provide a forum for people to parade their frailties in public. In the sacrament of Reconciliation the forgiveness of God is available. God's healing and compassion and forgiveness are available to each one of us daily in the sacrament of his love. The sacrament of Reconciliation is the way to freedom.

Declaring For Christ

Readings: Jer 20:10-13; Rom 5:12-15; Mt 10:26-33

There is a sting in the tail of today's Gospel! If we claim to be Christian, then witnessing to that fact by word and deed is part of our Christianity.

There was a famous scholar in Trinity College, Dublin by the name of Mahaffy, who, when asked was he a Christian, replied, 'Yes, but not offensively so.' He meant that he did not allow his Christianity to interfere with the society he kept and the pleasures he loved. Sometimes we say to other people that we are Church members, but not to worry about it too much, that we have no intention of being different. We are prepared to take our full share in all the pleasures of the world; and we do not expect people to take any special trouble to respect any vague principles that we may have. On the other hand there was another famous Dublin man by the name of Frank Duff, the founder of the Legion of Mary, who claimed that 'a Legionary should be twenty-four hours on duty'. He meant that witnessing to Christ was not so much something you did, rather it was someone you were. Your proclamation to being a Christian was a real way of life.

Here in today's Gospel is laid down the double loyalty of the Christian life. If a person is loyal to Jesus Christ in this life, Jesus Christ will be loyal to this person in the life to come. If someone is too proud or fearful to acknowledge that Jesus Christ is their Master, then there are consequences in the life to come. It is the plain fact of history that if there had not been men and women in the early Church who, in face of death and agony, refused to deny their Master, there would be no Christian Church today.

The Church of today is built on the unbreakable loyalty of those who held fast to their faith. We can deny Christ by our silence. Again and again life brings us the opportunity to speak some word for Christ, to utter some protest against evil, to take some stand, and to show what side we are on, and we fail through fear. This is particularly true in Ireland today. The 'silent majority' we hear spoken of are those who believe, good people, who are fearful of speaking out. Who wants to be ridiculed by the media or their peers? It is easier to keep silence than to speak. It makes for a quiet life. But such a silence is a denial of Jesus Christ. It is probably true that far more people deny Jesus Christ by cowardly silence than by deliberate words. We can deny him by our actions. We can live in such a way that our life is a continuous denial of the faith that we profess. It is true that 'actions speak louder than words'.

The witness of a life lived for Christ may be the most effective way of proclaiming the Gospel. A special prayer was composed for the Lambeth Conference of 1948, which began: 'Almighty God, give us grace to be not only hearers, but doers of your holy word, not only to admire, but to obey your doctrine, not only to profess, but to practise your religion, not only to love, but to live your gospel'.

That is a prayer that every one of us would be well to remember and continually to use.

Here is laid down the double loyalty of the Christian life. If a person is loyal to Jesus Christ in this life, Jesus Christ will be loyal to this person in the life to come. If a person is proud to acknowledge that Jesus Christ is their Master, Jesus Christ will be proud to acknowledge that this person is his servant. The Christian can never escape the duty of being different from the world. It is not our duty to conform to the world. We are to be in the world but not of the world.

Letting Go To God

Readings: Job 3:1, 8-11; 2 Cor 5:14-17; Mk 4:35-41

The storm frightened the disciples. Even the fact that Jesus was in the boat with them wasn't enough. They needed more reassurance than that.

American Carmelite poet Jessica Powers had a great faith in God as Sustainer. Two years before she entered the Carmelite order she wrote a poem, 'The Kingdom of God', the last verse of which goes like this:

> There is a Tenant here.
> Come home, roamer of the earth, to this room and find
> a timeless Heart under your own heart beating,
> a Bird of beauty singing under your mind.

The snows of worry, anxiety and suffering at times pile high in the human heart and limits can be reached. Does God care? Will God intervene? Jessica has another poem that tries to answer this question. She came from Wisconsin, born of Scotch-Irish stock. She loved nature. In the winter the snows fell heavily in her part of the country. In this poem she looks at the human person as a cedar tree in the snows:

> I clasp this thought: from all eternity
> God who is so good looked down upon this tree
> white in the weighted air,
> and of another cedar reckoned well.
> He knew how much each tree, each twig could bear.
> He counted every snowflake as it fell.

The compassionate Jesus was sleeping in the boat when a storm blew up. Whether waking or sleeping he was the 'timeless Heart under the heart of the anxious disciples'; although he was sleeping his providential care was present to them in a way they didn't understand.

'And can any of you by worrying add a single hour to your span of life? If then you are not able to do so small a thing as that, why do you worry about the rest?' (Luke 12) Jesus is sleeping. A sleeping person is unnoticed but nevertheless very much present. The sleeping person is not talking, advising and directing the affairs of people. But he is there – available. God does not go around interfering with the lives of people. He is not obtrusive. The greatest gift of God is our free will – free to do and free not to do. Much of the pain of the world is due to the freedom God has given us. Freedom to drive aeroplanes into office blocks, freedom to stand by and gaze as others starve. But God is there, always available to support, sustain and encourage when needed. His conscious presence in our lives does make a difference.

Insecurity frightens people. We need to see the path ahead. Threading on unfamiliar ground, without a road map, confuses people. Following Christ can be a bit like that. People can talk a little glibly about 'letting go and letting God'. I have done so myself. This letting go demands of us a faith in God's providential care for us. Jesus asked the disciples, 'Why are you so frightened? How is it that you have no faith?' It seems to me that Jesus was trying to tell them he was in charge of every situation. We even cling to our sins because we are afraid to let go of our 'comfort blanket'. What would we do without it? Could we manage? Today's Gospel is gently probing the anxious hearts of the disciples to see if the faith is there to rely on God alone. It's an invitation to me as well!

Who Do The Crowds Say That I Am?

Readings: Zech 12:10-11; Gal 3:26-29; Lk 9:18-24

Jesus predicts his forthcoming passion and death. The confession of Peter is a comfort and a joy to him.

'Jesus was praying alone with his disciples.' Prayer is self-revelatory. God speaks to us through the circumstances of our daily lives. It looks like this incident was the fruit of the prayer of Jesus. He knew that the time of his final journey and his death were approaching. Everything was building up to the crescendo of the passion, death and resurrection. What was his prayer to the Father on this occasion? How was it that the question 'Who do the crowds say that I am?' arose immediately after prayer?

We can go through life without asking ourselves fundamental questions. Who am I? What is the purpose of my life? Is there an afterlife? What things do I know to be true? Did Jesus want to know what the impact of his life and ministry had been? Did he want to know if there was any comprehension of his Messiahship? Peter's spontaneous confession must have been a real joy to the ears of Jesus. He was recognised as 'the anointed One of God'. This was a personal discovery, as all faith is. There is a saying that 'God has no grandsons'. Faith cannot be simply given to another. It is a personal journey of discovery. I cannot have my mother's faith or my father's. I must discover it for myself. Peter knew not just with the use of reason but with the depth of faith that 'Jesus was the anointed One of God.'

It would have been hard for the disciples to understand the place of suffering in the life of Jesus. Over and over again he had mentioned that he had a destiny to fulfil that involved suffering. (Luke 9:22; 17:25; 24:7) He said, 'I must go to Jerusalem and die.' The entire Gospels portray Jesus as a man who went to his death knowingly and willingly. The words and expressions that he used, especially in the so-called 'Passion predictions', indicate this. It is also significant that these 'predictions' occur during a period of withdrawal and prayer. Jesus was not willing to compromise. I suppose in theory he could have resorted to violence. He was not willing to tailor his words to suit the authorities. The only alternative was to die. In these circumstances death was the only way to serve the community. It was the only way of witnessing to the Kingdom, the only way of speaking to the world. It is through his paschal mystery that the message of Jesus most vividly finds expression. It is also through his passion and death that Jesus has put some shape and meaning on the pain of the world.

Jesus had a destiny to fulfil. His inescapable vision, throughout his life, was to accomplish the will of the Father. For this he came into the world. We, too, have to find a vision for our lives. This vision will be most effectively accomplished when we try to discern what the Father's will is for each one of us. 'Am I living according to God's will?' We seek God's will in the circumstances of our daily lives. God speaks to us through our lives when we ask him, 'Lord, what are you telling me through this or that particular incident? How do you want me to react or respond to this or that situation?' We will find answers to these questions through praying about the circumstances of our daily lives.

Twelfth Sunday in Ordinary Time

Anyone Who Welcomes You Welcomes Me

Readings: 2 Kings 4:8-11; Rom 6:8-11; Mt 10:37-42

Life-giving people are conscious that it is the little things of life that make the difference.

Cardinal Hume died recently. On one occasion in the 1970s I invited him to address a meeting here in Dublin. He readily agreed. Although I had never actually met him I knew his face well. He arrived in the Terminal building of the airport with a small case and a black coat, rather green with age, over his arm. When I identified myself, his first words were, 'My goodness, I didn't expect anyone to meet me.' He had no sense of his own importance. He really didn't expect anyone to meet him!

To pay respect to an ambassador is the same as to receive the person he or she represents. To welcome with love the messenger of a friend is the same as to pay respect to the friend. There was an uncanny feeling that the late cardinal's lack of self-importance allowed the person he represented to shine through. I think that is what Jesus is saying in the Gospel today. 'Anyone who welcomes you welcomes me.' If one is a true person of God, to receive him is to receive the God who sent him. In a very real sense the priest stands 'in persona Christi' – in the person of Christ. He stands at the altar 'in persona Christi'. He stands in prayer before the face of the Father on behalf of the people 'in persona Christi'.

It is generally acknowledged that there is a crisis in the priesthood and religious life in the Western world. Is it a crisis of faith? Is it a lack of generosity? Is it that the priest feels isolated and alone? Is it a lack of appreciation and affirmation? I do not know the answers to the above. Recently I helped a young girl, an alcoholic, and her boyfriend, who were in very bad shape. I was deeply touched when some days later a grubby parcel was dropped through the letterbox. Inside was a note, full of atrocious spelling and grammar, and a little marble and gold statuette of St Francis. This little 'thank you' gift, from those people on the very margins, meant so much to me. It affirmed me in my priesthood. The same happened at Christmas time. For the first time in thirty-two years I received a gift from a couple I didn't really know thanking me for my preaching every Sunday.

H. L. Gee has a lovely story. There was a boy in a country village who, after a great struggle, reached the priesthood. His helper in his days of study had been the village cobbler. The cobbler, like so many of his trade, was a man of wide reading and far thinking, and he had done much for the boy. In due time the boy was allowed to preach. And on that day the cobbler said to him, 'It was always my desire to be a priest but the circumstances of my life made it impossible. But you are achieving what was closed to me. And I want you to promise me one thing – I want you to let me make and cobble your shoes, for nothing. I want you to wear them in the pulpit when you preach, and then I'll feel you are preaching the gospel that I always wanted to preach standing in my shoes.' Beyond a doubt the cobbler was serving God as the preacher was, and his reward would one day be the same.

The great beauty of today's Gospel passage is its stress on simple things. The Church and Christ will always need their great orators, their great shining examples of sainthood, their great teachers, those whose names are household words; but the Church and Christ will also always need those in whose homes there is hospitality.

The Healing Ministry Of Jesus Christ

Readings: Wis 1:13-15, 2:23-34; 2 Cor 8:7-9, 13-15; Mk 5:21-43

The tender compassion of Jesus for the sick and distressed is beautifully illustrated in today's Gospel.

Jesus is confronted by two tragic cases: one is a young child on death's door, the other a haemorrhaging woman, a longtime sufferer. Jesus, as usual, is moved with compassion in the face of such suffering.

The healing ministry of Jesus needs to be set in the context of the time he stood up in the synagogue and proclaimed what he was about.

> Jesus stood up to read the lesson. The roll of the prophet Isaiah was given to him. He opened the roll and found the passage where it is written, 'The Spirit of the Lord is upon me because he has anointed me to bring the Good News to the poor. He has sent me to announce release to the captives, and recovery of sight to the blind, to set at liberty those who have been bruised, to proclaim that the year which everyone is waiting for has come.' . . . He began to say to them, 'Today this scripture has been fulfilled in your ears.'

Jesus' ministry was one of healing – of minds, hearts and bodies. The mission of the apostles was the same. When Jesus sent out the Twelve he commanded them, 'Heal the sick, cleanse lepers.' (Matthew 18:8) Many times before he healed, Jesus posed the question, 'Do you believe I can do this for you?'

'Daughter!' he said to the woman in today's Gospel, 'Your faith has cured you! Go, and be in good health, free from the trouble that was your scourge.' He said to the ruler of the synagogue, 'Don't be afraid! Only keep on believing!' Every time Jesus healed anyone it took something out of him. Here is a universal rule of life: we will never produce anything great unless we are prepared to put something of ourselves, of our very life, of our very soul, into it. No pianist will ever give a really great performance if he or she glides through a piece of music with faultless technique and nothing more. The performance will not be great unless at the end of it there is the exhaustion that comes of the outpouring of self. No preacher who ever preached a real sermon descended from the pulpit without a feeling of being drained of something.

If we are ever to help people, we must be ready to spend ourselves. The greatness of Jesus was that he was prepared to pay the price of helping others, and that price was the outgoing of his very life. We follow in his steps only when we are prepared to spend, not our substance, but our souls and our strength.

There emerges the strange and poignant fact that Jesus' disciples had never realised that it cost him anything at all to heal others. One of the tragedies of life is the strange insensitiveness of the human mind. We so often fail to realise what others are going through. Because we may have no experience of something, we never think what that something is costing someone else. That is why we so often hurt others, worst of all those whom we love. We would do well to pray for that sensitive, imaginative insight that can see into the hearts of others.

The passage about the healing of the young girl is a story of contrasts. There is the contrast between the despair of the mourners and the hope of Jesus. 'Don't bother the Teacher,' they said. 'There's nothing anyone can do now.' 'Don't be afraid,' said Jesus, 'only believe.' There is the contrast between the unrestrained distress of the mourners and the calm serenity of Jesus. They were wailing and weeping; he was serene and in control. Why this difference? It was due to Jesus' perfect confidence and trust in God. The worst human disaster can be met with courage and gallantry when we meet it with God. They laughed him to scorn because they thought his hope was groundless and his calm mistaken. But the great fact of the Christian life is that what looks completely impossible with humans is possible with God. What, on merely human grounds, is far too good to be true, becomes blessedly true when God is there.

The Call Of Discipleship

Readings: 1 Kings 19:16, 19-21; Gal 5:1, 13-18; Lk 9:51-62

Christianity is a radical call to follow Jesus. It does not allow for a minimalist interpretation of the Gospel message.

I can recall a Spanish bishop once saying that 'what we preach in the West is a minimalist interpretation of Christianity'. The perceived wisdom is that a good Catholic is one who goes to Mass regularly, occasionally to the sacraments, tries to lead a reasonable life without hurting anyone, and maybe throws in the odd prayer. Today's Gospel is frightening. It challenges our perception of 'armchair' Christianity root and branch. A disciple is one who is prepared to 'burn his or her boats' and trust in Jesus alone. The old life is left completely behind.

The disciple is one who is dragged out of relative security, into a life of insecurity; from a life that is predictable and observable, into the world of mystery and the spirit; out of the realm of the finite, into the world of infinite possibilities.

The life of discipleship has at its core an attachment to the person of Jesus Christ. The call is not to a Church, a set of rules, even a way of life, no, it is a call into an intimate relationship of love with Jesus. Even in human love people talk about being 'consumed with love'. At other times they talk of being 'besotted' or 'burning with love'. More extreme language is employed when people talk of being 'madly in love'. Many saints had this stance towards Jesus.

St Thérèse experienced God's love as 'waves of infinite tenderness'. In an unpublished poem she wrote:

You, the great God, whom all heaven adores,
you live in me, a prisoner night and day;
the whole time your gentle voice implores me,
you keep on saying, 'I am thirsty…. I thirst for love'.

The great medieval mystic Julian of Norwich used the imagery of fire.
In T.S. Eliot's poem 'Little Gidding' her now-famous words are quoted:

And all shall be well, and
All manner of things shall be well.
....
When the tongues of flames are in-folded
Into the crowned knot of fire
And the fire and the rose are one.

Marriage is a covenant, a promise and a contract between two people
in love. With God there can also be a type of spousal or covenant love.
In the past, religious sisters described themselves as 'brides of Christ'.
There is a deep truth behind what seems to us like archaic language.
We are called to follow Christ. We are summoned to an exclusive
attachment to his person. We tend to laugh at people who want to
enter into pre-nuptial agreements. 'In the event of a breakup this is the
way things will be divided' the agreement goes. We ask how can people
really love each other if there isn't a deep level of trust whereby one
relies on the other to be faithful for life. The people in today's Gospel
were trying to set limits to their love. They wanted to set conditions
before they were willing to follow Jesus, much in the way of 'pre-
nuptial agreements'. That wasn't the way of Jesus.

Suffering

Readings: Zech 9:9-10; Rom 8:9, 11-13; Mt 11:25-30

People have struggled with the reality of suffering from the beginning of time. Some see it as a confirmation of their atheism. Others see it as the discipline of the Lord. Either way, suffering tears open the human heart and exposes its depths.

On Thursday last I got an urgent phone call. Patrick, whom I had known well as a youth-club member, had committed suicide. Patrick's development had been arrested at a fairly early age. He didn't grow to be a football-playing, disco-loving youngster like his peers. Because he was different he became the subject of intense bullying by his companions. He retreated into a world of gnawing isolation. He was alone and afraid. Then one day he climbed a tree. He attached the steel cord he was carrying to the tree and the other end to his neck – and jumped! His family was plunged into a world of bitter suffering. No explanations were possible, none were offered. It was people like Patrick's parents that Jesus was addressing when he said, 'Come to me, all you who labour and are overburdened.' In Patrick's death a wall of mystery confronted me. The lonely isolation of the bereaved is a strange world of unknowing.

Martin, my namesake, had everything going for him. He had a loving, supportive family. With a good education behind him, the world was his oyster. Or so we thought! Three years ago Martin was caught red-handed peddling hard drugs in a Dublin nightclub. Even with the benefit of hindsight, his parents couldn't detect any signs of drug addiction in his behaviour. I have visited Martin a number of times in prison. His former affluent lifestyle didn't prepare him for the harshness of prison life. He can't take it and constantly calls for counselling and help. The life of his family has been turned upside down. His mother constantly frets. His father has retreated to deal with the issue in silence. Their pain is palpable.

Suffering tears open the human soul and exposes its depths.

One of my favourite passages of scripture is from St Paul's letter to the Romans:

> Suffering produces endurance;
> Endurance produces character;
> And character produces hope;
> And hope does not disappoint us because God's spirit is poured
> into our hearts through the Holy Spirit who has been given to us.

I think suffering is part of the journey. Very few escape. Suffering makes or breaks us. There were two special prisoners in Auschwitz. One was an Austrian, Viktor Frankl, a professor of neurology and psychiatry who wrote the perennial bestseller, *Man's Search for Meaning*. This book is bursting with hope. The other was the wonderful Italian novelist Primo Levi. His novels are nihilistic and pessimistic. Levi never really recovered from his suffering and eventually ended his own life. In the case of Frankl, suffering, initially endured, later moulded and shaped his character into something beautiful. Levi resisted. He suffered the guilt of the survivor and never recovered.

In an utterly mysterious way the hand of God can be in suffering, shaping the human heart. The compassionate heart is often the one that has suffered. Sheila Cassidy, who was captured and tortured in Chile during the Pinochet regime, admits that she was a changed person through her experience. Suffering has been called 'the discipline of the Lord'. I know that's not easy to accept. It may be that God, as Father, disciplines us through suffering. Not that he causes it but that he permits it to happen. He doesn't interfere. It was through the cross that he achieved the victory.

Jesus Experiences Rejection

Readings: Ezek 2:2-5; 2 Cor 12:7-10; Mk 6:1-6

Before God we are all equal. We get our dignity, not from wealth, prestige, fame, but from the fact that we are all sons and daughters of the Father.

Some things never change. In the society in which Jesus lived, money was the second most important value. The first was prestige. 'In the oriental world to this day prestige is more important than any other factor and people will commit suicide rather than forfeit it.' In the Gospel today one can see with the mind's eye the Nazarenes turning up their noses at Jesus. 'This is the carpenter surely ... and they would not accept him.' The society of Jesus' time was so structured that everyone had a place on the social ladder. Nothing at all was done or said without taking the status or rank of the person concerned into account. An insult from someone superior to you would be accepted, even expected! An insult from an equal would be so humiliating as to make life impossible. Status and prestige were based upon ancestry, wealth, authority, education and virtue. They were signified and maintained by the way you dressed and were addressed, by whom you entertained socially and who invited you to their table and by where you were placed at a banquet or where you sat in the synagogue.

From where does our dignity come? The book of Job tells us that 'Naked I came from my mother's womb and naked I will return'. We all came into the world with nothing. So is it the family we were born into that makes us important? Or is it the amount of money or position our fathers or mothers had that gave us our place in society? We all get our dignity from being sons and daughters of the Father. We get our dignity from our Baptism. An equal dignity to all. 'God has no favourites.' Popularity, fame, wealth, position are all shallow veneers that are easily scraped away on death. 'The Lord gave, the Lord has taken away – blessed be the name of the Lord.'

When the disciples asked Jesus who was the greatest he called a child over and said, 'Unless you change and become like little children you will never enter the kingdom of heaven' – a sober thought indeed! Children in the society of Jesus had no status at all – they did not count. Jesus' concern was that these little ones should not be despised and treated as inferior and because of his compassion they were, in his eyes, of extraordinarily great value.

Again it is interesting that Jesus said, 'Those who humble themselves will be exalted.' The Kingdom of God then will be a society in which there will be no prestige and no status, no division of people into inferior and superior. Everyone will be loved and respected not because of education or wealth, or ancestry or authority or rank or virtue or other achievements, but because they, like everyone else, are a person and a child of God. So Jesus was accorded nothing but contempt in his own town. 'They would not accept him.' Jesus experienced that same sort of treatment meeted out to the homeless, drug addicts, the old, the poor, the unemployed. Jesus gained an intimate experience of rejection. He was there before us!

Rejection is particularly hurtful. In most cases the one rejected is blameless. Put yourself in the skin of a refugee, an economic migrant, an asylum-seeker. See yourself queuing up at the Department of Justice, Equality and Law Reform hoping against hope that you will be given asylum. Then a rejection comes. You have no one to turn to. Where can you go? Who will befriend you? Jesus felt even worse because he was rejected by his own.

The Pepsi-Cola Generation

Readings: Isa 66:10-14; Gal 6:14-18; Lk 10:1-12

While Christians largely remain silent about their faith in Jesus, vast sums of money are spent marketing ideas and products that contribute little to the sum of human happiness.

In the spring of 1986 Pepsi-Cola concluded what by any standards was an extraordinary business deal. The company agreed to pay the twenty-seven-year-old pop singer Michael Jackson nearly $15 million to appear in two of its television commercials and to provide creative consultancy on a third. For 180 seconds of screen time, plus the advice, Jackson was to earn twice as much as the idol of the time, Marlon Brando, could command for a full-length film. The production costs for the advertisement were another $2 million, and added to this was the television time to air the advertisements, amounting to another $50 million worldwide. All this to sell what is little more than an aerated water!

It seems a little unedifying to say that the Gospel of Jesus Christ has to compete in the market place with the Pepsi-Colas of this world. But that is the truth of it. The 'global village' is a maelstrom of voices all competing for attention. The fact that Christians remain silent about Jesus means that the name that brings salvation is unknown. Jesus said to the seventy two, 'Go on your way; behold I am sending you like lambs among wolves.' They were being sent into a world that was looking for a worldly Messiah, and for a Kingdom that would supplant the power of the Roman occupier. The world of Jesus, like our own today, didn't really want a purely spiritual message. John had preached that 'the Kingdom of God is at hand', but the message was hardly understood, even by those closest to Jesus.

The instruction to the disciples was to travel unencumbered. They were not to be worried about what they were to wear or how they looked. Being unencumbered meant travelling with a heart that was free of any attachments that might affect their freedom to preach the gospel. It is interesting to compare the instructions of Jesus with those of Fr Ignatius of Loyola, the founder of the Jesuits. He said to his first recruits, 'Try to make friends with the leaders of the opposition and with those who have most influence among heretics and wavering Catholics and loose them from their errors through wisdom and love.' The Jesuits appeared like angels of light in the dingy and demoralised scene of the sixteenth century. Care for the sick, alms for the poor, prison visiting, threadbare cassocks, sermons of fiery yet charitable zeal – all this at the time seemed nothing short of sensational. And yet it wasn't far from the instructions Jesus gave. It gave a witness that onlookers found compelling.

The message the disciples were to bring was one of peace. The peace of Christ is not based on the absence of conflict or on tranquillity alone; it is based on the promise and assurance that in Jesus we have a friend and a saviour; it is based on the faith that ultimately 'all things work together unto good for those who love God'. The peace of Christ is a little like the sea when a stiff bleeze is blowing: on the surface there may be agitation and waves but the deeper one goes the calmer and more tranquil is the sea. The Christian may and probably will suffer discomfort and distress but the peace of Christ cannot be taken away from one who has placed all their trust in God. I can recall officiating at the funeral of a young child where the mother talked about 'giving her beautiful young child back to God'. I marvelled at her faith and peace in the midst of intense pain. That, I think, is what the peace of Christ is all about.

The Sunday Sermon

Readings: Isa 55:10-11; Rom 8:18-23; Mt 13:1-23

How do I listen to and respond to the Word of God that I hear every Sunday at Mass? Do I allow my life to be influenced by God's word to me? These are the issues dealt with in today's Gospel.

Modern human relationships place a premium on listening. The Gospel of today's Mass focuses on this point – how we listen, accept and respond to the Word of God. The Word of God we hear in church is unlike what we read in the daily newspapers, popular magazines, weighty reports or hear even in the most impressive speech. Christians believe that the scriptures are the inspired Word of God. They are God's Word to us. We talk of the Old and New Testaments. A 'testament', in meaning, is not unlike the will a person makes before they die. In a will a person disposes of their money and property. On occasions a will also includes other desires or directives of the deceased. The Old and New Testaments are God's legacy to us – his will, his desires, his commands and hopes for us his people. It is easy to appreciate, therefore, the importance of the readings in the Sunday Mass. What is God saying to me today? How are his words encouraging me, inspiring me, correcting me? Are there changes I need to make in my life to bring it into conformity with God's will for me? We can either close or open our hearts to God's Word. Do I ever consider taking the missalette home and reflecting on the Word that I have read and heard explained at Mass?

There are people who are negatively disposed towards the Sunday sermon. Their starting point is to try to detect the errors or the points they disagree with. Then there is the ploy of 'selective inattention' – this is the person who only hears what he or she wants to hear. Such a person has an inbuilt mechanism to filter out those parts of the readings or sermon that make them feel uncomfortable.

It is possible that Jesus spoke this parable of the sower on the shores of the Sea of Galilee, perhaps in sight of a farmer actually sowing in the distance. Jesus may have called his listeners' attention to what was happening. 'Look at that sower in the field scattering the seed.' They could see clearly what he was using as the basis of his parable. So many of his parables were related to life as it was lived in the Palestine of his day. The parable, as Jesus used it, was spoken; it was not read. Its impact had to be immediate, not the result of long study with commentaries and dictionaries. It made truth flash upon a person as the lightning suddenly illuminates a pitch-dark night.

Generally speaking, a parable will have only one point. A parable is not an allegory; an allegory is a story in which every detail has an inner meaning, so it has to be read and studied; a parable is heard. The parable is aimed at the hearers of the Word. If we take the parable as a warning to hearers, it means that there are different ways of accepting the Word of God, and the fruit that it produces depends on the heart of the one who accepts it. The fate of any spoken word depends on the hearer. There are people into whose minds the Word has no more chance of gaining entry than the seed has of settling into ground that has been beaten hard by many feet. There are many things that can shut a person's mind. Prejudice can make one blind to everything one does not wish to see. The unteachable spirit can erect a barrier that cannot easily be broken down. Sometimes an immoral character and a person's way of life can shut their mind. There may be some truth that condemns the things they love and that accuses the things they do; and many refuse to listen to or to recognise the truth that condemns them, for there are none so blind as those who deliberately will not see.

Repentance Is A Grace Without Words

Readings: Amos 7:12-15; Eph 1:13-14; Mk 6:7-13

'So they set off to preach repentance.' To repent means to change one's mind and to fit one's actions to this change.

The story of Dietrich Bonhoeffer is well known. He was martyred by the Nazis in 1945. He voluntarily returned to Germany, knowing full well that in continuing to proclaim his faith he was signing his own death warrant. His books, in particular *The Cost of Discipleship*, have had an enormous influence on generations of Christians. In one of his letters from prison he wrote: 'The Christian, unlike the devotees of redemption myths, has no last line of escape available from earthly tasks and difficulties into the eternal, he must drink the earthly cup to the dregs and only in his doing so is the crucified and risen Lord with him, and he is crucified and risen with Christ'.

We read today: 'So they set off to preach repentance....' Repentance is a death ... a death to self. Repentance is the first demand of the gospel. It was the message of John the Baptist even before Jesus began to preach. The change is not necessarily from robbery, theft, murder, adultery and glaring sins. The change may be from a life that is completely selfish, instinctively demanding, totally inconsiderate, the change from a self-centred to a God-centred life – and a change like that hurts. I think it is the pain of repentance that brought Bonhoeffer to mind. Again he wrote: 'When Christ calls a man, he bids him come and die'.

We think of repentance as an act rather than a journey. We have seen it as doing something rather than receiving something. By tying repentance to the sacrament of Reconciliation (Confession) we have set it in a moment in time. We have mirrored the question of the evangelical 'Are you saved?' rather than seeing repentance as a spirituality of reconciliation because repentance is a life's journey. The Dominican author Simon Tugwell noted in his analysis of the Ways of Imperfection: 'the first work of grace is simply to enable us to begin to understand what is wrong'. And one of the first things that is 'wrong' is that we are not 'in control'; we do not have all the answers. Our inability to change using our own power alone is a powerful first lesson in repentance.

I think we saw the sacrament of confession as a magical formula, a panacea with instant properties. We had the words without the grace. Repentance is a grace without words. Facing the sheer truth of our powerlessness in the face of wrongdoing makes available the fundamental spiritual insight that insists on the necessity of *kenosis* – the ancient Greek word that signifies an 'emptying out'. Expressed in modern vocabulary we are talking about the need to surrender. That is the rub! As they say 'let go and let God'. To repent means to change one's mind and then to fit one's actions to this change. Repentance means a change of heart and a change of action. The change of heart comes first. It is bound to hurt, for it involves the bitter realisation that the way we were following is wrong. It is bound to disturb, because it means a complete reversal of life. That is precisely why so few people do repent – for the last thing most people desire is to be disturbed.

Lady Asquith, in a vivid phrase, speaks of people who 'dawdle towards death'. So many people do that. They resent all strenuous activity. Life for them is 'a land where it is always afternoon'. In some ways the positive, vivid, swashbuckling sinner who is crashing his way to some self-chosen goal is a more attractive person than the negative, nebulous loiterer who drifts spinelessly and without direction through life. The sacrament is a staging post on the journey of repentance. Because every sacrament is 'an act of Christ' and forgiveness is received, it is Christ's forgiveness, and it is an important action in the pilgrimage of repentance.

Moved With Compassion

Readings: Deut 30:10-14; Col 1:15-20; Lk 10:25-37

Compassion is a much politicised word. It is a slightly glamorous and highly charged word, which can mask the reality illustrated in today's Gospel.

Compassion is on trial. It is a word that has become politicised into meaninglessness. It has been highjacked by the publicists and publicity seekers. I run scared when I hear this word used on political chat shows. The beauty of compassion (to suffer with) is that it is invariably hidden. Maura is a friend of mine. When her father contracted Alzheimer's disease she resigned from her well-paid job to give him full-time care. With never a complaint but a heart full of love, she cared for him until he died. That is compassion. The Bradys live in a neat suburban home. Well-trimmed hedges and a manicured lawn are indications of a house-proud family. John next door was paralysed through a terrible motor accident. The Bradys knocked their back garden wall down to facilitate ease of movement for John and his wheelchair from one house to the other. That is compassion. In a high-rise apartment complex in Boston I came across Lorenzo, a sad old man with a gaping wound in his throat. His lay-about sons were living off his Social Security cheque. All the time I was in Boston Maria tended to him with tenderness. His wound was bathed, the filth of his room was cleared away, the necessities of life obtained. All done with love. That is compassion. Compassion places high demands on the giver. It is giving without measure.

The priest and the Levite were unwilling to set aside the law of defilement in the interests of love. Their 'image' and their functions took precedence over the injured person. The Samaritan in today's Gospel hadn't the training or sophistication of those who passed by. He was a simple person, though hated by the Jews.

Compassion is more than 'doing things' for a person in need. It means looking into another soul and listening to the pain. It means experiencing some of that pain yourself. Compassion is trying to take some of the cross from the back of another person and feeling the weight on your own shoulders. Love unpins real compassion. This is an intertwining of the head and the heart that embraces the brokenness of the other. The Greek word for compassion is far stronger than the English – it means intestines, bowels, entrails or heart, that is to say, an inward part from which strong emotions arise. It means an impulse that wells up from one's very entrails, a gut reaction. The Gospel today says the Samaritan was 'moved with compassion'. We sometimes say 'my heart went out to him'. The suffering of the poor and oppressed had a powerful effect on Jesus. Compassion is a 'feeling', even a glamorous word. Yet when translated into practical action the cost can be high and painful for the giver. Like love, it is primarily a decision.

There are other places in the Gospels where we read of the compassion of Jesus: 'He was moved with compassion for the crowds and he healed their sick'. (Matthew 14:14) 'He was moved with compassion because they were like sheep without a shepherd'. (Matthew 9:36) 'Do not cry,' he said to the widow's son at Nain.

'Go and do likewise' Jesus tells the scholar of the law. We are to love others as we love ourselves. Wouldn't Christianity change the face of the earth if we Christians took the Gospel seriously?

Fifteenth Sunday in Ordinary Time

The Weeds And The Wheat

Readings: Wis 12:13, 16-19; Rom 8:26-27; Mt 13:24-43

Things are not all black and white. The spiritual life is a learning to live with paradox. It is holding opposites together and still living in hope.

Last night I came home and talked to a young boy and girl who were 'shooting up' heroin in the church porch. As she frantically searched for a vein in her arm, the pretty twenty-year-old girl said to me, 'I never thought I would be doing this in front of a priest.' The young boy told me he had obtained four As in his Leaving Certificate and 'now I am reduced to this'. She needed £60 a day to feed her habit. He needed £100. The crime and the pain and the wrecked lives were not what they planned for themselves. Like the farmer sowing the good seed, they too started out with hope. They were good young people, but somehow weeds or darnel began to sprout in the field of their young lives. So it is with all of us.

Jesus is comparing the human soul to a field sowed with good seed by the farmer. The farmer is full of hope that the crop he will reap will be a full and bountiful one. How like the human condition that is! Our marriage will be the best one ever. Our priesthood will be anointed and generous. We will be caring, sensitive and loving people. We will be the best of fathers/mothers. We will be different. Before I left the young addicts the boy said, 'Father, will you say a prayer for us?' I prayed with them both. I could see the huge areas of generosity and love in their lives. They were not all bad. The good seed was also visible.

Every life is a mixture of light and darkness, sin and virtue, good and evil. Every human life is a paradox. Jesus knows this. 'Let them both grow till the harvest,' he said of the weeds and wheat growing in the field. Isn't that peculiar coming from Jesus? Learning to live with paradox and still retaining hope in the mercy and grace of God is the pilgrim journey of most people. People condemn themselves and are condemned by others because there are areas of their lives that are disordered. Each of us carries a shadow – acknowledging it, embracing it and seeking healing for it is part of life's journey for the Christian. We were raised on the scripture, 'Be perfect as your Heavenly Father is perfect'. We strove to be perfect. We sweated and strained and worried when we were less than we ought to be. We feared the punishment of God. But only God is perfect. The goal set for us, based on a mistranslation of scripture, was unrealisable. Many people simply gave up the struggle and abandoned themselves to the darkness. They considered that following Christ was an impossible dream or only for the chosen few.

The good news is that God loves imperfect beings. I am imperfect. God loves me. A spirituality of imperfection suggests that there is something wrong with me, with you, with the world, but there is nothing wrong with that, because that is the nature of our reality. God comes through the wounds – the sin – the vulnerability – the pain. Our very sins, our sickness, are precisely what bring us closer to the reality that no matter how hard we try to deny it, we are not the ones in control here. And this realisation, inevitably and joyously, brings us closer to God. Western theology has been very linear in its thinking. Things were always right or wrong, good or bad, sinful or virtuous. There was no admission of any shades of grey. No place for struggle, for searching. We always wanted to know exactly where we stood with God. Was our insurance policy fully paid up? Were we in the clear? The spiritual life is not quite like that. It admits of greyness. The parable of the wheat and weeds is an encouragement to all of us when we are willing to admit to our darkness and learn to live with paradox.

The Desert Within

Readings: Jer 23:1-6; Eph 2:13-18; Mk 6:30-34

The encounter with self, the journey inwards, is a difficult journey and it demands courage.

I recently visited an alcoholic friend who was undergoing one of his periodic 'drying out' sessions in a psychiatric hospital. I asked him how he was feeling. Immediately he launched into an account of the group sessions he was attending, his individual counselling sessions, his proposed release date, his companions, and other details of life in the hospital. 'But how are you feeling about the whole thing?' I asked. 'How do you mean?' he replied, 'haven't I just told you?' I persisted, 'Are you feeling angry, ashamed, frightened, guilty, fearful?' But he couldn't really understand what I was getting at. He wasn't yet prepared to enter the lonely place, the desert, mentioned in today's Gospel. The encounter with self, the journey inwards, is a difficult journey and it demands courage. But it is in this desert journey that I am most likely to meet Christ.

In his book *Why do Christians Break Down?* William Miller writes: 'I break down because I am afraid to admit that evil, unacceptable, inappropriate tendencies, still exist within me, even though I have committed myself to the way of Christ, and I cannot accept them as being truly a part of me'. When I think of deserts I think first of all of the desert within. I think of the mystery of the human person, always searching, questioning, always wanting to know. I think, too, of desolation. Recently I had a phone call from a wonderful woman, mother of a suicidal child. Her terrible desert experience touched me.

She was so alone, struggling with this awful worry. A wife, soon to be bereaved as her husband dies of terminal cancer, is in the desert. So too is the drug addict who said to me, 'Father, I have a hole in my soul.' The homeless often have a hunted look, darting eyes, expecting the worst, looking for enemies, never at peace – in the desert.

I think of Jesus and his familiarity with the desert. It was there that he wrestled with the demons of temptation and won the victory. I think of today's Gospel and in a way it fills me with foreboding.

The desert within is the place of silence, where we confront ourselves and meet the Lord. Poet Jessica Powers puts it like this:

> Deep in the soul the acres lie
> of virgin lands, of sacred wood
> where waits the Spirit. Each soul bears
> this trackless solitude.
>
> The voice invites, implores in vain
> the fearful and the unaware;
> but she who heeds and enters in
> finds ultimate wisdom there.

Jesus invites the apostles to come away 'to a lonely place all by yourselves and rest for a while. We all need some silence in our lives. We need space – space to pray, to reflect, to retreat, to renew. Life is so busy. The desert is the place to rethink our attitudes and review our values. Unless I take hold of myself and shake the pillars of my rigidity, which so nicely protect my security, I will remain precisely where I am: secure in my familiar position, but troubled in my innermost self with vague but chronic dissatisfaction, filled with unfulfilment and longing for something 'more'. The encounter with self is best facilitated with the help of a spiritual adviser. We all need someone who will hold the mirror so that we can see ourselves more clearly. We can be the worst judges in our own case. A person who refuses to take time out for prayer and reflection will remain unfulfilled and live in holy discontent. There is such a deep level of wisdom in today's Gospel.

Hospitality

Readings: Gen 18:1-10; Col 1:24-28; Lk 10:38-42

We all need a 'safe port in a storm'. The house of Martha, Mary and Lazarus at Bethany was such a house for Jesus.

One of the most famous priests in Australian Catholic folklore is Fr Patrick Hartigan, whose parents came from Lissycasey in County Clare around 1864. Fr Hartigan wrote under the pen name of 'John O'Brien'. When his book of poems, *Around the Boree Log*, was published in 1921 it was an instant success and it is now established as an Australian classic. The tradition of hospitality was deeply rooted in the Irish emigrants, especially those who lived in the Australian outback. Our Gospel today hones in on the theme of hospitality.

> Bedad, he'll have to stay the night; the rain is going to pour
> So make the rattling windows tight, and close the kitchen door
> And bring the old lopsided chair, the tattered cushion, too;
> We'll make the stranger happy there, the way we used to do.
> The years have turned the rusted key, and time is on the jog
> Yet spend another night with me around the boree log.

One can almost smell and feel the cosy hospitality described by Hartigan. Here was a home that was also a sanctuary; his was a 'safe place' to be in. The happiness of the visitor was central. A person in trouble, or confused by fear or doubt, would experience this as a place of comfort protected from the gales of life. Such a place was that little house on the main Jericho Road at Bethany for Jesus. The faces of

Martha, Mary and Lazarus were always ready to greet Jesus. We all need a 'safe port in a storm'. For most people this will, hopefully, be the family home. The house at Bethany had an open door.

We live in a busy, busy, busy world. We are identified by what we do. Everyone is trying to prove him or herself – to whom? For what? Our newspapers are full of stories about stress and how to cope. Even holidays have to be a busy time. Maybe Martha was infected with the workaholic syndrome? Anyway she was a bit tetchy about having to do all the chores. Martha obviously wanted to please Jesus by having a good meal ready.

Jesus is pleased with Martha but he refers to something more spiritual, namely, the need of giving 'undivided attention to the Lord' (cf. 1 Corinthians 7:35) – an important aspect of hospitality. The stranger or visitor needs a listening heart that will embrace his or her story. Could it be that Jesus needed an attentive ear so that he could retell the frustration and joys of his ministry? Maybe he needed to complain a bit! In Martha Jesus found an 'anam chara'.

One must set one's heart on the Kingdom of God (Luke 12:31) rather than worry about other things. Jesus is gently emphasising that no matter how burdensome our worldly concerns are, we need to have time to listen to the Lord with undivided attention. All of us need time for prayerful reflection in our lives. The founder of Alcoholics Anonymous, Bill Wilson, wrote once that 'we must find some spiritual basis for living, else we die'. How can this be done without reflection?

There is the story of the little Jewish child who went up to the rabbi and asked, 'How come, Rabbi, that God does not speak to us today? He spoke through Moses, Abraham and all the patriarchs and prophets; why does he say nothing now?' The rabbi gently bent down to the little boy and whispered into his ear, 'Because today we do not bend down low enough to listen.' Our pride stops us from bending down low enough and the noisy world in which we live can stifle the voice of God unless we take time in his presence. Perhaps that's the message of this story.

An Inclusive Church

Readings: 1 Kings 3:5, 7-12; Rom 8:28-30; Mt 13:44-52

Thankfully the Church is not a gathering of the elect. It is a community of all who believe in some way. The Church cannot discriminate, it is open to all.

Albert Nolan is a priest working in South Africa. About fifteen years ago he was elected Master General of the Dominicans world-wide. This is a prestigious position of power. I believe a person elected to this position is referred to as 'the White Pope'. He refused the position. Albert returned to South Africa to continue his pastoral work among the disadvantaged. He wrote a book called *Jesus before Christianity*. What an intriguing title? Jesus before Church – before titles like Your Eminence, Your Grace, Your Lordship, Monsignor, Canon, even Father! Jesus before power and penalties; Jesus before Christianity! Nolan writes powerfully of the ministry of Jesus, who broke through all barriers of ritual exclusion practised by the Jewish hierarchy. The ministry of Jesus was at the margins. The special focus of his care and attention were those ostracised by the religious élite of the day. Today's Gospel reminds me of people like Albert Nolan and Dietrich Bonhoeffer, people who lived and preached the pure Gospel of Jesus (before Christianity). The example of fishing was so familiar to everyone. The Sea of Galilee, then as now, was a fruitful place to fish. It is in the nature of the drag-net that it does not, and cannot, discriminate. It is bound to draw in all kinds of things in its course through the water. Its contents are bound to be a mixture. If we apply that to the Church, which is the instrument of God's Kingdom upon earth, it means that the Church cannot be discriminative but is bound to be a mixture of all kinds of people, good and bad, useless and useful. To me, that is the glory of the Church. It has time for everyone, especially the sinner. There is an old down-and-out man who shuffles around the part of the city where I live. He lives rough. Not for him institutional care or any contact with authority – civil or religious. He is a serious alcoholic and unable to care for himself. He smells! Beneath the grubby exterior is a person I have grown to appreciate and love. A prayerful person, he hates to miss daily Mass. I love to think that Mickey is a true son of God and son of the Church. The presence of people like him is the glory of the Church.

There have always been two views on the Church – the exclusive and the inclusive. The exclusive view holds that the Church is for people who are good, people who are really and fully committed, people who are quite different from the world. Do we sometimes give that impression? Is the Church only for the clean, well-scrubbed, state-of-grace person? There is an attraction in that view, but it is not the New Testament view, because, apart from anything else, who is to do the judging, when we are told that we must not judge? (Matthew 7:1) It is not any person's place to say who is committed to Christ and who is not. The inclusive view feels instinctively that the Church must be open to all, and that, like the drag-net, so long as it is a human institution it is bound to be a mixture. That is exactly what this parable teaches. But equally this parable teaches that the time of separation will come when the good and the bad are sent to their respective destinations. We are not asked to involve ourselves in that separation. Individually we may choose our own heaven or hell but the final separation is a matter for the justice, mercy and love of God.

In the meantime we are to be like Solomon, praying for an understanding heart, as we seek to choose the Good in all our daily lives.

+ the author of Ps 118 That's why I love your commands more than finest Gold.

These parables put the great Gospel teaching another way 'Seek first the kingdom of God What do you treasure most? For where your treasure is, there will your heart be also

Greatness

Readings: 2 Kings 4:42-44; Eph 4:1-6; Jn 6:1-15

When we bring the little we have to Jesus we may be providing material for a miracle.

We are sceptical people! We refuse to believe that miracles can happen. If miracles do happen, we don't recognise them. I have seen miracles of love. Miracles happen quietly in hospitals, in night shelters, perhaps even in board rooms. It was Andrew who brought that lad to Jesus, and by bringing him made the miracle possible. No one ever knows what will come out of it when we bring someone to Jesus. If parents bring up their child in the knowledge and the love and the fear of God, no one can say what mighty things that child may some day do for God and for people. Think of people like Leonard Cheshire, bomber pilot and friend of the severely handicapped, or Jean Vanier, naval officer and founder of the L'Arche communities for the mentally disadvantaged, or Nelson Mandela, lawyer, prisoner and global reconciler. They all started out as ordinary people like you or me.

Andrew did not know what he was doing when he brought that lad to Jesus that day; he didn't know what Jesus would do, but he trusted that the offerings of the small boy would somehow be transformed. There is a tale of an old German schoolmaster who, when he entered his class of boys in the morning, used to remove his cap and bow ceremoniously to them. Someone asked him why he did this. His answer was: 'You never know what one of these boys may some day become'. He was right – because one of them was Martin Luther.

Think of Martin Luther King in his famous 'I have a dream speech' of 3 April 1968: 'I've been to the mountain top ... I've looked over and I've seen the promised land. I may not get there with you, but I want you to know tonight that we as a people will get to the promised land. So, I'm happy tonight. Mine eyes have seen the glory of the coming of the Lord'. King's famous speech was peppered with biblical allusions and with religious faith. Miracles of equality among the races happened because Martin Luther King made himself available to God. He was the Andrew of his time, or the loaves and fishes!

There is a contrast between Andrew and Philip. Philip was the man who said, 'The situation is hopeless; nothing can be done.' Andrew was the one who said, 'I'll see what I can do; and I'll trust Jesus to do the rest.' People like Dietrich Bonhoeffer, Mother Teresa, Jean Monnet, Sheila Cassidy, Pope John XXIII, have made a difference because they trusted in God to do something, and they co-operated. The boy's offering of bread and fishes was small in material terms. Jesus needs what we can bring him. It may not be much but he needs it. It may well be that the world is denied miracle after miracle and triumph after triumph because we will not bring to Jesus what we have and what we are.

When we want comfort in sorrow, when we want strength in difficulty, when we want peace in turmoil, there is no one so wonderful as Jesus, and we can talk to him and walk with him and open our hearts to him. But when he comes to us with some stern demand for sacrifice, with the offer of some cross, we are not at all happy. When we examine our hearts, it may be that we will find that we too love Jesus for what we can get rather than what we can give. The people in today's Gospel wished to use Jesus for their own purposes and to mould him to their own dreams. They were waiting for the Messiah, but they were looking for some impressive leader who would be king and conqueror. They wanted someone to put down the Roman occupiers. They probably thought 'If we can harness him and his power to our dreams, things will begin to happen'.

An aspect of this miracle that is seldom commented on is that of community. These people had traipsed together around the Lake of Galilee. As many as five thousand of them sat down without a murmur. They were together as a people. We call the Church the 'People of God'. But do we live as a people? Does our Sunday celebration together unite us in our care for one another? Are we characterised by our love for one another as we ought to be?

Teach Us To Pray

Readings: Gen 18:20-32; Col 2:12-14; Lk 11:1-13

In times of difficulty there appears to be a deep-seated need in the human heart to reach out for help to a force or forces beyond oneself.

Joe Simpson, an experienced mountaineer, faced an appalling situation in his attempt to scale the Siula Grande in the Peruvian Andes. On the descent he fell into a deep crevasse. His climbing companion, Richard, couldn't hang on to him any longer and cut the rope that was Joe's only lifeline to continued existence on this earth. It seemed like inevitable death. In *Touching the Void*, the taut and gripping account of his dilemma is vividly described. No mention of God. But Joe hoped fervently that his aunt in Liverpool was praying for him and that her prayers would be heard. Through a pilgrimage of excruciating pain Joe survived.

Brian Keenan in his extraordinary book, *An Evil Cradling*, describes his captivity for four and a half years in the cellars of Beirut. He professed himself an atheist to a Muslim inquirer before his capture. And yet he could write this: 'It was becoming increasingly difficult to hold our own minds in balance. On each occasion when these prayers [from their Muslim captors] would begin it was as if we were being inoculated with their hysteria. As hard as these men prayed I called out to God to shield my own mind from the contamination of this holy insanity . . . . Somewhere in my head as I prayed and ached and moaned, I heard these words 'Forgive them, for they know not what they do'.

On 3 December 1974 the door to Anne Maguire's London house was forced open by plainclothes policemen and she was arrested on suspicion of involvement in the Guildford IRA bombing. This was the beginning of an appalling human nightmare that resulted in an innocent woman spending eight years in jail for a crime she didn't commit. Her faith never left her. The prison authorities refused her permission to attend her son Vincent's wedding in 1982. She related: 'that day was one of the hardest of my sentence'. She devised a unique wedding gift for Vincent. 'I'd had two sets of rosary beads sent in and had them blessed by a priest. I said fifteen decades of the Rosary on each one and sent them to Vincent and Kathy with a letter regretting that neither Paddy [her husband who was also imprisoned] nor I could be with them on their big day.'

The request of the apostles to Jesus to 'teach us to pray' isn't difficult to understand. They knew, as many of us do, that we cannot make it on our own! They saw Jesus praying. They wanted to be able to pray too. Prayer is the cement that binds the relationship between God and us. I work with a group called Retrouvaille who help people suffering the pain of a marriage in trouble. We know the primacy of true dialogue in the human relationship. Such dialogue is healing. It's not that different in our relationship with God. St Thérèse in her autobiography put it simply: 'I tell God what I want quite simply… and he always manages to understand me'.

The greatest intercessory prayer was the prayer of Jesus on the cross. He hung between God the Father and the sins of humanity. He placed himself in the breach. His prayer was acceptable to the Father. When we pray for our own or others' needs we do something similar. We position ourselves between the problem or the pain, and the Father who is all merciful and kind. We become intercessors. When strife in Northern Ireland was at its height one Anglican clergyman, Reverend Cecil Kerr, established a house of intercession in Rostrevor. Year after year, as bombs exploded and good people died, a stream of intercessory prayer was directed to the Heavenly Father. I suspect, although I will never know, that this prayer played as significant a part in the Peace Process, as the worthy efforts of politicians and combatants.

The Light Of God's Love Can Never Be Extinguished

Readings: Isa 55:1-3; Rom 8:35-37; Mt 14:13-21

The second reading of today's Mass reassures us that 'nothing can come between us and the love of God'.

Thérèse of Lisieux, the French saint, commonly known as the Little Flower, died in 1897. She pioneered what has become known as 'the little way' to Jesus – doing the ordinary things extraordinarily well for love of Jesus. During the last eighteen months of her life she experienced extreme doubts against her faith. In fact, according to one author, 'in her heart she suffered a complete loss of faith'. She was plunged into such a spiritual darkness that she spoke of being capable of blasphemy. In the end her physical distress and spiritual weariness became so intense that she warned her sisters not to place anything poisonous nearby in case she might commit suicide! In the end all she could say was that 'behind the dark cloud my sun is still shining'.

I never tire of saying that 'religion is a relationship'. It is a relationship with the God who loves us – a love relationship. 'I have loved you with an everlasting love and I am constant in my affection for you.' To some extent we Catholics have pedestalised the Church, perhaps at the expense of our relationship with God. The institution may have become an obstacle rather than a help. As a result, many good Catholics have been devastated by recent happenings in the Church. Abuse of power, sexual scandals, theological divisions, liturgical experimentation, and many other things have shaken the faith of people.

Today's second reading has solid help and reassurance for us. In this reading we are told that 'nothing can separate us from the love of

Christ'. Certainly the Catholic Church is going through a crisis of seismic proportions. What should our response be? In verses 38-39 Paul makes a list of terrible things that might presume to separate us from God. But no. Here is a vision to take away all loneliness and all fear. Paul is saying: 'You can think of every terrifying thing that this or any other world can produce. Not one of them is able to separate the Christian from the love of God which is in Jesus Christ. Of what then shall we be afraid?'

My relationship is with God. And in the midst of the deepest darkness I know, like Thérèse, that 'behind the dark cloud my sun is still shining'. The light of God's love can never be extinguished.

As a postscript we need to remember that the Catholic Church has weathered trials even greater that those it is experiencing today. For instance, Avignon, a city in southern France, served for a time as the residence of two antipopes, Clement VII and Benedict XIII. During this long period in the 1300s it became the gathering place for some of the worst members of medieval society and was called a sewer by Petrarch because of its filth, disease and prostitutes. It was a place of debauchery and division. The Church has always been in constant need of reform and that happens again and again through the power of the Holy Spirit.

The Transfiguration

Readings: Dan 7:9-10, 13-14; 2 Pet 1:16-19; Mk 9:2-10

Within the cloud 'the mystery of God' is revealed. Jesus is reassured that his mission leads to death and ultimately resurrection and glory.

Two clouds, one of destruction, the other of hope. Sixty-six years ago the world's first atomic bomb destroyed the Japanese city of Hiroshima. The plane that carried the Hiroshima bomb was named the *Enola Gay* after the mother of the pilot, Colonel Paul Tibbets. Captain William Parson of the US navy, who was also on board, described the flash of the explosion as being as brilliant as the sun. Reconnaissance planes reported that, four hours after the explosion, nothing could be seen of the city but a pall of smoke and fires all round. A vast mushroom cloud rose ten miles into the sky. The city was vaporised! This was a shattering moment in history, now all but forgotten. This cloud filled humanity with dread and the threat of its use again fuelled nearly fifty years of the Cold War.

In the Gospel we have another, much more benign, cloud – a cloud of hope. The presence of God is regularly connected with the cloud. It was in the cloud that Moses met God. It was in the cloud that God came to the tabernacle. It was the cloud that filled the Temple when it was dedicated after Solomon had built it. And it was the dream of the Jews that when the Messiah came the cloud of God's presence would return to the Temple. (Exodus 16:10; 19:9; 33:9; 1 Kings 8:10; 2 Maccabees 2:8) The descent of the cloud is a way of saying that the Messiah had come, and any Jew would understand it like that.

The transfiguration of Jesus came at a turning-point in his life. Peter had just recognised Jesus as the Messiah, and Jesus went on to teach his disciples about his coming death and resurrection. Then he went up a mountain (traditionally thought to be Mt Hermon) with Peter, James and John. There they saw Jesus transformed by a heavenly glory, and Elijah and Moses talking with him. The experience ended with a voice from heaven, similar to that at the time of Jesus' Baptism, which said, 'This is my Son, whom I have chosen – listen to him.' Moses and Elijah represented the two major parts of the Old Testament, the Law and the Prophets. By their presence they showed that all was fulfilled in Jesus. Peter wanted tents to be put up, to make the experience last. But that was not the point. The Transfiguration confirmed the rightness of the way Jesus had chosen. It pointed to the glory that would one day be his. But before that time he had to die on the cross. The disciples did not understand this until after the Resurrection. I think there are other issues here.

Jesus had a system of evangelisation, a 'circle of caring', that has relevance for today. He didn't hope to reach everyone in Israel. He fostered degrees of relationship with people. Peter, James and John were very special. They shared the intimacy of his inner life – here at the Transfiguration and, of course, in Gethsemane. Then he had the twelve with whom he spent time alone, as we saw in a recent Gospel. They were 'special friends'. Then he had the seventy-two who enjoyed a relationship of discipleship with him. Then he had the women who were special and the crowds who followed him and listened to his teaching.

Today Jesus is sharing a very special moment with his very personal friends. They would play a pivotal role in his mission of spreading the good news after he died. Then there is the mystery attached to this incident. Commentators are puzzled by discrepancies in place and time in the Gospel accounts. There is speculation as to the real significance of this event. In a way it is surrounded by the 'silence of mystery'. Only in the end, when our partial knowledge ceases, when we see God 'face to face', will we fully know the ways by which God has guided his creation to that definite Sabbath rest for which he created heaven and earth. (*Cathecism of the Catholic Church*)

Money Makes The World Go Round?

Readings: Eccl 1:2, 2:21-23; Col 3:1-5, 5-9; Lk 12:13-21

Do we own money or does it own us? Money can separate us from family and friends and from the poor and dispossessed.

English author George Orwell wrote a book about poverty in London in the 1930s, entitled *Keep the Aspidistra Flying*. In it, the central character, Gordon Comstock, adapted one of the most famous passages on love in the Bible, from St Paul's letter to the Corinthians. He replaced the word 'love' with 'money'. This is how it read:

> If I speak in human and angelic tongues but do not have money, I am a resounding gong or a clashing cymbal. And if I have the gift of prophecy and comprehend all mysteries and all knowledge; if I have all faith so as to move mountains, but do not have money, I am nothing. If I give away everything I own, and hand over my body so that I may boast but do not have money, I gain nothing.

Perhaps the Great American Depression of the 1930s illustrates more than any other event in contemporary history the vice-like grip money can get on the human heart. Steel magnate Charles Schwab, despite his millions and the security of his Manhattan palace, freely confessed: 'I'm afraid. Every man is afraid'. J. David Stern, a wealthy newspaper publisher, became so terrified that he later wrote in his autobiography: 'I sat in my back office, trying to figure out what to do. To be explicit, I sat in my private bathroom. My bowels were loose with fear'. Calvin

Coolidge sadly told a friend: 'I can see nothing to give ground for hope'. Money was all they had and the thought of the loss of it paralysed them with fear and dread.

The Gospel today is not necessarily aimed at those who are rich but rather at those who put their hope and their future in the accumulation of wealth. It is also aimed at the malice of covetousness. If the person in today's Gospel had been 'wise', he would have been 'rich' towards God, that is, had his mind fixed on the things of God. This does not mean being indifferent to the things of this world, which have their important place. The question is 'Do we own money or does it own us?' Is it such a priority that things like friendship, family, voluntary work for others, are all subjected to our need to make more and more money?

> The covetous man is never satisfied with money, and the lover of wealth reaps no fruit from it; so this too is vanity. Where there are great riches, there are also many to devour them. Of what use are they to the owner except to feast his eyes upon? Sleep is sweet to the labouring man, whether he eats little or much, but the rich man's abundance allows him no sleep. (Ecclesiastes 5:9)

Many rich people use what they have accumulated to relieve the distress of others. Some place a priority on providing employment for people, thereby raising the quality of life for all. Others become patrons of the arts and sciences. Still others help the handicapped.

Storing treasure in heaven is a metaphor for attempting to lead a Christ-like life in this world. To have one's heart in heaven (12:34) means to be inspired by God, who is love. To be 'rich' with God means to share his life of love. Poverty or detachment from material things is not an end in itself. It is the means by which a person truly possesses these things in receiving them as God's gift to be shared with others. The only antidote to covetousness is a gratitude that is realised in generosity.

Peter – The Impetuous Friend Of Jesus

Readings: Kings 19:9, 11-13; Rom 9:1-15; Mt 14:22-33

After the feeding of the multitude Jesus sent his disciples away. John tells us that the crowd wished to come and make him a king by force. There was a surge of popular acclamation, and in the excited state of Palestine a revolution might well have begun there and then. It was a dangerous situation, and the disciples might have complicated it, for they, too, were still thinking of Jesus in terms of earthly power.

When he was alone, Jesus went up into a mountain to pray; and by this time the night had come. This was not the first time that Jesus retired alone for prayer. It was his prayer that strengthened him to fulfil the will of his Father and face the inevitability of his passion and death. The disciples had set out back across the lake. One of the sudden storms, for which the lake was notorious, had come down, and they were struggling against the winds and the waves, and making little progress. As the night wore on, Jesus began to walk round the head of the lake to reach the other side. Matthew has already told us that when Jesus fed the crowds he made them sit down on the green grass. By that we know it must have been the springtime. Very likely it was near the Passover time, which was in the middle of April. If that is so, the moon would be full. Jesus, walking on the high ground at the north of the lake, clearly saw the boat fighting with the waves, and came down to the shore to help. It may describe a miracle in which Jesus actually walked on the water. Or, it may equally mean that the disciples' boat was driven by the wind to the northern shore of the lake, that Jesus came down from the mountain to help them when he saw them struggling in the moonlight, and that he came walking through the surf and the waves towards the boat, and came so suddenly upon them that they were terrified when they saw him.

In the hour of the disciples' need Jesus came to them. When the wind was contrary and life was a struggle, Jesus was there to help. In life, the wind is often contrary. There are times when we are up against it and life is a desperate struggle with ourselves, with our circumstances, with our temptations, with our sorrows, with our decisions. At such a time no one need struggle alone, for Jesus comes across the storms of life, with hand stretched out to save, and with his calm, clear voice bidding us take heart and have no fear.

There is no passage in the New Testament in which Peter's character is more fully revealed than in the second part of today's Gospel. It tells us three things about him. Peter was given to acting upon impulse and without thinking of what he was doing. It was his mistake that again and again he acted without fully facing the situation and without counting the cost. He was to do exactly the same when he affirmed undying and unshakeable loyalty to Jesus (Matthew 26:33-35), and then denied his Lord's name. And yet there are worse sins than that, because Peter's whole trouble was that he was ruled by his heart; and, however he might sometimes fail, his heart was always in the right place and the instinct of his heart was always love. Because Peter acted on impulse, he often failed and came to grief. It was always Jesus' insistence that a person should look at a situation in all its bleak grimness before taking action. Jesus was completely honest with people; he always invited them to see how difficult it was to follow him before they set out upon the Christian way. But Peter didn't finally fail, for always in the moment of his failure he clutched at Christ. The wonderful thing about him is that every time he fell, he rose again; it must have been true that even his failures brought him closer to Jesus.

The Bread Of Life

Readings: 1 Kings 19:4-8; Eph 4:30-5:2; Jn 6:41-51

The 'bread of life' sustains and nourishes us because it is a meeting with Christ.

When I was a kid we lived on the periphery of the city, an idyllic sort of place. From my bedroom window I could see cows being milked, by hand, morning and evening. Now it is engulfed by concrete. One day, during a game of cowboys and indians, I was tied tightly to a tree. My companions ran off. There I was, all alone, unable to move hand or foot! I had been abandoned. I began to cry, frightened that no one would come and release me. Eventually I managed to slither free and ran crying home to my mother. That was the first time I realised what being 'the bread of life' was all about! My mother took me on her knee consolingly. She reassured me that she cared and wouldn't let anything bad happen to me. She was 'the bread of life' for me then. Have you someone in your life who is the 'bread of life' for you?

When Jesus said he was the 'bread of life' he was telling us that he wanted to enter our lives with an intimacy that was nourishing and life-giving. On another occasion he said 'I am the way, the truth and the life'. That word 'life' is full of meaning – life-saving; life-giving; life threatening; life-sustaining. Life with Christ who is the origin and source of our being is life-giving. But it can only be so if we allow Jesus to be the daily 'bread of life' who sustains us.

When Jesus said he was the bread of life he was reassuring us that he would always be there no matter what. His love would never fail. He left us himself in the Eucharist, always approachable. My father was a

Clareman. As a youngster I remember he brought us to Kilbaha is see the famous 'ark'. During the famine, that part of Clare – Cross, Kilbaha, Carrigaholt – was under the jurisdiction of an uncompromising landlord, who brought in Protestant teachers from England and had every place in which the priest said Mass, razed immediately. Large sections of the parish apostatised. A number of priests had died of famine fever. Those who remained struggled in their apostolate. The ark was built. It was only a small square box, about eight feet by eight feet, on wheels. The box was drawn on to the shore and into the water. Here the landlord had no jurisdiction. The priest said Mass inside the open box, over the sea, facing the shore, where eventually people began to gather. Little by little the people began to return to the sacrament and sacrifice of the Mass. The 'bread of life' – the 'bread that comes down from heaven, so that a person may eat it and not die' – nourished the people once more. Through ingenuity and faith a new beginning became possible.

The following story may be apocryphal. The last Chief Secretary of Ireland was a man named Augustine Birrell. It is said that he was asked by London to report on the level of faith and practice in Ireland. His reply was a one-liner: 'It is the Mass that matters'. Yes, it was the Mass that mattered.

Within the past two years I have had the opportunity of celebrating Mass at two Mass rocks, one in the Bog of Allen and the other on the Toher Pádraig. I experienced the spirit of my ancestors hovering about on both occasions. I knew that 'the ground on which I stood was holy ground'. It was on this ground, in times of danger and poverty, that my ancestors were nourished in the faith that was handed down to me. The 'bread of life' promised in today's Gospel transforms us and makes us more Christ-like. Every sacrament is an 'act of Christ'. When a priest baptises it is Christ who baptises. This meeting in the Eucharist is with Christ.

Death, Where Is Your Sting?

Readings: Wis 18:6-9; Heb 11: 1-2, 8-19; Lk 12:32-48

Despite the wonderful achievements of humankind, one mystery remains that no computer can solve – the mystery of death. Only faith has any answers in the face of the last great trauma of life.

There is an old story of a jester who sometimes had very wise things to say. One day he said something so foolish that the king handed him a staff, and said to him, 'Take this, and keep it till you find a bigger fool than yourself.' Some years later the king lay ill and very near to death. He asked his servants, family and friends to gather by his bedside as he wished to say a personal 'goodbye' to them. When the king finished speaking the jester stepped forward and asked the king a question: 'I know that during the course of your lifetime you made many important diplomatic visits to other countries. On each occasion you sent servants and court officials ahead of you to prepare the way for your visit. May I ask what preparations you have made for this final journey that you are about to undertake?' The king was nonplussed. 'I'm sorry!' replied the king, 'I have made no preparations.' 'Then,' said the jester, 'take this staff with you, for now I have found a bigger fool than myself.'

Some people leave everything until the last minute. I once had a friend who considered it a matter of pride always to check in at the last possible moment for a flight. He delighted in being last. The confrontation with death is the last possible human trauma each of us has to undergo. Most go unprepared. Humanly speaking we shrink from death. The finality of the clay frightens us. At times the faithful die in fear.

Can we separate death from life? Isn't the Christian perspective that of a pilgrimage, with death a gateway into a new and different phase of the journey? Our fear of death comes not from dying but from life and our own sense of failure about how we have lived it. In our contemporary culture I have been surprised at how often I have been asked 'Is there a heaven?' or 'Is there an afterlife?'

I believe there is an old Celtic myth that says that God has cut a shape in the sky to fit neatly the contours of every human person. This hole in the sky is our 'resurrection' place, prepared for us since the beginning of time. Life is a search for that 'resurrection' place, so that when the ultimate call comes we will be standing right where God wants us to be! Through this hole or space we will be brought neatly up into nirvana, the 'other world', or heaven. There is a simple truth here. All of life is a preparation for death. 'Being ready' is not the massive task of packing one's suitcases but of living in the way we would wish to die. We are preparing for that place where 'he will wipe away every tear from their eyes, and death shall be no more, neither shall there be mourning nor crying nor pain any more, for the former things have passed away.' (Revelation 21:4)

America Carmelite poet Jessica Powers has a magnificent poem on death and heaven, entitled 'The Homecoming'.

> The spirit, newly freed from earth,
> is all amazed at the surprise
> of her belonging: suddenly
> as native to eternity
> to see herself, to realize
> the heritage that lets her be
> at home where all this glory lies.

We do not know when the Second Coming of Christ will be. The Gospel today is reminding us to be always in a state of preparedness.

Healing

Readings: Isa 56:1, 6-7; Rom 11:13-15, 29-32; Mt 15:21-28

Jesus often asked for faith before he worked a healing. In today's Gospel a most unlikely person approached Jesus and her request for her daughter was answered.

The inextricable link of love that binds a parent to a child is a jewel in life's mysteries. A prisoner at Dachau gives us a glimpse of what the death of a child means. 'We were shaken to the depths of our soul,' he recalled, 'when the first transports of children's clothes arrived – we men who were inured to suffering and to shock had to fight back the tears.' Later they saw yet more thousands of shoes belonging to children who had been liquidated. 'This was the most terrible thing for us, the most bitter thing, perhaps the worse thing that befell us.'

Many years ago a husband and wife and their newborn baby were in a house I was visiting. The evening progressed in eating, conversation and music. At one stage the mother went to check on her baby who was sleeping safely in her cot upstairs. That was the beginning of a heartrending trauma, after which I knew the depths of the bonds between parents and their child. The child was not sleeping as everyone imagined. She had died alone. A young, unformed life snatched away in a dramatic cot death. A time of understandable anguish and pain followed.

The Canannite woman of today's Gospel was an outsider, a foreigner. A Canannite was a person with whom Jews would never have been on friendly terms. In fact the Canannites were the ancestral enemies of the Jews. In addition, Jesus, for once, was outside Jewish territory. He may have gone there to gather his resources for what he knew was to come. This woman must have heard of Jesus and his healing powers. Absolutely nothing was going to come between her and the possibility of her little child being cured. She loved her child deeply. Her cry is one of anguish: 'Have pity on me, Lord, Son of David! My daughter is tormented by a demon'. Sickness seeks anywhere and anyone who is likely to provide healing.

The Irish are great at 'slagging'. It is a gentle, humorous form of wit, endearing in its own way, which is used to ridicule at another's expense. Rather than harm being intended, it is often a quirky way of showing endearment. When Jesus said, 'It is not right to take the food of the children and throw it to the dogs', the intention may not have been insulting, as the coldness of the words suggest.

Here was a woman of faith. 'Lord, help me.' She knew Jesus could and she had faith that he would make her child well again. How many times was Jesus moved by faith to work a miracle? Many times he asked, 'Do you believe that I can do this for you?' An affirmative answer brought a healing. Faith is far more than wishful thinking. It is more even than hope. It is the assurance that Jesus can and will help in every situation. Faith such as this can move mountains.

There were times when Jesus asked for both a positive faith and persistence in prayer. Miracles do happen. Sr Briege McKenna described her own healing like this: 'The only prayer I said was "Jesus, please help me". At that moment, I felt a hand touch my head and thought it was the priest who had come over to me. I opened my eyes and no one was there, but there was a power going through my body. It's difficult to describe the feeling, but I often describe it this way: I felt like a banana being peeled. I looked down. My fingers had been stiff, but not deformed like my feet. There had been sores on my elbows. I looked at myself. My fingers were limber, the sores were gone, and I could feel that my feet in sandals were no longer deformed. I jumped up screaming, "Jesus, You're right here!" '

Religious Symbols Have Lost Their Meaning

Readings: Prov 9:1-6; Eph 5:15-20; Jn 6:51-58

For many people the symbolism of eucharistic worship is meaningless. Does it have to be like this?

At the height of the depression, in 1937, the McDonald brothers opened a small cinema, but it quickly went bust. As far as they could tell the only business making money at the time was a nearby hot-dog stand run by a man named Walker Wiley. So they opened a stand near the Santa Anita racetrack. They did well from the start. McDonald's are now on course to turn the Big Mac into a global brand to rival Coke. The February 1999 opening of McDonald's in Tbilisi, Georgia marked the 115th country to play host to those trademark golden arches. The group's 25,000th restaurant world-wide opened in August 1999. The golden arches have become a symbol for quick service, cleanliness and quality junkfood. The symbol is recognised everywhere. The holiday that changed the face of international highways occurred in the summer of 1951. Kemmons Wilson took his family on vacation. They had real difficulties finding suitable places to stay. Day by day on the trip, Wilson became more irritated, until he finally turned to his wife Dorothy and announced he was going into the hotel business. He saw Bing Crosby's Holiday Inn on television and that was the beginning. At one point he was building a new Holiday Inn every two and a half days. The Holiday Inn symbol, with its distinctive script, is recognised for cheap, no-frills holiday accommodation world-wide.

Symbols and chants contain meaning. The 'You'll never walk alone' chant from the kop at the Liverpool football ground is recognisable to fans world-wide. Religious symbols are meaningless to many people today. The tiny wafer and drop of wine used at Mass don't speak to them. Neither do vestments, or rituals, which are so specifically religious that a non-church-goer simply doesn't understand. I was speaking to a sociologist recently. He had just completed a survey of young people aged 17-25 on faith and culture. He told me that young people have lost the language and vocabulary of faith. The symbols and the language of liturgy are incomprehensible to a growing number of people. Nevertheless, where these symbols retain their meaning, perhaps for those who attended the Tridentine Rite, the devotion is obvious.

The Eucharist is referred to as a sacrament, a sacrifice, or as a sacred meal. I'm pretty sure what is meant in each case, but what about those who still attend church or indeed those who don't? The new liturgy regards the bread and wine not just as objects but gifts, what earth has given and human hands have made. The bread and wine are part of the whole ritual of self-giving. They are brought to our altar, as signs of our existence, for through them we wish to place in the hands of our Maker our entire existence, the bread of our labour and the wine of our joy. But this is less obvious when there is no offertory procession or when it is done in a careless and sloppy manner.

Church people could be partly responsible for symbols losing their meaning. There is a spiritual thirst. The ersatz bitterness of material goods alone is not satisfying. In Ireland, new centres for Buddhist meditation and alternative spiritualities are burgeoning. I know of two in County Clare alone – in the Burren and near Broadford.

In a favourite book of mine the authors make this salient point: 'For God is not only present in the Eucharist. "I was hungry and you gave me food. I was thirsty and you gave me drink. I was a stranger and you made me welcome, naked and you clothed me, sick and you visited me, in prison and you came to me." Until we find him there, we cannot find him in the Eucharist, or in his Word, or in the Church, or, for that matter, in ourselves.' So much of what Christ did was in the context of a meal. Feeding the multitude; the wedding feast; his meals with sinners. Then there is a feeding of the people in the desert. Here in this quote we see the essentially communitarian dimension of eucharistic worship.

There Is A Price To Be Paid For Tough Love

Readings: Jer 38:4, 8-10; Heb 12: 1-4; Lk 12:49-53

Discipleship is costly. Following Jesus may bring division, even among family and friends. 'Can we drink the cup that he drank?'

It is natural to recoil from suffering. Sometimes we observe the lives of others and envy them because they seem so happy and trouble free. Is any life immune from suffering? This Gospel seems so out of tune with the Beatitudes or with the promise of Jesus, 'My peace I leave with you, my peace I give to you'. Jesus knew what he was about to face – Jerusalem, suffering, rejection, and the cross. And so he was anguished. The human cost of what he was to face frightened him. The 'baptism with which I must be baptised' was the baptism of the cross. In suffering we always remember that Jesus has been there before us. He too entered through the gateway of suffering and knows the cost. The great spiritual writer Henry Nouwen wrote: 'Finding new life through suffering and death: that is good news'. This message is so counter-cultural as to be inexplicable in the post-modern mind. Our scientific age is geared towards the elimination of all suffering.

Catholics today seldom speak of 'actual grace'. The *Catechism of the Catholic Church* defines grace as 'the free and undeserved help that God gives to us to respond to his call to become his children'. The Church has always taught that there is available to us an 'actual grace'; that grace or help that comes from God at the moment and time when we most need his help. Therefore, God is present in a special way with his power at times of suffering. We do not have to face suffering alone. We can, and usually will be, afraid at the thought of having to suffer but when the time comes God is there. 'The Lord is kind and full of compassion.' The Lord, therefore, is 'suffering along with us'.

How is it that Jesus says he came to bring division? There is a paradox here. A paradox of compassion. 'The one who saves his life will lose it; the one who loses his life will save it.' This means that the person who is always willing to compromise to hold on to the 'comfort zones' of his or her life will lose it. In following Jesus there is a price to be paid. Sometimes the price is high. People like Martin Luther King, Maximillian Kolbe, Oscar Romero and others were willing to lose their lives in order to obtain the pearl of great price – eternal friendship with Jesus. Today, when even families are divided on matters of faith and belief, losing one's life for the sake of Jesus can be a reality. Families can be and are divided. These divisions are painful, particularly for parents and grandparents. Jesus could see this possibility. He was asking for love without compromise.

The Gospel will make demands on us. The cross will inevitably cross our path. To be a disciple will cost us something. These sacrifices are the stuff of love. We are 'laying down our lives' not for an ideal, a Church, a set of values, but for a person who 'loves us with an everlasting love'. There is a price to be paid for 'tough love'.

Twentieth Sunday in Ordinary Time

Thou Art Peter

Readings: Isa 22:19-22; Rom 11:33-36; Mt 16:13-20

The authority of the Church is seen as curbing personal freedom, whereas the opposite ought to be the truth. The law of Christ is the law of love, giving us the freedom to choose the good.

John the Baptist had a magnetic effect on many people. Herod Antipas wasn't the only person who was intrigued by this exceptional man. He was so exceptional that people would not have been surprised if he had returned from the dead. Elijah was one of the greatest prophets. He was to be the forerunner of the Messiah, as Malachi had predicted 'Behold I will send you Elijah the prophet before the great and terrible day of the Lord comes'. To this day the Jews expect the return of Elijah before the Messiah comes. Jeremiah was also predicted to come, returning the ark and the altar of incense before the coming of the Messiah. People were perplexed by Jesus. In John's Gospel a number of individuals recognised Jesus as the Messiah and the crowd once tried to make him king. Who was he? Where had he come from and why?

Then the profession of faith comes from Peter: 'You are the Christ, the Son of the living God'. Jesus Christ the Messiah. Simon's confession of Messiahship is attributed to divine revelation rather than to his own human insight. The Hebrew word 'Messiah' (with its Greek equivalent 'Christ') just means someone anointed by God. In biblical terms a Messiah meant more. He was a God-sent rescuer who bursts into a crisis to sort things out. A longing for a Messiah arises particularly when a people groan under a foreign oppressor, look back wistfully to past glories and yet cling to a creed that tells them they are God's special people. Once Napoleon gave his verdict on Jesus: 'I know men,' he said, 'and Jesus Christ is more than a man'.

The phrase 'upon this rock I will build my Church' is a disputed one. The *Jerome Biblical Commentary* claims that 'it is highly doubtful that Jesus himself used the word [ekklesia], which became the common designation of the Christian community in the epistles'.

The granting of the 'keys' to Peter was a clear indication of the conferring of authority on him. His position within the apostolic band became unique. Peter was to be the beginning of the New Israel, the new people of God, the new fellowship of those who believe in his name. The Pope of the day succeeds in this office of ruling and teaching with authority.

The 'nobody is going to tell me what to do' attitude sees the exercise of authority as personally limiting. But the law of Christ, as interpreted by the Church, is essentially liberating. It is to set us free so that we have the freedom to choose. Those who decry the role of authority are essentially conformists. They need the same designer labels, irresponsible sexual behaviour, indulgence in alcohol, because it is part of an ethos of conformity that fits most comfortably with their view of how life should be lived at this time. The inability to say no indicates not more freedom but less. The law of Christ is a law of love. It helps us to be free. It is difficult for people in an individualistic age to appreciate the nature and role of authority. There is an unwillingness to accept authority, especially within the spiritual sphere.

The Church built on the faith of Peter and empowered by the Holy Spirit will endure. We have the promise of the abiding presence of God with the Church. This can lead Churches into a position of arrogance. The world is divided into 'them' and 'us'; we being the elect. All that is outside the fold of the Church is the 'world', which invariably is seen as tainted. The abiding presence of God with the Church is like the morning sun falling on a rose; it opens it out to a new day of living, a new day of giving pleasure to others. The Church has to be open to the world, always looking for signs of the transcendent in people, places and events. The Church of its nature is essentially missionary.

The Church

Readings: Isa 22:19-23; Rom 11:33-36; Mt 16:13-20

The Gospel reading of today's Mass contains one of the most controversial passages of scripture, which has divided Christians since the Reformation.

Because we live in a very individualistic world, fewer and fewer of us are willing to take orders from anyone. 'I can make up my own mind'; 'I don't need the Church telling me what to do.' Even the Ten Commandments cut little ice with many people. How you can accept the Bible and not the Ten Commandments baffles me – but that's another story! The command of Jesus to his disciples was to 'go and teach all nations'. The Church teaches only out of obedience to the command of Jesus. Traditionally this passage of scripture, in the Roman Catholic tradition, has always been interpreted as conferring powers upon Peter – the power of binding and loosing. It also conferred on him a spiritual primacy of leadership. This power and primacy was intended by Christ to endure and so we have the apostolic succession of the Papacy. The *Catechism of the Catholic Church* puts it like this: 'The Lord made Simon alone, whom he named Peter, the "rock" of his Church. He gave him the keys of his Church, and instituted him shepherd of the whole flock. The office of binding and loosing which was given to Peter was also assigned to the college of apostles united to its head'. The conferring of the 'keys' is a clear statement of a position of leadership and authority. The key was the symbol of the office of the master of the palace, the highest of the officers of the Israeli court; so Peter is clearly declared to be the leader.

The binding and loosing probably refers to the power of including or excluding from the Christian assembly. Whatever it means it clearly confers power, spiritual power. If one accepts the Roman Catholic understanding of this passage of scripture one is conscientiously obliged to give respect and obedience to the clear and traditional teaching of the Popes on serious matters of faith and morals. The term 'mother' has been used of the Church. It has always seen itself as a teaching Church. Its teaching task is a motherly one. It teaches because of the command of Jesus, but also out of love for the People of God. It is difficult to adopt the 'pick and mix' approach to Catholic teaching on faith and morals and still continue to call oneself a Catholic.

The *Catechism* itself points out the primacy of conscience as the ultimate arbiter of our actions. When Jesus used the word 'church' he was hardly thinking of an institution or organisation with buildings and offices and services and meetings and a multitude of activities. The word in the sense used by Jesus would be more like what we call 'fellowship' or 'community'. It was a fellowship of believers. When the term People of God was used to describe the Church, a shiver of excitement went through the whole Church. A new model of Church was emerging, we thought. Much of the Catholic 'package' of beliefs, attitudes and practices that we inherited in our Catholic upbringing was shaped at a time when the Church was the centre of Western society and when its authority was unquestioned. It may have been that we had our parents' faith! Today people have to seek the truth with a sincere heart. It isn't just a matter of returning to the past. However we understand the Church, it is there to help us seek and find the truth and is understanding of the difficulties and questions that puzzle the modern mind.

The Risk Of Being Shut Out

Readings: Isa 66:18-21; Heb 12:5-7, 11-13; Lk 13:22-30

'Armchair Christianity' is hardly a guarantee of salvation.

Jesus declares that entry to the Kingdom can never be automatic but is the result and the reward of a struggle. 'Strive to enter through the narrow gate,' he said. The word for striving is the word from which the English word agony is derived. The struggle to enter is intense and lifelong. In asking this question the Jews assumed that the Kingdom would be excluded to the Gentile and that they alone would be saved.

It is easy to think that, once we have made a commitment of ourselves to Jesus Christ, we have reached the end of the road and can, as it were, sit back as if we had achieved our goal. When I was in the seminary I can recall our spiritual director saying time and time again 'Not to go forward in the spiritual life is to slip back'. In my work in Retrouvaille, for people who are suffering from the pain of a marriage in trouble, we set a plan for the participating couples that stretches over several months. We know full well that the process begun on the Retrouvaille weekend has to continue if there is to be any hope of success. There is no finality in the Christian life. A person must be going forward or necessarily he/she goes backward.

The Christian way is like climbing up a mountain towards a peak that may never be reached in this world. It was said of two gallant climbers who died on Mount Everest: 'When last seen they were going strong for the top'. Inscribed on the grave of an Alpine guide who had died on the mountain-side were the words: 'He died climbing'.

In her wonderful book, *The Past is Myself,* Christabel Bielenberg writes of the struggle to live in Nazi Germany during the war:

Our best years were sliding past – years which could have been well spent, years that were being thrown away; whispering, cadging, simulating, hating, hoping, stoking away at some inner flame, keeping alive an ever-dwindling faith that somehow, sometime, something would prevail which was good and which was right.

The Jesuits used to talk of 'agere contra', the need to 'act against' oneself in the spiritual life. Others called it 'self-denial'. It is a necessary struggle, as all of us are infected by Original Sin.

Those who are very prominent in this world may have to be very humble in the next. Those whom no one notices here may be the princes of the world to come. There is a story of a woman who had been used to every luxury and to great respect. She died, and when she arrived in heaven, an angel was sent to conduct her to her house. They passed many a lovely mansion and the woman thought that each one, as they came to it, must be the one allotted to her. When they had passed through the main streets they came to the outskirts, where the houses were much smaller; and on the very fringe they came to a house that was little more than a hut. 'That is your house,' said the conducting angel. 'What,' said the woman, 'that! I cannot live in that.' 'I am sorry,' said the angel, 'but that is all we could build for you with the materials you sent up.'

The Great Challenge

Readings: Jer 20:7-9; Rom 12:1-2; Mt 16:21-27

Today's Gospel is central to the Christian life but anathema to the world of luxury and pleasure that many live in. Can we make sense of it?

To deny oneself is to say 'no' to self and 'yes' to God. The cross is at the centre of the Christian life as it was at the centre of the life of Jesus. Today's Gospel is challenging because it is counter-cultural. It is presenting a way of life that is against the ethos of the times we live in. Think of the lines from the book of Sirach, 'When you come to serve the Lord prepare yourself for trials'. This is off-putting when trials are what we do not want in our lives. We are almost conditioned to seek the easy way out – the way of the most pleasure and the least pain. Further, the book of Sirach claims that 'as gold is tested in fire, worthy men are tested in the crucible of humiliation'. I believe the image being presented is that of a gold-refiner. All the impurities come to the surface under intense heat and are removed. The refiner knows the process is finished when he can see his own perfect image in the gold. The trials in our life could be the refiner's hand moulding us into the image of Jesus.

'Then Jesus said to his disciples: "If anyone wishes to come after me, let him deny himself, and take up his cross, and let him follow me. For whoever wishes to keep his life safe, will lose it; and whoever loses his life for my sake, will find it. For what shall a man be profited if he shall gain the whole world at the penalty of the price of his life? Or what will a man give in exchange for his life?" ' Here we have one of the dominant and ever-recurring themes of Jesus' teaching. These are things that Jesus said to people again and again (Matthew 10:37-39; Mark 8:34-37; Luke 9:23-27; 14:25-27; 17:33; John 12:25). He confronted them with the challenge of the Christian life.

Jesus is suggesting that we deny ourselves, not necessarily in a negative way by giving up things; we can deny ourselves by putting the wishes and needs of others before our own for the sake of the Kingdom of God. In every life lived with integrity there are necessarily elements of self-denial. Think of the demands made on many parents, on bread winners, on those caring for a sick relative, on those who are old and feeble. To deny oneself means in every moment of life saying no to self and yes to God. In Hebrews we read: 'Endure your trials as discipline; God treats you as sons, for what "son" is there whom a father does not discipline? If you are without discipline, in which all have shared, you are not sons but bastards'. Discipline is necessarily part of growing up. Some discipline we impose on ourselves. Other forms of discipline are imposed on us from without. The pains of life, the sufferings that come our way, could be the discipline of the Lord; God moulding and shaping us (perhaps for greater things). Very often it is those who have experienced suffering who in turn become compassionate healers. One has only to think of an organisation like AA.

The Christian life is a life of sacrificial love. The Christian may have to abandon personal ambition to serve Christ; it may be that he or she will discover that the place where they can render the greatest service to Jesus Christ is somewhere where the reward will be small and the prestige non-existent. The Christian will certainly have to sacrifice time and leisure and pleasure in order to serve God through the service of others.

Today is a real time of trial for us Catholics. There is an air of confusion about, a loss of morale, a sense of disillusionment. Facing these challenges demands accepting the cross with joy. Luke, with a flash of sheer insight, adds one word to this command of Jesus: 'Let him take up his cross daily'. The really important thing is not the great moments of sacrifice, but a life lived in the constant hourly awareness of the demands of God and the needs of others. The Christian life is a life that is always concerned with others, more than it is concerned with itself.

Standing Outside The Fold

Readings: Deut 4:1-2, 6-8; Jas 1:17-18, 21-22; Mk 7:1-8, 14-15, 21-22

By teaching as he did against exaggerated legalism Jesus placed himself in opposition to the elders and risked the indignity of ritual impurity.

At the time of Jesus, the law of Moses was virtually smothered by a plethora of minute interpretations and applications of the law by the rabbis, which constituted the 'tradition of the elders'. The ritual washing before meals was one such 'tradition'. The religious leaders of Jesus' day very often appeared to give more importance to these human-made traditions than to the law itself. Jesus saw this as the reappearance of the hypocrisy and formalism condemned by Isaiah. The Pharisees and the scribes were worried about anything unclean passing through the lips ('this people honours me with their lips'), but they were little concerned with what happened in the heart ('but their heart is far from me'). Although it may not seem so now, this passage, when it was first spoken, was well-nigh the most revolutionary passage in the New Testament.

Jesus has been arguing with the legal experts about different aspects of the traditional law. He has shown the irrelevance of the elaborate hand washings. He has shown how rigid adherence to the traditional law can actually mean disobedience to the law of God. But here he says something more startling yet. He declares that nothing that goes into a person can possibly defile him, for it is received only into the body, which rids itself of it in the normal, physical way. So much for not eating pork! In effect, Jesus was saying that things cannot be either unclean or clean in any real religious sense of the term. Only persons can be really defiled; and what defiles a person is his own actions, which are the product of his own heart. This was new doctrine, shatteringly new doctrine. The Jew had, and still has, a whole system of things that are clean and unclean. With one sweeping pronouncement Jesus declared the whole thing irrelevant. Jesus takes advantage of this dispute with the Pharisees and the scribes to teach the true meaning of purity.

Let us look at the things Jesus lists as coming from the heart and making a person unclean. He begins with 'evil designs'. Every outward act of sin is preceded by an inward act of choice; therefore, Jesus begins with the evil thought from which the evil action comes. Next come 'fornications'; later he is to list acts of 'adultery', but this first word is a wide word – it means every kind of traffic in sexual vice. There follow 'thefts', 'murders' and 'adulteries', and their meaning is clear.

Then comes 'covetous deeds'. This comes from two Greek words meaning to have more. It has been defined as the accursed love of having. I suppose in modern parlance this is the 'shop till you drop' syndrome. It is not just the desire for money and things; it includes the desire for power. Plato said, 'The desire of man is like a sieve or pierced vessel which he ever tries to, and can never fill.' It is that lust for having which is in the heart of the person who sees happiness in things instead of in God. The list continues but it is really a call to examine not so much how we keep the rules, but rather to search our hearts; to seek out our evil intentions and designs. Scripture says 'Where your treasure is, there is your heart also.' What is the so-called treasure in my life? Where is my heart?

This passage of scripture demonstrates that Jesus was prepared to step outside the laws of ritual purity. He was prepared to suffer the personal indignity of being considered unclean. He was placing himself with the poor, the dispossessed, the people of no consequence. He was prepared to suffer the judgment of the elders and the scorn reserved for the ritually impure. His is the act of the prophet. Prophets are seldom the darlings of the power-brokers, whether in religion, business or politics. To go against the tide is to suffer personal indignity.

Behind The Façade Of Riches Lie Deep Human Needs

Readings: Sir 3:17-20; Heb 12:18, 19, 22-24; Lk 14:1, 7-14

The pain of the poor is the pain of always being dependent. The rich can insulate themselves from the discomforts of life but they too cannot escape the pain of the heart.

The rich have the capacity to insulate themselves from much of the pain of this world. They can travel First Class, sleep in five-star hotels, and eat in the best restaurants. They never know the insecurity of being without. Riches of themselves can be a façade behind which lurks hidden a trembling soul in need. It was only with the publication of Andrew Morton's book that the suffering of Princess Diana was revealed. The 'people's princess' was in pain! Recently the wholesale slaughter of the Nepalese royal family by one of their own shocked the world. The dead included Dipendra, 29; his parents, King Birendra, 55, and Queen Aishwarya, 51; and other members of the family. The lonely life of reclusive oil billionaire and aviator Harold Hughes has been well documented. Gianni Versace, arguably the world's most ostentatious and famous fashion designer, was shot outside his apartment in 1997. The same happened to famous rock star John Lennon in 1980. Phil Graham, the owner of the *Washington Post*, and adviser to Presidents, shot himself. Riches are no protection against pain. The true history of humankind is the history of suffering, something about which one finds precious little in the history books!

The pulse of rich and poor beat equally with joy and pain. Beneath the skin, all hearts look for love and security. Behind the designer labels, the stretch limousines, even the bodyguards, is a soul searching for love and acceptance. Sometimes the rich patronise or look down on the poor. They feel their stature confers privileges on them by right. They flaunt their riches as if the phrase from Job, 'naked I came from my mother's womb and naked I shall return', would or could never happen – at least to them! In our world the paths of rich and poor seldom cross. Misunderstanding, prejudice, even fear, arises between rich and poor; who, beneath the façade of their rags or their riches, experience the same deep human needs. The principal suffering of the poor, in the time of Jesus and today, is shame and disgrace. The poor are dependent upon the 'charity' of others. That is a special kind of suffering. There are some who seem destined to be 'inferior' by state. This shouldn't be.

The Gospel is asking that the cataracts of prejudice be removed from the eyes of both rich and poor. We are being asked to look behind the masks, to listen with our hearts and then with our heads. We must see the dignity of the human person irrespective of our positions in life. We are being asked to recognise that all is 'gift'. Talents, money, family, health, goodness, life itself, is a gift ultimately from God. Humility is acknowledging what God has done for me. 'My soul glorifies the Lord and my spirit rejoices in God my Saviour. For He who is mighty has done great things for me. . . .' The top seat or the lower one doesn't matter. One often experiences pomposity in senior church-people. Cardinal Hume was not one of these. I recall going to meet him at the airport one day and being taken aback at his genuine surprise that anyone would come out to meet him. He felt awkward about being 'important'. God had given him a real gift of humility. This type of humility will lead us to take the 'lower seat' without needing to be called up higher.

To Love Without Measure

Readings: Ezek 33:7-9; Rom 13:8-10; Mt 18:15-20

In the second reading today we are invited to love. This is 'tough love'. It is a love that requires us to act against ourselves for the love of God.

Perhaps all the teaching of Paul can be summed up in the words of today's epistle: 'If you love your fellow men you have carried out all your obligation'. Love is the supreme virtue but it encompasses and includes every other virtue.

There was a song by the Beatles in the 1960s, entitled 'All you need is Love'. This is true and it is false. It is true in so far as each one of us needs to love and to be loved. If we do not experience some sort of warm and satisfying relationship with another human being, we remain incomplete. Life without friendship is never wholly human. To be special to another person is a source of wholeness. The deep longing of the human heart is for love and acceptance. It is also false, because the emphasis is on the 'you', the self. The love St Paul is speaking about here is unconditional, unselfish love. That is the love for which a price has to be paid. To love is to give. There are people today who claim that in recent years we have played down the fear of God, of sin, of hell. As a result people are willing to excuse themselves anything. Rationalisation masquerades as love, they would claim. There is some truth in this but there is no truth in it if the love we speak of is the love outlined by Paul in 1 Corinthians 13. Love is patient. When we experience hurt from others, the possibility to 'get our own back' is often there. We hold back without sulking. St Thérèse of Lisieux was thought to love some of the sisters in the community more than others. In truth, these were the ones who most irritated and annoyed her. She loved them in a special way. Tough love.

Love is kind. So much Christianity is good but unkind. So many good Church people would have sided with the rulers and not with Jesus if they had had to deal with the woman taken in adultery!

Love knows no envy. God has given each of us a beauty that is unique. The possessions, looks, good fortune of others, if they are from a source of envy, eat us up and distract us from the loving we have to do.

Love does not boast. The real lover cannot ever get over the wonder that he or she is loved. Love is kept humble by the consciousness that it can never offer its loved one a gift that is good enough.

Love is not inflated with its own importance. A person 'dressed in a little brief authority' can be a sorry sight. Why do prelates dress up and use archaic titles? I wish I knew. Love does not behave gracelessly. There is graciousness in Christian love that never forgets that courtesy and tact and politeness are lovely things.

Love does not insist upon its rights. In the last analysis, there are in this world only two kinds of people – those who always insist upon their privileges and those who always remember their responsibilities. Whenever we start thinking about 'our place', we are drifting away from Christian love. Love never flies into a temper. The person who is master of his temper can be master of anything. Love does not store up the memory of any wrong it has received. We have to open our hands and let go of past hurts in order to achieve wholeness. Christian love has learned the great lesson of forgetting.

Love finds no pleasure in evil-doing. There are times when we rejoice in another's evil simply because it makes us seem better. Taking pleasure in gossip about another's faults is not loving.

Love rejoices with the truth. There are times when we do not want to hear the truth!

Love can endure anything – any insult, any injury, any disappointment. It describes the kind of love that was in the heart of Jesus himself. If this is our charter for living, then the rules, the commandments, the fear will all be taken care of in our desire to love for the sake of Jesus.

There Is A Dialogue Deficit Between The Rich And The Poor

Readings: Isa 35:4-7; Jas 2:1-5; Mk 7:31-37

We are all equal in the sight of God. A visitor from another planet would find this difficult to discern in the affluent society we live in.

In most affluent countries there is a 'dialogue deficit'. The deficit is not just the absence of talking but of contact. People are beginning to speak of the yawning gap between rich and poor. For seven years I lived in the inner city. Almost nightly, homeless people, some of them drug addicted, slept in the church porch. One summer's evening I saw young boys, scarcely out of their teens, with one shoe off, injecting into their big toes. No other vein was available! Chronic alcoholics, some of them two-bottles-a-day people, walk about in a daze. It is terrifying. The broken, messed-up people try frantically to cope while the Mercs flash by. The two groups never meet! Never talk! They never have any, even the most cursory, contact with one another. There are no mechanisms available that would facilitate such a dialogue. Ostentatious wealth breeds resentment on the part of the disadvantaged.

A Christian's dignity does not come from the size of his or her house, the type of car that is driven, priority on the social pecking order, or the clubs one holds membership of, or where one's children go to school. Our ultimate dignity comes from who we are in relation to God – sons and daughters of the Father. The poor and addicted are our brothers and sisters. To translate that reality into practice is a challenge to everyone who bears the name Christian. It is through Baptism that we become sons and daughters of the Father. In the eyes of God we are all equal. 'There are no pockets in shrouds' my mother used to say. Wealth is as transitory as life itself. How true that is! As a people we are generous. We generally top the poll per capita when an international calamity hits the tubes. Giving at arm's length is good, but eyeball-to-eyeball dialogue and personal nurturing is even better.

I can recall a story told by Jean Vanier, that great shepherd of the disadvantaged. He was visiting a mental hospital in Paris accompanied by the medical superintendent. He noticed a young woman sitting facing the wall, immobile, unspeaking. He asked what had happened. The medical superintendent explained that she was admitted with a serious depression. While in hospital her mother died. It was decided not to tell her so as not to aggravate her condition. But a fellow patient who had heard about the death told her. She became autistic and totally withdrew into herself. Jean Vanier reached out to her and hugged her so that she could experience what he called 'body warmth'. He asked permission to take her to one of the L'Arche communities. There she experienced the healing warmth of a loving community. In time she regained her communication skills and in the end returned to live a full and fruitful life. The 'body warmth' of an individual or a loving community can be so healing.

Thankfully, the message of the first reading today is made flesh in the actions of Jesus. Jesus healed, not because he wanted to prove who he was, or to put on a display of power, but out of compassion for the suffering: 'The Lord is kind and full of compassion, slow to anger and rich in mercy'. If one is blind or lame, the disability is available for all to see. Deafness must be a real embarrassment. The deaf often speak in a hesitant manner. This was the case with the man in today's Gospel. Jesus' heart went out to him. At the time of Jesus, spittle was held to have curative qualities. I wonder did this action of Jesus in some way prefigure the sacrament of healing where oil is used? Anyway, Jesus brought healing and liberty to the deaf person. If Jesus is the same yesterday, today and forever, oughtn't we expect him to act in our lives?

Twenty-Third Sunday in Ordinary Time

Are We Willing To Pay The Price?

Readings: Wis 9:13-19; Phil 9-10, 12-17; Lk 14:25-33

As we grow into our relationship with God our giving will become more generous and free.

Early in the morning on Tuesday 6 July 1535, Sir Thomas More, Lord Chancellor of England, and one of its most powerful men, was led to the scaffold on Tower Hill in London. As tradition demanded, the executioner knelt and asked More's forgiveness for what he was about to do. More embraced and kissed him and gave him a blessing. He asked the people to pray for him and told them to bear witness that he should 'now suffer death in and for the faith of the Holy Catholic Church'. More said he died 'the king's good servant but God's first'. More died living out the ultimate implications of the Gospel of today's Mass.

On 4 December 1980, over three hundred years after the death of More, the body of Catholic lay missionary Jean Donovan was discovered. Jean Donovan had placed her life on a path from which there was no going back, not because she met her death in El Salvador, but because it was there that she met her calling. Jean was the girl next door. But a girl with a difference. A girl in her mid-twenties, motivated by God and love, who lived this out in the savagery of a Salvadorean civil war. It ended in her brutal rape and murder at the hands of the Salvadorean military. Jean died carrying out the prompting of Jesus in the Gospel of today.

It is tempting to think that these were very special people, people who were given gifts and graces not available to you or me. It is easy for the 'armchair' Christian to dismiss people like More and Donovan as somehow part of history and not of real life. They made choices. We too have choices to make every day of our lives. Every day is a succession of choices from the moment we awake and decide to get up and figure out what we will wear that day. A rosary of choices is our lot, as it was for More and Donovan.

It is said that we become Christians through Baptism. The mere pouring of water or the recitation of the correct formula is not what makes a Christian. We become Christians by choice – by freely choosing Jesus and following in his footsteps. An inherited faith is no faith. Like all following of Jesus, we also freely choose to live out the implications of that following as best we can.

One of St Francis' first followers was a wealthy merchant of Assisi named Bernard of Quintavalle. Shortly after meeting they decided to go to Mass at the Church of St Nicholas and after Mass ask the priest to open the book of the Gospels for them three times. This is where the pages fell:

> If you wish to be perfect, go and sell all your possessions, and give to the poor and come follow me. Take nothing for your journey, neither staff nor knapsack, shoes or money. If any will come after me, let them renounce self, take up their cross and follow me.

In Jesus, the man and the message are inextricably intertwined. The life of Jesus was a pilgrimage to Calvary. Our humanity recoils from the renunciation of self and the acceptance of the cross, both so central to following Jesus. There is no 'cheap grace'. The radical cost of discipleship is only learned in the context of our relationship with Jesus. As we grow into that relationship our giving will become more generous and free. There are times when we just won't measure up. Then we call on God's mercy and forgiveness in our human weakness.

Forgiveness Is Healing

Readings: Sir 27:30-28:7; Rom 14:7-9; Mt 18:21-35

Lack of forgiveness holds two people in bondage. How can we pray the Lord's Prayer and hold bitterness in our heart?

I don't often cry. But I can well remember that May day in 1994 feeling the warmth of my tears as they trickled down my face. I was watching the inaugural address of Nelson Mandela on television. Erect, proud, but above all forgiving, were the impressions he made on me. Recently released, after a horrible thirty years in jail, this is what he said: 'The time for healing has come. The moment to bridge the chasms that divide us has come. The time to build is upon us. We have triumphed in the efforts to implant hope in the breasts of the millions of our people. We enter in to a covenant that we shall build the society in which all South Africans, both black and white, will be able to walk tall, without any fear in their hearts, assured of their inalienable right to human dignity – a rainbow nation at peace with itself and the world'.

There was another time I cried. That was when I heard the extraordinary words of forgiveness on the lips of Gordon Wilson after the horrible Provisional IRA bombing of Enniskillen. His beautiful daughter Marie had been bitterly snatched from him. Among his first words were ones of forgiveness for her murderers and a pledge of daily prayers on their behalf. What a man! When the Pope recovered after being shot in May 1981, among his first visits was to the Regina Coeli jail in Rome to offer forgiveness to his potential assassin. There is something noble about forgiveness. As I was typing this sermon a man rang up. 'What are you doing?' he asked. 'I am writing a sermon for next Sunday,' I replied sheepishly. 'It is about forgiveness.' His reply was immediate. 'Sure, if we don't forgive we die.' Wisdom comes from unexpected quarters.

Against the tapestry of these recent incidents we hear the words 'Father, forgive them for they know not what they do'. Jesus walked over the threshold of forgiveness before us. Where there is lack of forgiveness, two people are in bondage. One closes the door on the inside, denying access to the other. The other cannot enter the bolted door. Lack of forgiveness is like a cancer. It involves a playing and replaying of real or supposed hurts. It festers and intensifies as long as the hand of forgiveness is withheld.

How can we change our heart if it is filled with bitterness and lack of forgiveness? Praying sincerely for the person who has hurt you and wishing for them all that God wishes for him or her often produces dramatic results. It is so hard to pray for a person and at the same time harbour bitterness and resentment. The Lord's Prayer is frightening. In this great prayer we ask God to forgive us in proportion and to the extent that we forgive others. No one is fit to pray the Lord's Prayer so long as the unforgiving spirit holds sway within their heart. If a person has not put things right with others, he or she cannot put things right with God. Forgiveness is healing.

I can recall preaching about forgiveness at a prayer meeting about twenty years ago. I thought nothing of it until a woman approached me the following week. 'You preached about forgiveness last week,' she said. 'I did,' I replied. 'I was moved by your sermon.' She explained, 'I have a brother in Australia with whom I hadn't spoken for eleven years. We broke up over a family quarrel. Last week after the meeting I went home determined to ring my brother. Imagine my great joy when he answered the phone and broke down at the prospect of a reconciliation. We talked for over an hour. There was no thought of the telephone account! Most wonderfully,' she concluded, 'he is going to come home next year for a holiday.' What a wonderful miracle!

The Messiahship
Of Jesus

Readings: Isa 50:5-9; Jas 2:14-18; Mk 8:27-35

The disciples and indeed the Jews were looking for a different sort of Messiah. The words of Jesus were a disappointment to them and difficult for them to appreciate.

When Jesus asked 'Who do you say that I am?', Peter realised what he had always known deep down in his heart. This was the Messiah, the Christ, the Anointed One, the Son of God. No sooner had Peter made this discovery than Jesus told him he must tell no one of it. Why? Because, first and foremost, Jesus had to teach Peter and the others what being the Messiah really meant. Who do you say Jesus is? An adult faith demands that we ask that question of ourselves.

Throughout all their existence the Jews never forgot that they were God's chosen people. Because of that, they naturally looked for a very special place in the world. In the early days they looked forward to achieving that position by peaceful means. They dreamed of a day when another king of David's line would arise. But as time went on it became clear that this dreamed-of greatness was unlikely to be achieved by peaceful means. Their history was full of subjugation. The ten tribes were carried off to Assyria and lost for ever. They were conquered by the Babylonians, the Persians, the Greeks, the Romans. So far from knowing anything like dominion, for centuries the Jews never even knew what it was to be completely free and independent. The time that preceded the coming of the Messiah, they believed, was to be a time when the world would be torn in pieces, and the physical and the moral order would collapse. The Messiah they were looking forward to would be a bit of a revolutionary.

The word Messiah and the word Christ mean the same thing. Messiah is the Hebrew and Christ is the Greek for the Anointed One. The Messiah was God's anointed king. It is important to remember that Christ is not a name; it is a title. With the coming of the Messiah the Jews who were dispersed all over the world would be gathered into the city of the new Jerusalem. Palestine would be the centre of the world and the rest of the world subject to it. Israel would rejoice to see her enemies broken. Even the dead Israelites were to be raised up to share in the new world. Finally, there would come the new age of peace and goodness which would last for ever.

Think of Jesus set against a background like that. No wonder he had to re-educate his disciples in the meaning of Messiahship; and no wonder they crucified him in the end as a heretic. When Jesus connected Messiahship with suffering and death, he was making statements that were, to the disciples, both incredible and incomprehensible. All their lives they had thought of the Messiah in terms of irresistible conquest, and they were now being presented with an idea that staggered them. That is why Peter protested so violently. To him the whole thing was impossible. Why did Jesus so sternly rebuke Peter? Because Peter was putting into words the very temptations that were assailing Jesus. Jesus did not want to die. This was the devil tempting him again to fall down and worship him, to take his way instead of God's way. It is a strange thing, and sometimes a terrible thing, that the tempter sometimes speaks to us in the voice of a well-meaning friend. We may have decided on a course that is the right course but one that will inevitably bring trouble, loss, unpopularity, sacrifice. And some well-meaning friend tries with the best intentions in the world to stop us. It is quite possible for someone to love us so much that they want us to avoid trouble and to play it safe. 'He called the crowd to him, together with his disciples, and said to them, "If anyone wishes to come after me, let him deny himself, and let him take up his cross, and let him follow me." ' This part of Mark's Gospel is near the heart and centre of the Christian faith. There is the almost startling honesty of Jesus. He never tried to bribe people by the offer of an easy way. He did not offer people peace; he offered them glory.

More Joy In Heaven

Readings: Ex 32:7-11, 13-14; 1 Tim 1:12-17; Lk 15:1-32

Today's Gospel is consoling to the sinner. It also illustrates the willingness of Jesus to cross religious barriers to embrace the pain of the sinner.

The name Omarska may mean nothing to you. It was the Serbian concentration camp where Muslims experienced the venomous hatred that sadly, all too often, springs from religious divisions. One former detainee wrote: 'During the two and a half months I was there I saw about 600 bodies. None of them were shot. They had been beaten to death; they used heavy metal cables, or bars. Every morning a van used to come by and collect the bodies'. Religious hatred tends to be merciless and absolute. It can be among the Hindus and Muslims of India, among the Islamic fundamentalists of Egypt or Algeria, and among Orthodox Serbs and Bosnian Muslims and Catholic Croats of former Yugoslavia.

This same bitterness was demonstrated when in July 1998 a car bomb tore the heart out of the busy and peaceful market town of Omagh in County Tyrone. It indiscriminately killed and maimed men, women and children. Once more, religious differences, with a veneer of political justification, caused the suffering of the innocent. The British Prime Minister called it 'a blast of evil'.

Today's Gospel opens with bitter religious divisions. It was an outrage to the scribes and Pharisees that Jesus associated with men and women who, by the orthodoxy of the day, were labelled as sinners. To have a daughter marry one of them was like exposing her bound and helpless to an enemy. At that time the Pharisaic regulations laid it down that 'when a man is one of these people, entrust no money to him, take no testimony from him, trust him with no secret, do not appoint him guardian of an orphan, do not make him the custodian of charitable funds, do not accompany him on a journey'. It was a deliberate Pharisaic aim to avoid every contact with 'sinners'. They were shocked to the core at the way in which Jesus made friends with people who were not only rank outsiders, but sinners. By befriending people such as these Jesus had made himself ritually impure. He was defiled!

The parable of the lost sheep was turning everything the Pharisees believed in, on its head. For them the death of a sinner was a matter for rejoicing. Here was Jesus telling them that sinners were especially loved by him. By example, he was telling us that religious barriers were to be crossed – at any price. He, the compassionate one, excluded no one from the scope of his compassion and love.

Shepherds at the time of Jesus were personally responsible for their sheep. If a sheep was lost the shepherd must at least bring home the fleece to show how it had died. A shepherd would risk his life for his sheep. Many of the flocks were communal flocks, belonging, not to individuals, but to villages. There would be two or three shepherds in charge. Those whose flocks were safe would arrive home on time and bring news that one shepherd was still out on the mountain-side searching for a sheep that was lost. The whole village would be watching and when, in the distance, they saw the shepherd striding home with the lost sheep across his shoulders, there would arise from the whole community a shout of joy and of thanksgiving.

That is the picture Jesus drew of God; that, said Jesus, is what God is like. God is as glad when a lost sinner is found as a shepherd is when a strayed sheep is brought home. As a great saint said, 'God, too, knows the joy of finding things that have been lost.'

It is easy to think of the joy of the woman when at last she saw the glint of the elusive coin and when she held it in her hand again. God, said Jesus, is like that. The joy of God, and of all the angels, when one sinner comes home, is like the joy of a home when a coin that has stood between them and starvation has been lost and is found.

The Wonderful Promises Of God

Readings: Isa 55:6-9; Phil 1:20-24, 27; Mt 20:1-16

When we are sad or rejected, as the Jews were in Babylon, there are still the wonderful promises of God to console and strengthen us.

In the end President Habibie had to back down. As I write this there is relief in the besieged UN compound in the capital Dili where a thousand refugees are sheltering. East Timor had been convulsed with conflict, many killed, houses burned to the ground, people loaded on trucks and forcibly taken away. It has happened before in this century – the Holocaust, Rwanda, the Balkans and now East Timor. But it also happened before that. The Jewish people were taken into captivity in Babylon. Psalm 137 captures their feelings: 'By the waters of Babylon we sat and wept when we remembered Zion, On the aspens of the land we hung our harps though there our captors asked of us the lyrics of our song, and our despoilers urged us to be joyous "Sing for us the songs of Zion" ' Around the sixth century before Christ the Babylonian forces sacked and took Jerusalem. Large numbers of surviving citizens were settled in Babylonia, and the territory of Judah was placed under a governor. The exiles seem to have been moved to Babylonia itself, living in various towns and villages as well as in the capital city. While their captivity was not harsh, many had a deep longing to return to their homeland.

The reading from Isaiah (55:6-9) is a beautiful and consoling one written for a people in exile. 'Seek the Lord while he is still to be found, call to him while he is still near. Let the wicked man abandon his way, the evil man his thoughts. Let him turn back to the Lord who will take pity on him, to our God who is rich in forgiveness; for my thoughts are not your thoughts, my ways not your ways – it is the Lord who speaks'. Even in this world of plenty there is a sense of homelessness. 'Of always being a stranger at love's side' as one poet put it. There is a 'loneliness of mystery' about life itself. The pilgrim journey of life throws us into darkness and back to light again. The death of a loved one, failure in marriage, unemployment, disappointment in one's children, the results of our own sinfulness, a car accident – there are so many things that bring pain and darkness. On the other hand the joy of celebrating an anniversary, a victory, new life, are bright lights. All go to make up life as it is lived today.

We are, in one sense, sharing the exilic experience of the Jews in Babylon. If we are sensitive at all to the warmth of God's love we will be pained by any wilful separation from him. Even in exile there is hope. There is always a silent presence, an active, interested spectator, who wills our well-being, sharing life with us. God never abandons us. Our reading today is a plea from a compassionate God to return to him, so that he can lavish us with his life-generating love.

Many of the Jews in Babylon were becoming absorbed into the pagan culture that they were surrounded by. They didn't want to return home. Isn't that so true of us today? We prefer the darkness! Isaiah is gently reminding them of the God they worshipped in Jerusalem. He is asking them to remember where they came from, spiritually as well as physically. Revisionism in history and social comment can deceive us. We can be deceived into believing that the past was all black, harsh, forbidding. For many it was not so. They learned of God's love at the table of their bedside. They knew the consolation that the forgiveness of sins brings, they were fed with that special meeting with Christ in the Eucharist. We should not forget where we came from. The invitation from God, through the prophet Isaiah, is couched with gentleness. He reminds them of the presence 'while he is still near'. He reminds them of the welcome their return will generate. 'Turn back to the Lord who will take pity on him.'

Last week Peter attempts to distort the lordship of Jesus. He is rebuked. JC follows F, not man's will.

This week the apostles attempt to distort discipleship, once again by following man's will, not God's.

...wer

Readings: Wis 2:12, 17-20; Jas 3,16-4:3, Mk 9:30-37

Some years ago a German psychologist wrote that there is in each one of us a will to power. Is this what the disciples were arguing about as they followed Jesus?

Many years ago I read a book entitled *The Psychology of Character*, by an author named Rudolph Allers, a German psychologist. He claimed that in each person there are two dominant traits – the will to power and the will to community. There is something in each one of us that tends towards the desire to exercise power. This is most obviously present in a person who is a bully, or arrogant. But power can be exercised by manipulation; by withholding praise or encouragement; even by silence. It can be unwisely used at times in families, communities, political parties, industries. Of course, what happens goes unrecognised for what it is, namely, a desire to get one's own way, invariably at the expense of others. Power and responsibility are very close bed-fellows. When they fall out, dysfunctionality arises.

In the Gospel the disciples asked one another 'Who is the greatest?' Who had the most power? Who among them exercised the most influence – over Jesus? over others? An element of competitiveness was entering into the apostolic band! Human nature never changes! It was strange that this was the burning question, especially after the example they had seen Jesus set. Yet in their heart of hearts they knew they were wrong. When he asked them what they had been arguing about they had nothing to say. It was the silence of shame. They had no defence.

It is strange how a thing takes its proper place and acquires its true character when it is set in the eyes of Jesus. So long as they thought that

or passive resistance at best or passive aggression. at worst

To welcome is to wash feet and
welcome (serve) children, bottom of [?] children

"The greatest among you
must be the servant of all".

The will for others not self
must win out the inner conflict.

Ab Lincoln expressed it well
"I look for the day when
the love of power
will give way to the
power of love."

A society is judged
on how it treats its
most vulnerable members

✳ Whatever the reason.
Jesus uses this display of
human selfishness to give a
teaching on care for others.
He turns an ugly moment into
a moment of tenderness + child

seen, the argument about
but when that argument
is it was seen in all its
when it is found, it is

face of conflict is: 'How
my own way in the light
really important thing is
ts or rows. If we took
it would make all the
lid, we asked, 'Could I go
of everything we said, we
us was listening to me?',
be saved from doing and
t there is no 'if' about it.
s presence. God keeps us
e ashamed that he should

e every performance she
ray, 'God, help me to sing
e only power we have
n being a son or daughter
The disciples had been
ey had not nurtured that
Whatever gifts God has
ourselves alone. We keep
ntact with the God who

Life Is A Series Of Choices

Readings: Am 8:4-7; 1 Tim 2:1-8; Lk 16:1-13

The parable of the unjust steward has always caused problems for the scripture scholars. A willingness to choose God first, and a refusal to compromise on Gospel values, runs through the reading.

Nothing ever changes in the human heart. Its deviousness and capacity for duplicity was there from the time of Adam and Eve. The Gospel today portrays a number of rogues working on different levels. The steward has 'squandered his master's property'. We are not told how. Like most rogues he wants to cover his tracks and secure his future in the comfort to which he has become accustomed. He calls in two debtors and slices a huge amount off their debt to the master. The 'one hundred measures of olive oil' is equivalent to about two and a half years of wages; the 'one hundred containers of wheat' is equivalent to about seven years of wages. These are whopping debts! By forgiving the debt the servant is reasonably assured of the security he craves. Doesn't it all sound so familiar?

There are two key phrases in the Gospel. The first is: 'The children of this world are wiser in their generation than the children of light'. I see the so-called children of this generation every morning. They are driving to work in BMWs at 7 a.m. Most will not expect to return home until the late evening. For many of them there is the thrill of the chase, the desire for money and advancement, the job satisfaction that goes with entrepreneurial activity – this is what motivates these so-called children of this generation. On the other hand they have a work ethic that is taken seriously, there is the desire to create employment, they often put their talents at the service of the community. They work hard and they play hard. Jesus is telling us that those who profess the gospel and are in a relationship of love with him, need to look at people who are highly motivated. Be as enthusiastic about witnessing to Jesus in your life and in your words as they are about things of the world.

The second key phrase is 'No servant can serve two masters'. Where does our relationship with God fit into the whole scheme of things in our lives? Have we a bottom line? It is said that 'everyone has their price'. Are there any issues in my life about which I am unwilling to compromise? 'Seek first the Kingdom of God and everything else will be added' is the attitude that this Gospel asks of us. Put God first and God will look after you. Is that true of me? One outstanding figure of the twentieth century who was willing to put God above all was Reverend Martin Luther King. After his own home was bombed he said, 'Christian love can bring brotherhood on earth. There is an element of good in every person. No matter how low one sinks into racial bigotry, he can be redeemed. . . . Non-violence is our testing point. The strong man is the man who can stand up for his rights and not hit back.' With such an approach he outflanked the Southern legislators. He struck where an attack was least expected, and where it hurt most: at the South's Christian conscience. He didn't meet violence with violence but with love.

Prostitutes And Tax-Collectors Are Entering Heaven

Readings: Ezek 18:25-28; Phil 2:1-5; Mt 21:28-32

The theme of this Gospel is that 'actions speak louder than words'. The Christian life is the struggle to bring our daily lives into conformity with the faith we profess.

When I was living in the inner city, one bleak November day a knock came to the Presbytery door. A youngish girl, sad, woebegone and wet, was looking for help. Her boyfriend was in prison; her children had been taken from her; she was, as she said herself, 'on the game'. Worst of all she was a 'druggie'. She had lost everything – dignity, companionship, children and love. She was, in the ways of the world, 'a woman of no importance'. I wonder sometimes where she is now. People of my generation will remember the name of only one prostitute, that of Christine Keeler. Her well-known liaison with a government minister, Jack Profumo, toppled the Tory government of Harold Macmillan. It was a gala time for the newly emerging tabloid press. Prostitutes are invariably harassed, both by the legal system and the police. They are considered the flotsam of society, hardly worthy of anything but contemptuous dismissal. To be robbed of one's good name and forced to indulge in the humility of prostitution through need must be the ultimate in degradation. For the compassionate Jesus such people were special. The funeral of King Baudouin of the Belgians was attended by prostitutes. He was a holy man who tried to live with the heart of Jesus. I truly understand that Jesus in today's Gospel uses prostitutes as an example of those who said they would go their own way and then took God's way.

Jesus is taking the example of two flawed characters. The second son was a 'yes' man. The mask he wore was that of the ever-obedient and docile son. This person is always ready to appear obliging. I suppose the television series *Yes, Minister* was peopled by such characters. The churches are full of them – career clerics for whom the trappings of power and position are more important than the 'spirit and truth' contained in the scriptures. These people are coifed to the last and smell heavily of perfumed deodorant. These are the type of people who give great protestations of piety and fidelity, but their practice lags far behind.

The first son is a 'macho' type. He loves to appear a winner. He likes to compete, to be the man to strike a hard bargain – a tough negotiator. He never gives up. This man does good by stealth. A man with whom I am acquainted is not unlike the first son in today's Gospel. He appears too busy even to speak to you. His photograph is always in the newspaper, invariably in the high society section. I happen to know that this man gave one million pounds to a most deserving charity and there was never even a whisper about it in the media. This man says 'no' and then quietly, when nobody is looking, goes off to do the good deed!

Neither of the characters in the Gospel is anything but flawed. I recall when the Pope was in Ireland in 1979 he asked us a number of times to try to bring our practice into conformity with the faith we profess. The ultimate test of fidelity is to have words and actions in perfect alignment. Jesus teaches us what is right but doesn't judge us on our sin alone. The key is the end result, God's will or not. What this Gospel is saying is that 'actions speak louder than words'. It isn't a matter of saying 'yes' or professing creeds. If tax-collectors and prostitutes can enter the Kingdom of God, then there has to be hope for us all.

Exploiting Children

Readings: Num 11:25-29; Jas 5:1-6; Mk 9:38-43, 45, 47-48

This is a challenging Gospel. It is here 'the rubber hits the road'! Living as brothers and sisters to one another and caring for the 'little ones' is a real Gospel value.

Each Sunday we stand up and recite together 'Our Father ... but deliver us from evil. Amen'. The implications of this prayer are enormous. We have a common Father, a Father who loves us with an infinite love. In fact, a Father who loves us with the same love as he loves Jesus. 'As the Father has loved me so I have loved you,' Jesus said. We are drawn up into the community of love that is the Trinity. It isn't easy to accept love or to acknowledge that we are loved. A silent voice within whispers, 'If he/she only knew me they wouldn't or couldn't love me.' How could I be loved, scarred as I am by my sinfulness? And yet I am.

But this prayer has other implications. If we have a common Father we are brothers and sisters to one another! We share the same life – the life of Jesus! I was born into the Tierney family. I will always be a Tierney. This cannot be erased. Ever. A few days after I was born I was baptised in University Church in St Stephen's Green. I was reborn into another family – the family of God, the Church. This, too, leaves an indelible mark that can never be erased. This means that I am a brother and sister in Christ with all, but more especially with those who have been baptised. Now you see where the cup of water given in the name of Jesus comes in! It is the Christ in me reaching out to the Christ in the other person.

When I read the part of the Gospel today about scandal I went to the Internet and keyed in 'Children at risk'. I had my eyes opened about the suffering of children in our world. In the US many, many children are abducted each year by the non-custodial parent following a break-up in the family. They are the subject of the so-called tug-of-love stories beloved of the tabloids. Can you imagine their suffering? Or the many children who have to grow up with an alcoholic parent, with the fighting, bitterness and violence that invariably are present. How do they survive? I could hardly believe that child slavery exists. Young children are sent into the sweat shops of Asia to produce the designer clothes that we like to wear. Many of them are pre-teen, working long hours for paltry wages. Such are the sins of adults against the most vulnerable. How would you like your children to have to suffer this? Young boys, some hardly ten years of age, haul the heavy weapons of war as the boy-soldiers of Africa. They can fight before they can write! They can kill before they have lived themselves.

The scandal of adult greed, adult pride and adult power-lust is a tragedy. In many places in the world young boys and girls are forced to prostitute their bodies to satisfy the lust of adults who use and dispose of them as so much human debris! I am sure Jesus weeps over the little ones exploited in so many ways. How about the Western world? The indulgence and the pampering of so many children is surely damaging them. The latch-key kids of the Western world are equally exploited in the interest of money. In our own city young men have been kicked to death by their peers! What about the sexual abuse of children? Their innocence exploited to satisfy the warped lust of adults. This Gospel is a challenge to us to discern the ways in which we give scandal to those in positions of powerlessness over whom we exercise responsibility. Parents must equally discern how they are fulfilling their obligations of stewardship in relation to their children. There is much to think about.

There Was A Rich Man

Readings: Am 6:1, 4-7; 1 Tim 6:11-16; Lk 16:19-31

The Gospel today is about rich and poor but it is also about the choices we make in this life and whether we listen to God speaking to us through his Word.

The richest man in Britain is the Duke of Westminster, who tops the richest 100 list with a fortune of £4 billion. He may be Britain's richest man but Westminster knows only too well that you can't buy happiness. He was struck down by depression four years ago. The 200 acres he owns in London's Belgravia alone, could easily fetch millions. Perhaps the man in today's Gospel was the Westminster of his day?

At the other end of the spectrum is Eddie. A hopeless alcoholic who sleeps rough, winter and summer. Last year Eddie had to go to hospital. He was so unused to a bed, he insisted on sleeping on the floor under the bed. He has nothing except the clothes he wears. He is a lovely person, seldom giving offence. Occasionally he appears all spruced up and clean, indicating that he has been in prison for a time, usually for the misdemeanor of 'disturbing the peace'. Or there is John, the tragic human debris of a dysfunctional home. A row with his mother's 'live-in' boyfriend leaves him on the street. Soon he is on drugs, hopelessly imprisoned, his life spiraling downwards. John is in free-fall. He has nothing. He said to me, 'Father, I have a hole in my soul.' The Duke of Westminster is unlikely ever to meet the Eddies or Johns of this world. They are poles apart. But they did 'meet' in the Gospel we have just read!

Occasionally the word 'rich' is used pejoratively. Rich equals evil or sinful. Poor equals good and virtuous. In the Gospel today the rich man is not necessarily sinful, he is simply indifferent to the plight of Lazarus. A hardness of heart is suggested. Did the rich man step over Lazarus to enter his house? Incidentally, the name Lazarus means 'God helps', that is, one who is 'dependent on God'. The Gospel is not so much about rich and poor but about priorities in our lives and the choices we make. It is also about listening to God in his Word.

They both died. The 'nether word' of the reading need not necessarily refer to the Christian vision of heaven and hell. Indeed, the message of this Gospel can be rooted in the 'here and now', and deals with the consequences of the choices we make on a daily basis.

This vivid reading, with its talk of Moses and the prophets, is a timely warning to us to listen to the Word of God. For those who have been baptised and brought up in the faith, a plea of ignorance will hardly justify an acquittal, when the time comes for the record to be set straight. We have God's 'last will and testament' available to us in the Bible. His Word has been taught to us in school and through the teaching of the Church. The reading is asking us to listen to God's Word and respond to it generously. The rich man had other priorities and it is only in his suffering that he experiences a need for God. It is only in his suffering that he thinks of the other members of his family. He wants to warn them. Too late!

I remember someone once saying to me that the worst thing that could happen to us Christians is we could allow our hearts to be hardened. Repeated sinfulness and a carelessness about the things of God can lead to a hardening of the heart. Sin is no longer recognised as such. Where do we go from there?

The Lost Art Of Listening

Readings: Isa 5:1-7; Phil 4:6-9; Mt 21:33-43

We are asked to listen to the voice of God with the head and the heart.

It is hardly a coincidence that this parable is addressed to the 'chief priests and the elders'. The Sanhedrin was composed of the chief priest, scribes and elders. They were supposed to be people of impeccable character. 'You shall search from among all the people, able men, who fear God, men of truth, disdaining unjust gain, and you shall place them over the people.' (Exodus 18:21) As long as the Sanhedrin convened, it functioned as both supreme court and central legislative body for all Israel. These were important people whom Jesus was addressing. People of power find it difficult to listen.

I know of one very important executive in a multinational company to whom every response is choreographed. When he makes an appearance in Ireland, staff are told when to rise and sit. In minute detail they are advised how to respond when the chief executive walks in. How and when to clap is practised, as is the manner of speaking with this man! When leaders are treated in this fashion they become absorbed in illusions of grandeur. They have all the answers. There is no need for them to listen. A leader who fails to listen is 'surdus' (deaf), from which the word 'absurd' comes.

The first thing Jesus is pointing out is the failure of the spiritual leaders to listen to the voice of God speaking through the prophets. God speaks to us today. He speaks through the Bible, through the Church, through the world around us, through the circumstances of our daily lives. Do we 'bend down low enough to listen?' Listening to

God speaking to us and responding to the prompting of the Spirit is very central to our relationship with God. The patience of God is immeasurable. The glory of the human person is the freedom to say no, even to God. God will never force himself into a human life. He waits to be invited.

In the early chapters of the book of Revelation there are three of the most important doors in life. There is the door of opportunity. 'Behold,' said the risen Christ to the Church at Philadelphia, 'I have set before you an open door.' (Revelation 3:8) That was the door of opportunity by which the message of the gospel could be taken all over the world. God sets before every person their own door of opportunity. There is the door of the human heart. 'Behold,' says the Risen Christ, 'I stand at the door and knock. (Revelation 3:20) At the door of every heart there comes the knock of the nail-pierced hand, and a person may open or refuse to open. This door can only be opened from the inside. The opportunity is characterised by the successive servants who are sent to the vineyard. There is the door of revelation. 'I saw a door in heaven standing open,' says the seer. God 'wills all men to be saved and to come to the knowledge of the truth'. God offers to every person the door that leads to the knowledge of God and of life eternal.

Clearly Jesus lifts himself and distinguishes himself from the long line of servants (prophets) who were sent to the vineyard. He is someone special, the son of the owner. He is their last chance. I have often been asked by evangelical Christians whether I have 'been saved' or not. I know what they meant. For me, salvation is an ongoing process, not necessarily an instantaneous experience. I am in the process of being saved. But the evangelical Christian does have a point. One could ask 'Am I living in a real relationship with the Lord?' Have I made an adult commitment to Jesus? This is question we all have to ask ourselves.

Is There Any Such Thing As A Marriage?

Readings: Gen 2:18-24; Heb 2:9-11; Mk 10:2-16

Marriage is part of God's plan for men and women. It is lived out in the messiness of daily living.

Isn't marriage something that only becomes real in people who commit themselves to one another? Are any two marriages the same? Malachy and Angela McCourt had a squalid, sad, alcohol-seeped relationship, painfully brought to life in *Angela's Ashes*. Katharine Graham, arguably the most powerful woman in America as editor of the *Washington Post*, had a peculiar relationship with her husband Phil, which ended with his brutal suicide within earshot of his wife. Charles Dickens, a compassionate and caring person, who outwardly at least seemed happy, walked away from his marriage to Catherine to be with Ellen Ternan.

Then there was the little old man I discovered sobbing deeply in the encroaching gloom of Sword's Church in north County Dublin. His wife had died some weeks before; 'All I want to do is to die to be with her,' he told me. He loved her deeply. He didn't really want to live without her. Can any two marriages be the same? Is there a blueprint for a happy marriage? Men and women were designed for each other. The first reading indicates that men and women were made for each other and a man or woman alone is an unfinished person. They were not made to be alone.

There is generally an ache at the core of a person who is single, not by choice but by circumstances. Marriage, the committed relationship of man and woman, is very much part of God's providential plan for the human race. But the relationship is one of equality and complementarity. This is the way God wants it to be. At the centre of the integrated person is a pull, an attraction, towards the opposite sex. It is as if, deep within each heart, is buried a powerful magnet drawing the two together. They want to be one, and talk of eating each other.

But love of its nature spreads; it is an opening out to the world to embrace the 'other'. Sexuality of its nature is ordered towards the procreation of children. The rearing and caring for offspring is best accomplished in a committed or covenanted relationship. The young need love, stability, security, and this can best be provided within the context of marriage. So marriage is about love but more than love; it is about commitment.

Love is a feeling but it is more than a feeling, it is a decision. My feelings are fickle. One day I am frivolous and gay and on another grumpy and sad. I need something more stable than this on which to base my relationship. I need to decide to love this person today, despite either my own or the other person's feelings.

Sexuality is an intimate form of communication. By giving my body, mind and heart to another I am making a statement. I am saying 'I am yours, take me'. It is a sacred place of personal intimacy. But for a marriage to work, other forms of communication are needed. One form of communication is dialogue. Not talking with the head alone, but with the head and the heart. Not listening with the ears alone, but with the ears of my heart; listening to the nuances, the body language, the words, the feelings behind the words. Dialogue is an active listening and talking, which is done with respect and without judging.

Marriage is blighted by the 'if only' syndrome. If only he would come in time for his meals; if only he would give up the drink; if only she would stop nagging; if only she would discipline the children. The 'if only' syndrome forgets that there is only one person that you can change, and that is yourself. God is love. Where love is, God is. When a man and a woman love each other God is present. Every sacrament is an act of Christ. When a wife listens intently to her husband, when she is sensitive and kind, love is present – God is present.

Faith

Readings: Hab 1:2-3, 2:2-4; 2 Tim 1:6-8, 13-14; Lk 17:5-10

The apostles, who lived a life of intimacy with Jesus, ask him, 'increase our faith'.

In 1843 Marx, a Jew, wrote of religion like this: 'It is, the sight of the oppressed creature, the heart of a heartless world, the soul of a soulless environment. It is the opium of the people'. A French philosopher wrote a little earlier that religion 'is the art of making men drunk with enthusiasm, to prevent them thinking about the oppression committed by their rulers'. Some see faith as the preaching of 'pie in the sky when you die'. Faith, they say, is without substance, a sort of delusion. Today many people are simply indifferent about religion and matters of faith. In today's Gospel the apostles say to the Lord 'increase our faith'. What were they asking for? What is the nature of faith?

Ordinary life couldn't operate without some sort of faith. You buy a present for your wife, a watch perhaps, believing the maker's guarantee that it is reliable. Someone in the office asks you for a loan of twenty euros; you give it, secure in the knowledge that they will pay you back. You have faith in that person's reliability. I am typing this on a laptop computer, the working of which I simply cannot understand. Nevertheless, I have faith that it will do the job for me. Taking up a new job, trusting a colleague, entering a marriage, buying a computer, all demand a degree of faith in a person or a product. We believe all sorts of things that we ourselves cannot prove to be true or false. We trust them to be true on the evidence or word of another.

So, in the biblical sense, faith rests on the character of God. God keeps his promises. He can be trusted. In the Old Testament the prophets spoke of the Lord's 'steadfast love', his faithfulness to his people. They may wander away from him but he remains faithful.

The basis of New Testament faith is the life, death and resurrection of Jesus. If people 'believe' in Jesus they trust in the fact of what Jesus has done for them. Faith, then, is trust in what God has done, which results in a wholehearted commitment, trusting ourselves to him. This affects every area of our life.

But faith has to be more than that! We live in a world where things can be tested. We can weigh, measure, analyse, computerise, evaluate, put under a microscope, into a CAT scan, and get a result. Isn't faith more than simply blind trust? The *Catechism of the Catholic Church* says faith 'is a supernatural gift from God'. More importantly it adds, 'in order to believe we need an interior help of the Holy Spirit'. To make the jump from the empirical world – the world of see, touch and feel – into the world of the Spirit, the world of mystery, we need something more. That something more is the gift of faith. Believing is a free, conscious, human act, aided by grace. Faith is a personal, free act.

Faith is a gift that grows as it is exercised. It grows through prayer, spiritual reading, frequenting the sacraments, acts of charity. Our faith is nurtured within the context of a community – that is the Church. This faith is given to us, in embryonic form, at our Baptism. But faith is personal, therefore there comes a time when we have to say 'yes' to the gift received.

It is our faith that gives the answers to the deepest questions of life and death. Who am I? Why am I here? Where am I going? What's the good of my life? Ultimately, the walk of the Christian demands that one's life comes more and more into conformity with the faith we profess. Faith was important to Jesus. How often did he ask a petitioner 'Do you believe I can do this for you?' How many times did he say 'Go in peace, your faith has made you whole'?

Twenty-Seventh Sunday in Ordinary Time

The Wedding Feast

Readings: Isa 25:6-10; Phil 4:12-14, 19-20; Mt 22:1-14

We have been invited to a wonderful wedding feast of God's love. The table is laid, the room is prepared, God awaits our reply.

Being a Christian is not the same as being a black person, Chinese, or a graphic artist. It is not a name, it is a way of being. Being Christian is not a label that says 'made in heaven'. It is more. It is a way of being in relationship with Jesus. Relationships bring with them joy but also responsibilities. The parable of the wedding feast tells us that we have received an invitation to be in relationship with the King, but something is expected of us.

It reminds us that in the last analysis God's invitation is the invitation of grace. Those who were gathered in from the highways and the byways had no claim on the king at all; they could never by any stretch of imagination have expected an invitation to the wedding feast, still less could they ever have deserved it. It came to them from nothing other than the wide-armed, open-hearted, generous hospitality of the king. It was grace that offered the invitation and grace that gathered people in. Grace is a free gift of God. It is undeserved and unearned. Why should God love me? I know myself, my darkness, my sin. I know my unworthiness. God loves imperfect beings. God loves me as I am – right now. I am loved uniquely. 'I have loved you with an everlasting love and I am constant in my affection for you,' he tells us. But God loves me too much to want me to remain where I am. And so his grace is always prompting me forward to great things and deeper holiness.

Grace is a mysterious thing. I like to think of it as the invisible bond of love. You can't see, touch or feel it, yet when you are in the presence of the beloved you know it is there. It is the heart of the relationship. I suppose we are flattered when we get invitations from important people. I have to admit I am. I mark it in my diary and make sure I am appropriately dressed for the occasion. I try to keep the date. Do people know that they are invited to the heavenly banquet of God's unfailing love? Do they know that he wants, indeed expects, a reply to his invitation? In the parable of the wedding feast they all had good, even legitimate reasons for saying no. Because those who were invited didn't come, the party was opened to everyone. We talk about ourselves as the People of God, the invited ones. If we don't come there are consequences.

Do We Possess Money Or Does It Possess Us?

Readings: Wis 7:7-11; Heb 4:12-13; Mk 10:17-27

The readings for today are a challenge for the rich, but they are also a challenge for all of us, even those of us without much.

Little did American hotelier Leona Helmsley realise the implications of her now-famous phrase, 'only little people pay taxes'. Mrs Helmsley was right. It will only be the little people who pay taxes; the new barbarians will have a choice. Recently our major bank coughed up a whopping £90 million in unpaid DIRT tax, but only because it was caught! The chairman, defiant to the end, claimed innocence and implied that they only paid up 'for peace sake'. They just couldn't be bothered with the hassle. Our newspapers tell us that another batch of dot-com millionaires are being created, despite the fact that the chief executive of the company admitted that it was a loss-making operation, largely because of investment to reorganise, and good will and other write-offs. Our world revolves around money: making it, stealing it, trading in it and spending it, but above all looking for more. It is hard to see how the gnomes of Zurich, the 'suits' of Threadneedle Street or the moguls of Frankfurt or Wall Street will be interpreting the Gospel for today. They will hardly be impressed with the words of Jesus, 'It is easier for a camel to pass through the eye of a needle than for a rich person to enter the kingdom of Heaven'. It is unlikely that the people who will be in church today will need to hear the message of today's Gospel – most likely they will be poor!

The barbarians of global enterprises think nothing of pushing a nation's economy to the brink, and beyond. They do not identify with any particular country, and consequently they walk away from a country just as easily as they enter it. Companies have little loyalty. They will move to politically stable areas with a ready supply of educated workers, and most importantly with preferential taxation and regulation policies. We have benefited from this in recent years in Ireland but things could change just as easily!

The Christian message is hardly a whisper in the boardrooms of London, New York or Tokyo. And yet the example given by religious people is not without its influence. One has only to think of Mother Teresa, Mahatma Gandhi or the Dalai Lama.

Do we possess money or does it possess us? 'Where your treasure is, there your heart is also.' Where is our treasure? Are we consumed with making more and more money or with possessing more and more things? Can we do without the props we construct in our lives and rely on the Lord and his providence? The goal is holiness.

Walking the Gospel road can be a lonely journey. With the rapid change of times we can feel unappreciated and our message unheard. We all need a little affirmation. And yet the promises at the end of the Gospel reading today are an enormous source of consolation to us. If we have left much for Christ our reward is assured. This is not 'pie in the sky when you die' because by trying to do the will of God on a consistent basis we will experience the peace of Christ that goes with it. The gifts and fruits of the Holy Spirit will be evidenced in our lives. We will not have the constant worry that goes with the frantic search for more and more money. Our reward will be in this present time and, in the world to come, eternal life.

Giving Thanks

Readings: 2 Kings 5:14-17; 2 Tim 2:8-13; Lk 17:11-19

When Jesus healed the lepers, thanks came from the most unexpected quarter.

In 1939 Sergeant Major Robert MacCormack saved the life of his commanding officer, Major Harry Parkin, on a battlefield in France. Every year he received a letter of thanks on the anniversary of the incident. Parkin, an estate agent in Richmond, Yorkshire, wrote: 'Dear Bob, I want to thank you for the forty years of life which ordinarily I would not have had were it not for you. I am grateful to you. Regards Harry'. He never forgot to give thanks.

On his journey towards Jerusalem Jesus met a small band of lepers. Because of the contagious nature of the disease, lepers were obliged to stay fifty yards downwind from those people with whom they wished to communicate. They were outcasts with little hope of rehabilitation into the community. An impenetrable barrier of fear separated them from those they loved. At the time of Jesus the term leprosy covered all skin diseases. It was believed that bodily uncleanness was also the result of sin. Today, many fundamentalist Christians believe that the AIDS crisis is God's way of punishing the sinful!

Fr Peter O'Leary, in his autobiographic book *My Own Story*, tells of similar circumstances to today's Gospel during the famine in Ireland. Many people died without consolation or hope because their neighbours were afraid of catching 'famine fever'. He relates a particularly poignant story of a Cork couple from near Skibbereen, who left the workhouse and hobbled painfully home to die. They were only discovered some considerable time later because of fear on the part of the neighbours.

Try to put yourselves in the place of the lepers. It is interesting that there was a Samaritan among the group. Jews and Samaritans didn't mix. To do so would be to incur defilement for a Jew. Need and pain overcomes all barriers. They were together as people in need. If fear unites those naturally opposed to one another, shouldn't love do the same? The priests were the ones who would determine the fittingness of the healed lepers to return to the community.

Here it is not merely a question of our Lord's mercy towards the outcast, but the universal character of God's salvation. Just as the true charity of the Good Samaritan had shown up the inadequacy of priest and levite, so here the ingratitude of the nine Jews is shown up by the spontaneous return of the one they despised as 'an outcast'. Jesus' question, 'The other nine, where are they?', is, of course, rhetorical, not looking for information, but a striking expression of his indignation and disappointment. The Samaritan was the only one to give thanks. Thanks came from the least expected source.

Was the casualness with which the nine Jews received their bodily restoration an omen for our Lord of the obduracy with which his people as a whole would reject the salvation 'he was to accomplish in Jerusalem'? There is surely a lesson here for Christians, too, perhaps especially for 'born Catholics', not to let the great privileges that are theirs since Baptism sit lightly on them.

Twenty-Eighth Sunday in Ordinary Time

Taxation

Readings: Isa 45: 1, 4-6; Thess 1:1-5; Mt 22:15-21

'Is it lawful to pay the census tax to Caesar or not?' ask the Pharisees. The Christian is a citizen of two worlds and owes allegiance to both.

Those who are as old as I am will remember serious agitation against penal rates of PAYE taxation in Ireland in the Eighties. The salaried workers looked on as the self-employed evaded tax on a significant scale, while they had no escape-hatch in offshore accounts. Taxation is always a bone of contention between the ruler and the ruled. It was no different in the time of Jesus!

There were three regular taxes exacted by the Roman government in Palestine. There was a grain tax, whereby a person must pay to the government one tenth of the grain, and one fifth of the oil and wine that he produced; this tax was paid partly in kind and partly in a money equivalent. There was an income tax, which was one per cent of a person's income. There was a poll tax; this tax had to be paid by every male from the age of fourteen to the age of sixty-five, and by every female from the age of twelve to sixty-five. It amounted to a denarius – that is, what Jesus called the tribute coin. So nothing changes!

The Pharisees hatched a plot to trap Jesus. He was put, in the eyes of the Pharisees, between 'a rock and a hard place'. No matter what answer he gave he was in trouble! If he said it was unlawful to pay tax, then he was in trouble with the Roman authorities. If he said it was right to pay tax, then he risked been branded a quisling by his own people – collaborating with the enemy! For a Jew this was important not only for political reasons but for religious reasons as well. God was the only king. To pay tax to a foreign king was to usurp the rights of God and true religion. It must not be forgotten that the poor Jew also had Temple taxes to pay.

Every Christian has dual citizenship. Christians are also citizens of their country. Their taxes are important for the common good. Taxes maintain the fabric of a well-ordered society which cares for the least advantaged, maintains the infrastructure that is needed for the commercial life of the country, provides clean water for drinking and emergency services for times of need. The State provides public lighting and education. Not to pay one's taxes is to deprive others of the services they may be badly in need of. In a document from the Irish bishops entitled *Prosperity with a Purpose,* published in 1999, they say: 'The calibre of people who enter politics, business and the public service, and the development of a more tax-compliant culture, remain as critical to ensuring economic wealth, as they were to the generation of the present boom in the first place'. Good citizenship demands the payment of taxation. The moral climate at present says 'pay up, don't wait to be found out!'

The Christian has a dual allegiance; there are matters of religion and of principle in which the responsibility of the Christian is to God. When the citizen is convinced that it is God's will that something should be done, it must be done. So in the answer Jesus gave, 'Repay to Caesar what belongs to Caesar and to God what belongs to God', there is an implied claim that the civil ruler (Caesar) only rules by God's permission.

Spiritual Leaders

Readings: Isa 53:10-11; Heb 4:14-16; Mk 10:35-45

A good leader can spark a revolution. He or she can inspire sacrifice in the cause of an ideal. Little Rosa Parks from Montgomery, Alabama began something that made history.

On 1 December 1955, Mrs Rosa Parks, a 42-year-old coloured seamstress, was ordered by a Montgomery City Lines bus driver to get up and make way for some white passengers. She refused, was arrested and fined $10 under an Alabama law that made it a misdemeanour for any person to disobey a bus driver's seating instructions. Within forty-eight hours after Rosa Parks had been arrested, mimeographed leaflets were being circulated in Montgomery's coloured section, calling for a one-day boycott of the city buses. The strike was so successful that black leaders decided to continue it until their demands were met. The demands: that coloured people be seated on a first-come, first-served basis, without having to vacate their places for white passengers; that white bus drivers show more courtesy toward black passengers; that black drivers be employed on buses travelling through mostly Negro districts. The boycott continued, and was a staggering 95 per cent effective. A black motorist, working for the car pool, stopped to pick up an old woman who had obviously walked a long way. 'Sister,' said he, 'aren't you getting tired?' Her reply: 'My soul has been tired for a long time. Now my feet are tired, and my soul is resting.'

The single act of defiance by a simple woman sparked the beginning of the Civil Rights Movement that was to culminate in the Civil Rights Acts enacted in the late Sixties by President Lyndon Johnson. Rosa was prepared to pay the price. It took courage.

In the Gospel today Jesus is trying to teach the disciples the 'Rosa Parks doctrine'. Following Christ is not about power, or position, or seats at his right or left hand in heaven. It is about being willing to drink the cup of suffering that Jesus himself was to drink. They were looking for the 'perks' before paying the price! He was teaching them a first lesson in leadership.

Spiritual leader Lao Tzu summarised this predisposition when he said around 565 BC:

> A leader is best
> When people barely know he exists,
> Not so good
> When people obey and acclaim him,
> Worse when they despise him.
> A good leader is one, of whom, when the work is over,
> they will say 'we did it ourselves'.

Good leaders are willing to risk everything. They cling to nothing as a protection for themselves. They are not self-justifying or self-serving. Rosa made her protest not really for herself but for all the black people of the United States.

Mahatma Gandhi also learned the road of non-violent leadership: 'It is not non-violence if we merely love those that love us. It is non-violence only when we love those that hate us. Love of the hater is the most difficult thing of all. But by the grace of God even this most difficult thing becomes easy to accomplish if we want to do it'.

When leadership is limited to the exercise of power it is ultimately ineffective. In the past we punished people for stepping out of line, in the home, in school, in the Church, and many people were cowed for a time. Some were hurt and still bear the scars. People obeyed through fear. Thankfully we have moved to a new model of leadership. The servant model is effective because it is seen for what it is, 'a service of love'. Of course, good leaders need to set their own hearts on fire before they can hope to set the world ablaze.

Spiritual Nagging

Readings: Ex 17:8-13; 2 Tim 3:14-4:2; Lk 18:1-8

We are a people in need. We carry painful memories through life. Is this the way it is meant to be? God is asking us to be persistent in prayer. He will hear us.

Life is a roller-coaster. The dips can be bitter and painful; the highs can be moments of great pleasure and happiness. We bring our memories with us. The sharpest ones are often the most painful. Like the little child whose strongest memory is of the day she and her sister were brought to an orphanage by their mother, separated from one another, and later physically abused. She told her story on television when she was ninety-five years of age. A lifetime of suffering stemming from unhealed memories! On the same programme, a ninety-year-old spoke of the wonderful memories she had of her father, who every night, without fail, came to her bedroom, kissed her on the forehead and said, 'Good night, Alice, and God bless you.' We can carry the pain of separation, death, broken relationships, sin, failure, sickness, with us through life. Never utterly sad, but never truly happy either. Is this the way God wants it to be? I think today's Gospel provides hope and consolation. The Lord is saying: 'Don't be afraid to bother me with your needs and your disappointment. I will listen. Keep asking'. We are a people in need. The parable is suggesting that God will meet our needs if we are persistent in asking him.

The judge in the parable was one of the paid magistrates appointed either by Herod or by the Romans. Such judges were notorious. Unless plaintiffs had influence and money to bribe their way to a favourable verdict they had no hope of ever getting their case settled. These judges were said to pervert justice for a dish of meat.

The widow was the symbol of all who were poor and defenceless. It was obvious that she, without resources of any kind, had no hope of ever extracting justice from such a judge. But she had one weapon – persistence.

This parable is like the parable of the Friend at Midnight. It does not liken God to an unjust judge; it contrasts him to such a person. Jesus was saying, 'If, in the end, an unjust and greedy judge can be wearied into giving a widow woman justice, how much more will God, who is a loving Father, give his children what they need?'

That is true, but it is no reason why we should expect to get whatever we pray for. Often a father has to refuse the request of a child because he knows that what the child asks would hurt rather than help. God is like that. We do not know what is to happen in the next hour, let alone the next week, or month, or year. Only God sees time whole, and, therefore, only God knows what is good for us in the long run. That is why Jesus said we must never be discouraged in prayer. That is why he wondered if people's faith would stand the long delays before the Son of Man should come. We will never grow weary in prayer and our faith will never falter if, after we have offered to God our prayers and requests, we add the perfect prayer, 'Thy will be done'.

Being The 'Bread Of Life' For Another

Readings: Ex 22:20-26; 1 Thess 1:5-10; Mt 22:34-40

Jesus wants to nourish us with an intimacy we can hardly imagine. Through the eucharistic sacrament and sacrifice Jesus is the bread of life for us on an individual level and as a people.

Has anyone ever been the 'bread of life' for you? Think back. Perhaps you were seriously ill and it was the loving support of a special person that you remember most from that time. Maybe it was a time when you were in grave financial difficulties. Who was the person who bailed you out and gave you a new beginning? Was there a time when your marriage was in tatters and some person acted as a healing, reconciling agent? Did your mother or father hug you when you were small and encourage and praise you? If any of these things happened to you, wasn't that person 'the bread of life' for you at that time? When I think of the promise of Jesus to be the 'bread of life' for us I think he is offering to be our intimate companion on the journey of life.

Jesus wants to be close to us. We are his only child, unique as a fingerprint, created individually in his image – the image of love. We are uniquely loved by Jesus. We are the beginning and end of the assembly line of humanity – as if no one else existed. The presence of Christ in the Eucharist is the glory of our Church. But Jesus addressed not just one person but a crowd. They gathered around him at the lakeside in Galilee. So Jesus wants to be the 'bread of life' for us individually but also as a people. The celebration of the Eucharist is a community act. It is allowing Jesus to nourish us as a parish, diocese, Church. Have you ever noticed in that wonderful painting *The Last*

Supper by Leonardo da Vinci how the disciples are crowded around Our Lord? They are right up there with him, sharing his physical and eucharistic presence in common bread and wine in their native Aramaic. They even sang a hymn together. 'After singing hymns of praise, they walked to the Mount of Olives.' On Sunday we celebrate, communicate, listen, give thanks – as a community.

St Paul writes about eating and drinking unworthily, 'not discerning the body of the Lord'. We are the body of the Lord. When we go to Mass lacking a spirit of reconciliation, of forgiveness, or with enmity towards another person, we are 'not discerning the body of the Lord'. Jesus wants to nourish us through his Word, his sacrament and sacrifice. This happens at Mass. The desire of his heart is to be the 'bread of life' for us.

Thirtieth Sunday in Ordinary Time

The Journey Home

Readings: Jer 31:7-9; Heb 5:1-6; Mk 10:46-52

Many Catholics lead their lives estranged from the Church. Some are hurt by past experiences. God is waiting to receive with joy those who desire to make the journey home. 'Courage' he says to Bartimaeus in the Gospel today.

Near the end of the Second World War, while still in his middle twenties, John Howard Griffin began to lose his sight. He was told that his loss of sight would eventually be total. He wrote at that time: 'The sight of a pin, a hair, a leaf, a glass of water, the faces of strangers, these filled me with tremendous excitement. I took them in and bound them up in me'. Eventually John Howard Griffin became totally blind. In spite of this, he wrote novels, became proficient at music, and became a Christian. For twelve years he lived in a world of total darkness. This was the sort of darkness that poor Bartimaeus of today's Gospel experienced. Then in 1957 Griffin miraculously began to see again. A twelve-year blockage of the circulation of the blood to the optic nerve had suddenly opened, restoring his sight. His life became one of rejoicing in the sight that he had received back. He now knew his wife and children not just as voices or shapes but he experienced them more intimately through the gift of sight. He became a very famous person in the struggle for racial equality in America. He travelled through the deep south of America after dying his skin black and becoming like a Negro so that he could share the experiences of rejection and discrimination. He wrote the bestseller *Black Like Me* and threw himself into the civil rights movement until he died in 1980. Bartimaeus and Griffin shared the darkness and rejoiced in the restoration of sight. What a wonderful experience that must have been for both of them.

Of course, there is another kind of blindness. In a book entitled *The Road Home*, we find the stories of five Catholics, estranged from God and the Church, who find, as they put it, 'the road home'. I am amazed at the instruments God used to make the way easy for them to return to him. One of them read the wonderful autobiography of Thomas Merton, *The Seven Story Mountain,* and was so moved that she travelled with a friend to Gethsemane Monastery where her re-conversion began. Another signed up for a Marriage Encounter weekend and rediscovered the peace that only God can give. It was the chance encounter with two Mormons on her doorstep that started Jean thinking again about faith and God. Lee, whose marriage broke up, went on a Beginning Experience weekend, for those suffering the pain of loss through death or separation. This experience touched him so much that it sparked a desire to find again the God he had once loved and worshipped.

Sometimes the journey back is painful. The only requirement Jesus required was faith. This could hardly have been the full-blown faith of the believing Christian. Perhaps it was the tentative faith of a newly converted Francis of Assisi; 'Who am I God and who are You?' Perhaps the faith required is little more than a genuine desire for the truth. At every Mass we pray 'for all those who seek You with a sincere heart'. Surely those prayers will be answered. I could be the instrument God will use to help another to return to his love and mercy. Help me to be open to that possibility.

I am seldom the best judge in my own case. My free-thinking position on many things could possibly be a form of spiritual blindness from which I need to be cured.

The Pharisee And The Publican

Readings: Sir 35:15-17; 2 Tim 4:6-8; Lk 18:9-14

✱ Praise, Thanksgiving, contrition. Petition.

Today's Gospel is a wonderful story that has a lot to teach us about ourselves and our relationship with God. ✱

movements in prayer → Thanksgiving. The leper healed with ✱ intercession. The persistent widow today. contrition

I can understand the Pharisee in today's Gospel! There is a bit of him in all of us. I recall reading a book entitled *Making friends with Your Shadow*, in which the author, William Miller, said that facing 'your shadow' is a bit like drinking your own spittle! The expression is not very elegant but the reality invariably has some truth. Coming to grips with the evil side of oneself is no picnic. It may be a powerful and frightening experience. But true spirituality rests a great deal on knowledge of oneself. St Teresa of Avila said, 'The thought of one's sins is the bread with which all palates must be fed.' Our duplicity, our lust, our sloth, our pride, tell us of our brokenness. But our brokenness is a part of us. Martin Tierney is shaped and moulded by his virtue and his sinfulness, by the events of his life; his darkness is as much a part of him as that part that is sweet and light. The posturing of the Pharisee looks like he was trying to convince himself of his own virtue and did so by comparing himself with the failures of the publican. He just couldn't face his own reality. We do it all the time. Read a report in the newspapers of a rape or a robbery, a sex-abuser or a fraudster, and we preen ourselves a little; 'I may be bad but I am not that bad,' we say to ourselves. Of course the Pharisee forgot that goodness is a gift of God, not something we can achieve by our own cleverness or effort. The boasting of the Pharisee was a hollow echo, insubstantial, wafted away,

we do not save ourselves. Humility is the virtue from which all other virtues grow.

Only the humble know that salvation is of God, not of man, lest any man boast never to return. Notice that in his prayer the Pharisee makes no petition at all. Does he need God?

The 'publican' of the parable was one of the class who had bought the right to collect customs, were unashamedly profiteers, and accordingly both social and religious outcasts. The prayer of the publican, like his way of life, is poles apart from the Pharisee's. He has nothing but his guilt to talk to God about. His very stance, at a distance, with lowered gaze, expresses his total abasement before the Presence of God. He beats his breast, the seat of his heart, from which all evil comes. There is no thought in his mind of comparing himself with others. He can do no more than ask God for mercy. The publican's stance before God illustrates the scripture: 'a humbled, contrite heart you will not spurn'.

The Pharisee lost out. It is plain that the verdict of justification is on the side of the publican. It is only when we face our darkness, 'our sin', and admit that it is a part of us, needing exposure and healing, that forgiveness can be found. In addition, when we admit we are sinners we can stop pretending. We no longer have to wear a mask that we present to the world. We can be who we are – a mixture of 'weeds and wheat'. When we reach that point, a real pressure is lifted from our shoulders and we become free. It is easy to fall into the trap of believing that 'God only loves the good'. God loves all of me. God wants all of me. God sees the contradiction of my life. He loves me just the same.

The fact that both went to pray is significant. Even though the prayer of the Pharisee was self-justifying, there was some little spark in him that needed a relationship with God. They went to pray. We need to pray. It is just not possible to maintain a relationship with God or to deepen it without prayer.

Lord be merciful to me a sinner!

Spiritual Leadership

Readings: Mal 1:14-2:2, 8-10; 1 Thess 2:7-9; Mt 23:1-12

Recent Church scandals may have been the Lord's way of telling us that a model of leadership that did not reflect the compassionate leadership of Jesus needed to be changed.

The twentieth century, perhaps more than previous ones, is littered with the shattered reputations of fallen leaders. Among the most notorious are Stalin, Hitler, Idi Amin, Nixon, Clinton, Pol Pot. Some followed policies that left slaughtered millions in their wake. Others exploited the vulnerable, regardless of the consequences. Millions of people have perished as a result of their flawed leadership. But there were other tyrants in a minor league hardly worth mentioning.

Spiritual leadership is particularly open to exploitation. Jesus knew this. If religion is a matter of ostentation, or titles, or of rules to be interpreted only by experts, it ceases to be life-giving. If religion becomes burdensome and drained of the joy and hope that are so central to the love and worship of God, then we look to the leadership. Is a person helped by religion or haunted by it? Does it carry a person, or has the person to carry it? Whenever religion becomes a depressing affair of burdens and prohibitions, it ceases to be true religion. Orthodox Jewry loves the paraphernalia of religion. In Jerusalem one still sees the ultra-orthodox wearing their phylacteries. These are little leather boxes, strapped on the wrist and on the forehead; they have little compartments that house four passages of scripture.

The whole design of the Pharisees was to dress and act in such a way as to draw attention to themselves; the whole design of the

Christian should be to live the life intended for us by God and allow that life to be the only authentic witness to the truth of God's love. Any religion that produces ostentation in action and pride in the heart is a false religion. Jesus had little time for ostentation in religious matters. 'Anyone who exalts himself will be humbled and anyone who humbles himself will be exalted.' He told the people to listen to the scribes and Pharisees but not to be guided by their way of life.

Sometimes we judge our leadership harshly. We expect more of them than any human being is able to deliver. However exalted a position a person holds, he or she is still subject to circumstances and the changes of human life. He or she still has a mortal body, with all that body's weakness and pain. He or she is like a person with a precious treasure contained in an earthen vessel, which itself is weak. Of course the real characteristic of people is not their power but their weakness; the power of Christ is made perfect in weakness. In addition, every leader must remember that 'there but for the grace of God go I'.

Recent Church scandals have forced a change in the model of Church leadership. Weakness has been exposed in all its rawness. No person is above the frailty that comes with original sin. Leaders are beginning to understand this. A compassionate leadership is replacing the autocracy of old. Understanding is replacing a spirit of judgement. Hopefully, dialogue will replace the issuing of edicts. Good leadership is pivotal to the health of any Church. Perhaps the Lord in his wisdom is teaching us the hard way to walk in his footsteps and exercise leadership as a service.

Love Betrayed

Readings: Deut 6:2-6; Heb 7:22-28; Mk 12:2-34

Marriage break-up wreaks havoc in families. The betrayal of love and trust is one of the most bitter experiences of life.

I recently received a letter from a very old and dear friend. Joan and her husband Peter (not their real names) have been married for nearly forty years. Over the years I spent many happy days in their home, with their four children. My friend Joan wrote this to me: 'It was at this business conference that he met a woman and somehow got into an affair. I found out two months later. I started to suspect something was wrong, but each time I asked Peter he replied that there was nothing wrong. Eventually he told me he had met a woman and promised to get help and talk to someone he trusted.

However, he had already reached a point of no return and refused any suggestion of counselling, prayer or anything. When I said that it was adultery, he said, "No it's not, this is a relationship!" In August last year we went to Glasgow for our son's wedding, telling our children nothing. He had already decided he was willing to give up everything as he wanted this "woman" so badly. So last October he left and has had virtually no contact with myself or our children since then.

The whole thing has been so devastating for me, our children and our families. We had a great marriage, or so I thought. We both had a great faith in God and in his provision for us. I keep asking myself how could a man who believed so much in marriage and family and who had such a great faith in God throw it all up. Recently I have heard he is seeking a divorce. As far as I am concerned I made my marriage vows, and it is my intention, with God's help, to keep them. I still pray that he will return.'

On a recent television programme a divorced couple were together after seventeen years' separation. The tension and the recriminations began almost as soon as they started to speak. He was away from home a lot on business. She was left for up to two weeks at a time with the children. In her loneliness and isolation she began a series of affairs. He returned one day to find one of his wife's male partners in his home. She left. Divorce followed. This wasn't love. Neither was prepared to pay the price that love demanded of them. They also had an inability to dialogue at the level of feelings. They were adrift, floundering about, knowing nothing but their own personal needs, which were unsatisfied.

It is in giving that we receive. 'Greater love than this no man hath than that he lay down his life for his friends.' Love means listening – with the heart. Love means listening not just to the words but to the nuances, the gestures, the body language. Love means trying to understand rather than judge. Love means not taking the stance of a victim – 'poor me' – but trying to change yourself. Love means keeping sex alive. Love means learning how to handle conflict. Love means not allowing yourself to drift into a 'single married' lifestyle. Love means making time for talk. Love means all this and more.

The next time you go into a restaurant, observe the couples not talking. Invariably they will be the married ones! Why is this? Probably because the love they had in the beginning hasn't yet grown into friendship. We can never learn about love. Love, above all, is a decision and not a feeling.

No One Is Outside The Scope Of God's Love And Forgiveness

Readings: Wis 11:22-12:2; 2 Thess 1:11-2:2; Lk 19:1-10

The story of Zacchaeus is a great consolation to us. He was despised as an oppressor in the local community. 'Jesus looked up. . .' – that look became the beginning of a life-changing experience.

During the Great Irish Famine of the 1840s, many of the landlords, especially the absentee ones, were feared and hated by the peasantry. Acting on their behalf, in the collection of rents, were middlemen, agents and sub-tenants. They were the ones who often initiated the large-scale evictions that led to so much emigration and paupery. A constant battle of wits took place between the different groups. Although Irish, the middlemen were acting on behalf of a frequently English-based aristocracy, and were not liked by the people. The names of some of them, like Marcus Keane of the Vandeleur estates in Kilrush in County Clare, are still very strong in local folklore.

It was not dissimilar at the time of Jesus. The middle-class Jews who were in rebellion against Rome were themselves oppressors of the poor and the uneducated. In practice, Roman rule meant Roman taxation. For most Jews, paying taxes to the Roman overlord meant giving to Caesar what belongs to God, namely, Israel's money and possessions. Some of the tax-collectors grew rich. In his book *Jesus before Christianity* Albert Nolan writes: 'Considered in terms of compassion, the hardship of having to pay taxes to a Roman government instead of a Jewish government and the hardship of having one's religious sensibilities offended occasionally by the pagan intruder, were minimal in comparison with the hardships suffered by the poor and the sinners at the hands of their rich and virtuous fellow-countrymen'. Undoubtedly, a person like Zacchaeus, would have been despised in the local community. He was part of the machinery of oppression.

In the light of the above the Zacchaeus story is important. I am sure Zacchaeus climbed the tree out of curiosity. Stories of Jesus were doing the rounds. Who was he? What did he look like? Zacchaeus let his curiosity get the better of him. 'Jesus looked up.' A look from Jesus was a life-changing experience; that same look was to penetrate the heart of Peter, who went out and 'wept bitterly', and became a mighty man of God. Jesus looked up and said, 'Come down quickly, for today I must stay at your house.' Zacchaeus, the tax-collector, was not outside the scope and affection of Jesus. A life-changing look was enough. Zacchaeus' heart was changed. He was willing to repent, and to return well over and above what was required from his accumulated wealth. Jesus came to seek out and save what was lost. Here we have echoes of the parables of a few Sundays ago – the lost sheep and the coin. The people grumble . . . judgemental people, the self-righteous, the indignant, the holier-than-thou; they didn't like the idea of Jesus eating with tax-collectors and sinners. This was going against the law. Jesus always put love before law.

This Gospel brings together many of Luke's themes: Jesus offers salvation to all without exception; he seeks out the lost; he cares for the sinner; he goes to great lengths to encourage us along the way. He asks in return a form of discipleship that will be costly but will bring great joy to our hearts.

Thirty-First Sunday in Ordinary Time

An Invitation To A Different Kind Of Living

Readings: Mal 1:14-2:2; 1 Thess 2:7-9; Mt 25:1-13

In telling us that we do not 'know the day or the hour' we are being invited into a new life lived for God here on earth.

The following extract is from *The Theft of the Spirit – A Journey to Spiritual Healing with Native Americans* by Carl Hammerschlag.

In the stark desolate beauty of the Tusayan Plateau, in a village a thousand years old, the Parrot Clan chant prayers. In a ceremony from this timeless spiritual world of the Hopi, her words mingle with the penetrating sounds of reggae music from a pickup truck. Its teenage inhabitants, already drunk, are parked in front of a bootlegger's house not more than twenty yards from her. The Old Badger Clan chief who first blessed the Wupamo in New York moves towards them. Seeing the old man approach, they put their beer cans down behind them. After a brief exchange they turn off the music and return with him to the blessing place. They stand quietly by his side. One of the young men is his grandson. At the truck, he says: 'I will soon be gone from the world, Grandson. I have nothing to give you, no inheritance, no money, but I do have a trust fund. It's over here.' He drags the boy inside the circle of the Parrot Clan mother's prayer. Pointing at it, he leans over to his grandson. 'This is my trust, "this way" – "this way" will give you life. Everything else you think you have or want will go away – your truck, the bootleggers. This is your life right here in that Spirit Friend, in these prayers. This is the life of your family. If you give it away you will give up the spirit of your people.' There are tears in the boy's eyes, so I know the spirit in the mask still lives.

Fear of the unknown is natural. Death is the great unavoidable. It is the barrier no one has yet climbed over. 'It is appointed unto man once to die,' say the scriptures, 'and after death the judgement.' Nearing the end of the Church's year thoughts of death are presented to us in the readings. Heaven, hell, death and judgement – the great 'four last things' – are frequently anaesthetised from the mind. They cannot be eliminated!

In our heart of hearts we know that 'we do not know the day or the hour'. We have witnessed too many sudden deaths. Death by accident, by suicide, by cancer, are daily facts of life.

In the spring after Cardinal Newman's sister Mary died, he wrote to another sister about the nagging feeling of loss: 'The country is so beautiful – the fresh leaves, the scents, the varied landscapes. Yet I never felt so intensely the transitory nature of this world as when most delighted with these country scenes. Dear Mary seems embodied in every tree and hid behind every hill. What a veil and curtain this world of sense is! Beautiful, but still a veil'. (*Letters and Diaries*) Catherine McAuley, the founder of the Mercy Sisters, grew reconciled with the phenomenon of death. An onlooker at her death, Elizabeth Moore, wrote: 'I did not think it possible for human nature to have such self-possession at the awful moment of death, but she had an extraordinary mind in life and death'. St Thérèse of Lisieux imagined herself dying like a tired traveller coming to the end of a journey and falling over: 'Yes, but I'll be falling into God's arms,' she said.

But is it death that should concern us? Isn't it living well as a prelude to what is to come that matters most? 'So stay awake, because you do not know either the day or the hour' is an invitation to enter into a life lived for God and for others. It is an invitation, a summons rather than a warning, a call to examine how we are living. The reading at the beginning is not really about death, but about life. It is about thinking of what we would like to leave behind. How would I like to be remembered when I die?

God Loves A Generous Giver

Readings: 1 Kings 17:10-16; Heb 9:24-28; Mk 12:38-44

What a contrast; on the one hand Jesus criticises the religious leaders of his day, and on the other praises the poor widow for her generosity.

Leaders tend to be conservative. They inherit a system, a set of values, ways of doing things, that they are reluctant to let go of. They have a sense of protecting and conserving and handing on intact the legacy they themselves have received. They usually have closed minds. Gandhi, Martin Luther King, Nelson Mandela, Dietrich Bonhoeffer, are a few leaders who have stepped outside the straight-jacket of tradition to create something new. Pope John XXIII was such a man.

Leadership tends to protect itself in the name of protecting others. Jesus was aware of the oppression of leadership. The chief priests, elders, scribes and Pharisees were oppressors. The power that enabled them to dominate and oppress was the law. The law was the rules and regulations handed down to the Jewish people, both in the written word of scripture and in the oral tradition of the scribes. There were instructions and rules about every imaginable detail of life, secular, social and religious. Jesus was not opposed to the law. He was opposed to the way people used the law. The law was being made into a burden, whereas it was supposed to be a service.

The leaders and scholars of Jesus' time had first enslaved themselves to the law. This not only enhanced their prestige in society, it also gave them a sense of security. After enslaving themselves to the letter of the law, such people go on to deny freedom to others. Jesus wanted to ensure that the law would be the servant of people, not their oppressor. There are great personal dangers in religious leadership. One must reflect seriously on the use of such forms of address as 'Your Eminence', 'Your Grace', 'My Lord', 'Monsignor'. Are they at all appropriate in the age in which we live? Such titles damage the holder, and equally diminish the person using them. They pander to the desire for prominence and can convince ordinary sinful mortals that the leader is in fact far holier or more blessed than the others.

The person who enters upon office for the respect that will be given to him, has begun in the wrong way, and cannot, unless he changes, ever be in any sense the servant of Christ and of others. It is still possible to use religious connections for self-gain and self-advancement. This would be anathema to all that Jesus stood for.

In the Court of the Women at the Temple there were thirteen collecting boxes, called 'The Trumpets' because they were so shaped. They were for contributions for the daily sacrifices and expenses of the Temple. Many people threw in quite considerable contributions. Then came a widow. She flung in two mites. The mite was the smallest of all coins and was worth one-fortieth of one pence. And yet Jesus said that her tiny contribution was greater than all the others, for the others had thrown in what they could spare easily enough and still have plenty left, while the widow had flung in everything she had. In my experience, most people in need are little different to ourselves. Something happened that left them bereft of the things we take for granted. A dysfunctional family, abusive parenting, a failure in a relationship, a drink or drug problem, all throw up beautiful people in a mess. Prepare to give this Christmas to the organisations and groups who are dedicated to helping those in need. Real giving must be sacrificial. The amount of the gift never matters as much as its cost to the giver; not the size of the gift, but the sacrifice. Real generosity gives until it hurts. Real giving has a certain recklessness in it. The woman might have kept one coin; it would not have been much but it would have been something, yet she gave everything she had. There is a great symbolic truth here. It is our tragedy that there is so often some part of our lives, some part of our activities, some part of ourselves that we do not give to Christ. Somehow there is nearly always something we hold back. We rarely make the final sacrifice and the final surrender.

There Is A Homelessness

Readings: 2 Macc 7:1-2, 9-14; 2 Thess 2:16-3:5; Lk 20:27-38

Death is the unsolved riddle of life. In Jesus we have the promise of eternal life.

The topic of resurrection was a main point of contention between the Pharisees and the Sadducees and Paul plunged the Sanhedrin into disarray by mentioning the issue. (Acts 23:6-10)

After more than thirty-five years in the priesthood I still find death traumatic. The confrontation with finality, in the human sense, is always deeply painful, even if I have never met the deceased. The dark brown clay, mottled with stones, of the newly opened grave, somehow penetrates my soul. It isn't easy to be reconciled to the fact that this pulsating, loving, chatty human being who was known and loved, is having shovels of clay dumped on her. The readings of the funeral liturgy are assuring and comforting. They soothe the pain without healing it. However much we believe that 'the souls of the virtuous are in the hands of God' and 'no torment shall ever touch them', a gnawing grief clasps the heart in a vice-like hold. We have to deal with the Resurrection, which is pivotal to our Christian faith.

The resurrection of the body is a central doctrine of our faith. The *Catechism of the Catholic Church*, in answer to its question 'What is rising?', says: 'In death, the separation of the soul from the body, the human body decays and the soul goes to meet God, while awaiting its reunion with its glorified body. God, in his almighty power, will definitively grant incorruptible life to our bodies, by reuniting them with our souls, through the power of Jesus' resurrection'.

The human being is constantly looking forward. The next holiday, exam results, marriage of a relative or friend, new house, new experience; these are the sort of things that capture the human heart, which lives so much in the future. When one event happens we immediately turn to the next future expectation. The human heart is restless, never completely fulfilled. How can the finite human heart ever find fulfilment in this life? 'Thou hast made us for thyself O Lord and our hearts are restless until they rest in Thee,' wrote St Augustine.

Poet Jessica Powers, in her poem 'There is a Homelessness', writes:

> It is the homelessness of the soul in the body sown;
> it is the loneliness of mystery:
> of seeing oneself a leaf, inexplicable and unknown
> cast from an unimaginable tree ...

If the finite is embraced by the infinite and absorbed into it, fulfilment is accomplished. God is infinite love, infinite peace, infinite joy – he is everything that the heart desires. Heaven is the infinite embrace of God in that place 'where all tears shall be wiped away'.

Over the years I have attended at the bedside of the dying on many occasions. The end comes and everything changes and everything remains the same. The person before me is still Mary or James or Paula. The breathing has stopped. Something has gone!

I Will Give You A New Heart

Readings: Prov 31:10-13, 30-31; 1 Thess 5:1-6; Mt 25:14-30

The message of Ezekiel has an uncanny aptness for the times we live in. It gives hope to the soul. (Ezekiel 36:24-28)

When God first called Ezekiel, an Old Testament prophet, he was a refugee in Babylonia, married but with no career. He had been born in Jerusalem into a priestly house in the days of Josiah. When Josiah died, his religious reforms went with him, and the verdict of 2 Kings on each of his successors is the same: 'They did evil in the sight of the Lord'. The shocking new foreign paganisms that they brought in must have been a continuing subject for outraged debate in Ezekiel's priestly family home. Nothing changes! God called him to be a prophet and pastor to his people in exile in Babylonia. For the next twenty-two years he spoke God's words to the exiles and sent messages to the remaining people back home in Jerusalem. 'I will give you a new heart.' How we long for that as we struggle with our daily weaknesses!

When I was a clerical student, an Anglican bishop, John Robinson, published a book entitled *The Death of God*. It made a huge impact and was the subject of intense media interest. It wasn't that different in the time of Ezekiel. The theme that constantly emerges through the pages of Ezekiel is the 'otherness' of God. It is easy to try to bring God down to size, to make him simply a friend or a buddy. But God is still beyond our imagining. God is quite different from us. Like Bishop Robinson, Ezekiel lived in an age of disillusionment. It was easy to think that God was dead, or had at least forgotten to do anything. Life seemed a meaningless mess, with world affairs out of control and God's people suffering as a result. And yet Ezekiel's favourite name for God is 'the sovereign Lord'. For Ezekiel, God is sovereign, meaning that he is in overall control. Nothing slips through his fingers, nothing is forgotten.

The whole basis of Ezekiel's ministry is that the sovereign Lord has spoken to him and given him the key. The blurred images of the film make sense because Ezekiel has been given the soundtrack to explain it, straight from the heavenly Director. The wages of sin. The Israelites thought that because God loved them he would ignore their sin. Ezekiel saw that they were a people who ignored God's laws, trusting in secular powers and worshipping idols that claimed to bring material blessings and offered licence for lust. He stated clearly that their complacent idea of God was wrong. Ezekiel is a prophet for our time. He balances the notion of God's justice, with his mercy and power to renew.

The wonderful promises 'I shall cleanse you of all your defilement ... I will give you a new heart ... I shall remove the heart of stone ... I shall put my spirit in you ... you will live in the land ... you shall be my people ... I will be your God' are so encouraging. There are people who no longer believe that it is possible to love and serve God faithfully. There are people who run up the white flag of defeat and give themselves over to sinfulness. Ezekiel was addressing these words to the Jews in exile. Some had given themselves over to pagan gods. Some didn't even want to leave Babylon when the liberation came. They were a confused lot – just like us today. We have to believe and claim the promises of God. God's word is true and will not disappoint us. This reading is full of wonderful hope. But one clear thread is Ezekiel's concept of Spirit-filled renewal bringing life to the spiritually dead. His final vision is of the people of God ordering both their worship and their land according to his will; a praising, obedient people of whom it may be said 'the Lord is there'.

Expectant Vigilance

Readings: Dan 12:1-13; Heb 10:11-14; Mk 13:24-32

Thoughts of the Second Coming and of the destruction of Jerusalem are invitations to begin our annual spiritual stocktaking.

When Dostoevsky, the great Russian novelist, was sent to Siberia in the 1850s he was befriended by a Madame Fonvizina, who gave him a copy of the New Testament, which he cherished all his life long. As he lay dying he had his wife Anna read to him from it. 'I believe', he wrote in a letter to Fonvizina, 'that there is nothing more beautiful, profounder, more sympathetic, more reasonable, more courageous, more perfect than Christ, and not only is there nothing, but I tell myself with jealous love that never could there be'.

At home as I write this the news is of houses being saturated with the water from swollen rivers and roads becoming impassable. Strikes threaten our schools and transport system. Christmas is still too far away to lighten our spirits. The readings of today's Mass appear to fit appropriately into such a scenario of gloom. The destruction of Jerusalem, and the Second Coming of Jesus to judge the world, are matters we would prefer to avoid thinking about.

And yet, even facts that we humanly shudder from, have to be seen against the fact of a loving, caring God so beautifully outlined by Dostoevsky above. To forget that would be to risk despondency, leading to hopelessness. The theme of the reading today is of vigilance. Longmans Dictionary describes 'vigilance' as: to be alert, watchful, especially to avoid danger. It also says 'to keep watch' or 'to stay awake'. There is the vigilance of a mother at the bedside of a sick child;

there is the vigilance of waiting for examination results; there is the vigilance of the airtraffic controller gazing intently at the radar screen; the vigilance of the single-handed sailor in an Atlantic swell; these are tense vigils. There is also the vigilance of waiting to greet an old and dear friend returning home after years away. There is the vigilance of expectant parents waiting to greet their longed-for firstborn child.

The vigilance that is being asked of us is one of expectant faith. A vigilance that knows the deep love of God, as described by Dostoevsky, and that is assured of this, and yet is aware only too well of its own sinfulness. To be on vigil is not a passive activity. It is active, anxious, expectant, hopeful. The thought of the Second Coming and the consequent judgement is to encourage us to draw closer to the source of love, indeed to love itself. At this time of the year we are nudged ever so gently to do our annual spiritual stocktaking, to take a tally on how our relationship with Christ has developed over the past year. Where have we been and where are we going? It is a time of year when we might consider taking 'time out' for a day or a few hours to draw close once more to Christ – the tremendous lover.

A Sacred Place

Readings: Macc 3:19, 20; 2 Thess 3:7-12; Lk 21:5-19

The Temple in Jerusalem, whose destruction is foretold by Jesus in today's Gospel, was the focal point of all hopes, desires and aspirations of Judaism.

In the 1967 war against the combined forces of the Arab States, nothing so elated the Israelis as the capture of the biblical city of Jerusalem. The tough commando leader who took what was formerly the Temple area, and its remaining, so-called Wailing Wall, said: 'None of us alive has ever seen or done anything so great as he has done today'. And there by the Wall, he broke down and wept.

In 2000 Pope John Paul II touched the stones of the Western Wall, prayed, crossed himself, and placed a note asking for forgiveness in its cracks. In the note, the Pope asks God's forgiveness for sins against the Jews. The note's text, written on a Vatican letterhead and signed by the Pope, read: 'God of our fathers, you chose Abraham and his descendants to bring Your name to the nations.... We are deeply saddened by the behaviour of those who in the course of history have caused these children of Yours to suffer and, asking Your forgiveness, we wish to commit ourselves to genuine brotherhood with the people of the Covenant'. This was a most sacred act in a sacred place.

'Wherever I go, I go to Jerusalem.' And so it is for every Jew. The eternal message of Jerusalem accompanies Jews every day of their lives. Jews long for Jerusalem, the 'city of peace', to find their complete fulfilment. They mourn for its Temple, temporarily removed from its people. From the time it was dedicated by King David until the Romans destroyed it, Jerusalem was the focal point of the Jewish people. There were certain things that could only be done there; no matter where a Jew lived he or she would have to go to this holy city to do these things.

Imagine yourself in Jerusalem two thousand years ago. It is the festival of the Passover, and Jews from all over the world are coming to celebrate the holy season. They come from every direction, first by hundreds, then by thousands, and finally by hundreds of thousands. When the festival arrives a good portion of the entire Jewish population is concentrated in this one city. As far as the eye can see, the mountain slopes are covered with tents, where people will roast their Paschal Lamb, which in the time of the Temple was the focal point of the Passover service. 'God shall choose a place for his Name to dwell; there shall you bring your offering and sacrifices, your tithes and gifts.' (Deuteronomy 12:11) This place was Jerusalem.

The Gospel today (Luke 21:5-19) refers principally to the destruction of the Temple at Jerusalem, with obvious references to the end of the world. Christ's discourse on the End, or the 'Apocalyptic Discourse', as it is generally called, is found with certain significant differences in each of the first three Gospels. It is a difficult discourse to understand and interpret, in good part by reason of the fact that it contains references both to the destruction of Jerusalem and to the end of the world. The period preceding the final destruction of the Temple was a difficult one for the nascent Christian Church. Christians were tempted to follow what the many false Messiahs taught throughout Palestine. They needed to be people of perseverance and faith to survive. They would have to suffer social ostracism, perhaps persecution. It was in Christ that they would find the will and the grace to remain faithful to the end.

Sheep And Goats
– Christ The King

Readings: Ex 34:11-12; 1 Cor 15:20-26; Mt 25:31-46

When we come to be judged we will be judged on how we have loved.

There is a subtle apartheid operating in our country. It's not the division between country and city dwellers, nor between blue- and white-collar workers. In a way it's not even between rich and poor. There is a transparent wall whereby the haves and the have-nots never meet. The rich do help the poor, sometimes to the point of sacrificial generosity. But they never meet. There is a 'dialogue deficit' between the poor, the drug addict, the wino, and those who have come to be called 'suits'. Those who live on the bottom of the heap know, only through advertising and television, how the Mercedes-ensconced 'suit' lives his or her life. They have never entered the rich person's house or supped at their table. Nor have they ever joined in their recreation or visited their office or club.

The same is true of the rich. They know only too well of the poor. Some are very generous givers. But they know little of how poor people live or of the language they use. They know nothing of the scramble to make ends meet. They have never experienced what it is to have to save up for a pair of shoes, or queue for attention in the out-patients of a public hospital, or the humiliation of joining a dole queue. The 'dialogue deficit' is a gulf in which groups of people living side by side may know little about one another. The opportunity to dialogue just isn't there.

This brings me to the Gospel story of the sheep and the goats! 'I was hungry and you gave me no food.' This can hardly refer exclusively to food for the body. Every night around where I live the Simon Community come with food for the homeless. I have no doubt that much of this food comes from the generosity of the rich. But there is a deeper hunger: it is the homelessness and hunger of the heart; it is the loneliness of mystery. Sometimes the food that is needed most is a sign, no matter how feeble, that somebody cares. Those who are addicted have little interest in bodily food. Frequently, it is left uneaten and thrown away. A word of kindness is seldom refused.

Giving without hope of return. Occasionally the gesture of love will not even be reciprocated. Real love is unselfish love. 'I was a stranger and you made me welcome.' Have you room in your heart for someone else? Someone who may be smelly, occasionally rude? This person might even steal from you! The person who needs that room may even be a classical 'chancer' with a Grimms-fairytale complex! That's the test! Of course, the stranger may live next door, or work in the same office, or be in the same club! Who is the stranger that you need to make welcome? What you do for the least ... 'you do unto me.' What an extraordinary statement! It tells us something about God, about ourselves, about the stranger in our midst. Jesus identifies so closely with us that we are as one in his eyes. They say that in passionate love, the lover and the beloved want to devour one another, to become one! Jesus in his compassionate love for us considers that what we do to others we do to him. Why wonder how to love God? Jesus is in our midst 'in his distressing disguise', as Mother Teresa put it. It is frightening that the ultimate test is how we have cared for 'the little ones'. If we have to put a measure up to our lives, a plumb-line, a spirit-level, then the most important one is love. Have we loved?

The Ignominy Of Suffering

Readings: Dan 7:13-14; Rev 1:5-8; Jn 18:33-37

The quiet dignity of Jesus in the face of suffering is an encouragment to us. It was the dignity of presence, the dignity of knowing who he was in relation to his Father.

Group Captain Leonard Cheshire was, by any reckoning, one of the great human beings of our time. No other pilot in World War II came near his record of one hundred bombing raids. After the War, Leonard began to establish homes for severely disabled people. Cheshire Homes have been established in over fifty countries. Cheshire was an individual who lived close to God. Not long before he died he became captivated by the words of Jesus in Matthew's Gospel: 'My God, my God, why have you forsaken me?' Here was a cry of unimaginable loneliness – the experience of the absence of God. The fact that Jesus chose this road must have made the intensity of the pain all the greater. Jesus plumbed the depths of misery and pain. He was like us, though without sin. Leonard was greatly moved by this thought and its consequence for us. Our response, he said, 'must be to give nothing less than everything in return'. Today's Gospel demands the same response.

What we read today has something of the ignominy of suffering. Much suffering has an ignominy attached to it. Last night on television I saw atheltic young men groping to touch a button on their electric chairs, to which their accidents has consigned them. Potentially shattered – perhaps not? In the court of Pilate, Jesus is under the glare of the inquisitive and curious. There is a taunting resonance in the question of Pilate, 'Are you the King of the Jews?' When the powerful confront the impotent there is always the lurking danger of bullying.

The strong, rich and famous can allow themselves the luxury of arrogance.

There is a dignity about the response of Jesus. There is no fawning before he who has the power of life and death over him. There is no grovelling; rather the dignity of majesty, the dignity of a person who knows who he is and where he gets his dignity from. 'His kingdom is not of this world' must have made no sense to Pilate. Through his complete passion Jesus never lost his inner dignity. He was subject to indignities – the crowning with thorns, the scourging, the arrest, the journey, the crucifixion, the oil and vinegar to drink, the abandonment. Yet the dignity of his suffering penetrated the humiliation.

Even worldly kings have the dignity of breeding about them. A beautiful moment in my life was a one-to-one meeting with King Baudouin of the Belgians. In the course of a very long meeting he pulled from his pocket a book entitled *Abandonment to Divine Providence*. 'This is what I live by,' he told me. He went on to explain how his life was dedicated to the Lord through the service of his people. Under the trappings of high office was the simplicity of the saint. Jesus, throughout his suffering, retained the dignity of who he was. Jesus says that he came into the world 'to bear witness to the truth'. Subordinated to that was the observation that 'all who are on the side of truth listen to my voice'. There are other times when Jesus mentions the importance of truth. In John's Gospel 'the truth will make you free'. He also says 'I am the way, the truth and the life'.

Recently a man was released from jail after twenty-seven years for a crime he didn't commit. There were times when he could have got his freedom on parole, but no, he wouldn't take it. The truth had to prevail. The truth was his innocence. How easy it is for us to compromise the truth – about ourselves, about Jesus. The example of Jesus in today's Gospel is an encouragement to us always to stand firm in word and action. The truth is Jesus, who said that all who are on the side of truth listen to his voice.

This grace is there to help us. We are not alone.

Last Sunday in Ordinary Time

The Cross Is A Contradiction

Readings: 2 Sam 5:1-3; Col 1:12-20; Lk 23:35-43

'This day you will be with me in Paradise' is a promise that Jesus never abandons those who turn to him, even at the ninth hour.

I have a treasured book in my possession, entitled simply *Last Words*. This book records the last written words of the men who were executed in Dublin after the Rising of Easter Week 1916. Last words are poignant and always from the heart. They tell us more about a person than a library of speeches given in perfect health. In his play *Richard II*, Shakespeare writes 'the tongues of dying men enforce attention like deep harmony'. Joseph Mary Plunkett wrote these final words to his beloved Grace Gifford: 'That is all I have time to say. I know you love me and so I am happy'. Patrick Pearse wrote to his mother: 'Goodbye again, dear, dear Mother. May God bless you for your great love for me and for your great faith, and may he remember all that you have so bravely suffered. I hope soon to see Papa, and in a little while we shall all be together again. Your son, Pat'. James Connolly was executed in Kilmainham Jail on 12 May 1916. The surgeon who attended him asked him to pray for him and for those about to shoot him. Connolly replied: 'Yes, Sir, I'll pray for all brave men who do their duty according to their lights'.

The words from the cross have an added gravity because of Jesus' imminent death. 'This day you will be with me in Paradise' is the final reprieve for a guilty man who had only uttered one sentence: 'Remember me when you come into your kingdom'. Because death was so near, this sentence, only eight words long, gathers all the virtues of faith and hope and repentance. Like Zacchaeus and Peter before that, a look of compassion from Jesus was enough to change a human heart. I know that these words of Jesus were for time and eternity. They are for me, too, an assurance that Jesus is holding out the hand of friendship to me until the moment I breathe no more. Nobody is lost. There is always a last chance, and a last chance!

At this time the apostles must have been questioning one another: 'Is this all there is? Is this the end of the adventure with Jesus that we gave some of the best years of our life to?' Perhaps each one in his own heart was searching for meaning to what seemed a catastrophe. The whole project had ended in failure. Apart from the few who were healed, and the numbers who were inspired to change their lives, there was little left to show for their effort or for the work of Jesus.

The death of Jesus, the apparent failure of his life, flies in the face of everything that men and women have valued throughout the whole of history. What a tatty kingdom! The contradiction of Christianity is that the cross, a sign of defeat, is a symbol of victory. The cynical have always scoffed at Jesus on the cross; his throne was an incongruous one, incomprehensible to the unbeliever. His kingdom was not of this world and therefore wasn't recognisable except to those who looked with the eyes of faith.

Other Feasts

The Immaculate Conception

Readings: Gen 3:9-15, 20; Eph 1:3-6, 11-12; Lk 1:26-38

The only mother chosen by her son was Mary. Her freely given 'Yes' changed the course of human history.

We all carry within our heart a blueprint of the one we love. What seems to be 'love at first sight' is actually the fulfilment of desire, the realisation of a dream. We already have an ideal in us, one that is made by our thinking, our habits, our upbringing, of the sort of person we would like to meet and love. A tiny architect works inside the human heart drawing sketches of its ideal love, from the people it sees, from the books it reads, from its hopes and daydreams, in the fond hope that one person will become a reality for them.

God, too, has within himself blueprints of everything in the universe. A tree is truly a tree because it corresponds to God's idea of a tree. A rose is a rose because it is God's idea of a rose. Human beings, because they have been given free will, fall short of all that God wants them to be. We are subject to sin, which is not in accord with God's plan. There is actually only one person in all of humanity, from the beginning of time, who perfectly conforms to what God wanted her to be. That person is Our Lady, who figures in today's Gospel. He wanted her to be what she is, his own Mother.

If you could have chosen your mother, would you not have made her the most perfect woman that ever lived? One who would be the most gentle, merciful, kind and loving person possible? The only mother chosen by her Son was Mary. Today we are celebrating the Feast of the Immaculate Conception. If Mary wasn't immaculately conceived then we are saying that Christ came from a less-than-perfect woman. We are saying that he didn't pick a perfect woman to be his mother. (Luke 1:26-38) It doesn't seem to make sense.

In the light of the feast being celebrated, consideration of the Annunciation passage can be confined to two phrases: the angel's greeting, 'Rejoice, so highly favoured! The Lord is with you', and secondly, the promise that Mary will be overshadowed by the power of the Holy Spirit.

Mary's holiness comes from her being favoured, chosen by God as the mother of the Lord. In fact, the phrase 'full of grace' is rather cold and static when set beside the reverent, joyful greeting of the angel, full of wonder as he salutes her from whom the Son of the Most High was to take his flesh.

In Luke the promise of the angel that the Holy Spirit will come upon Mary and that the power of the Most High will cover her with its shadow, is a clear reference to her as the new Ark of the Covenant. There is an echo from the book of Exodus.

The Church teaches that Mary is not only the mother of Jesus but also the mother of the Church and therefore our mother. We pray through Mary to Jesus. We have at the side of the throne of Jesus an intercessor, immaculately conceived, highly favoured by God, fully one of us. Mary gives a freely chosen 'Yes' (fiat) to God's invitation to be the mother of his Son. In Mary alone a child waited not on nature but on the acceptance by his mother of the Divine will.

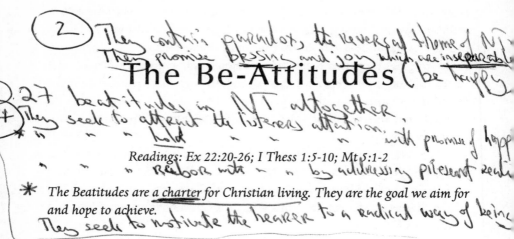

The Be-Attitudes

(handwritten annotations:) (2) They contain paradox, the reversal theme of NT. They promise blessing and joy which are inseparable (be happy)

(3) 27 beatitudes in NT altogether.

(4) They seek to attract the listeners attention. hold ... with promise of happy ... Reborn into ... by addressing present reali...

Readings: Ex 22:20-26; I Thess 1:5-10; Mt 5:1-2

The Beatitudes are a charter for Christian living. They are the goal we aim for and hope to achieve.

(handwritten:) They seek to motivate the hearer to a radical way of being

The Beatitudes, to my mind, have never had the centrality they ought to have had in Christian spirituality. 'Theirs is the Kingdom of Heaven' is the promise to the poor in spirit; those who mourn; the meek; those who hunger and thirst for justice; the merciful; the clean of heart and so on. Is this a promise of salvation? I think not. The phrase 'the kingdom of heaven' is found only in Matthew – thirty-two times. The more common phrase was the 'kingdom of God'. At no time did Jesus give a definition of this 'kingdom of God'.

In the context of the spiritual life the Kingdom is 'interior'; it is capable of growth and evolution, and from the individual it reaches out to others, to all humanity, to the whole world. Membership of the Kingdom is determined by one's relationship with Jesus Christ. What we are and what we do determine the Beatitudes or blessings in Luke and Matthew.

The poor in spirit. These are those whose agendas in life are not determined by outside forces like money, power or popularity. They have a willingness to change and are available to respond to the call of God, wherever it may lead. Such people are not encumbered by baggage. They travel light.

Those who mourn – not for the dead alone but for the evil and sin in the world. These are intercessors who place themselves between

God and the sin of the world, much as Jesus did on the cross. Through their prayers they stay the hand of evil.

The meek, the powerless, the *anawim*, are those whose hope is the Lord. These are those who recognise that ultimately all is gift and comes from God alone. Their hope is in him that ultimately 'all things work together unto good for those who love God'.

Those who hunger and thirst for righteousness are those who look for the final salvation that can only be achieved through God. For them life is a journey that entails working for justice and integrity as staging posts, as part of life's pilgrimage to ultimate salvation.

The merciful are the compassionate ones. Their heart is always open to receive the crippled and the lame. Their task is neither to praise nor blame but only to seek to understand. They do not stand in judgement over the world or bemoan its faith.

The pure in heart are those who follow the simple way, like St Teresa: 'To you alone, O Jesus, I must cling; and running to your arms, dear Lord, there let me hide; Loving with childlike tenderness'.

The peacemakers are those who work for wholeness in the person and the world. They seek to remove the barriers erected by racists. They are reconcilers who bring divided people together.

Those who suffer for righteousness are people like Sheila Cassidy, tortured in Chile under Pinochet, or Pat Rice in Argentina during the so-called 'dirty war'. These are people prepared to pay the ultimate price rather than compromise their integrity.

[handwritten notes:]

Start + finish

1) This Feast of All Saints +
b) tomorrows Feast of All Souls +
our commemoration of them are all linked by
states of acceptance of the plan of God for us
by common thread.
What the Saints enjoy +
what the Holy Souls anticipate
and what we are promised is all one + the
same reality that we have been sealed by
the love of God. That the beatific vision
is God's will for all whom he has called.

When Things Fall Apart

Readings: Apoc 7:2-4, 9-14; 1 Jn 3:1-3; Mt 5:1-12

Saints are people who have overcome fear. Fear is the emotion that prevents us from embracing the plan of God for our lives.

Retrouvaille is a programme to help couples who are experiencing the pain of a marriage in trouble. I work with a team in presenting this programme in Ireland. The healing process demands of couples a willingness to change. As the only person you can change is yourself, there is a natural reluctance, even when the pain in intense, to move from entrenched positions. I can understand this. At the root of this unwillingness is fear. In the course of a Retrouvaille weekend there is a presentation entitled 'To trust again'. To do this one must let go of fear.

Marriages don't have fixed charts to sail by. A marriage is a voyage of discovery. Before setting out one can only guess at what's out there. There are unfaced fears – like the early death of a spouse, falling 'out of love', unexpected illness, unemployment and so on. We have got to get to know fear, to look at it straight in the eye – not as a way to solve problems, but as a complete undoing of old ways of seeing, hearing, smelling, tasting and thinking. The truth is that when we really begin to do this, we're going to be continually humbled.

In a marriage in difficulty, when one or other of the parties is unwilling to face fear, invariably they are also unwilling to face change. This, in turn, leads to an unwillingness to trust again. This is true not only of marriage, but for everyone who is willing to undertake 'the journey inwards'. When I feel bogged down, or that my life is in a mess, it is because I have been fearful of the consequences that might result from the changes I know I have to make in my life. Fear is the buffer to leading a fuller life.

We habitually spin off and freak out when there's even a whiff of fear. We feel it coming and we check it out. It is only when there is nowhere to hide that we are willing to face fear. On a Friday night of a Retrouvaille weekend the couples arrive frozen in their fear of what they have let themselves in for. It is only because the pain has become unbearable that they have got to this point. Fear can also be tinged with hope, even excitement. It's a bit like a parachutist taking their first jump. He or she knows the parachute has been tested many times – but there is always the one in a million chance that it won't open. What then? When the parachutist jumps, the fear is left in the 'plane behind, in the exhilaration of floating gently down to earth.

What has this got to do with the Beatitudes? I think they are saying 'Blessed are those without fear'. These are those who are willing to accept, with joy, their meekness, humility, mourning, as 'blessed' states. They are really 'be-attitudes'. They are a decided stance towards life and are seen as blessed. For people like myself they are a vision to be embraced when the fear of 'letting go' is overcome. There are many such visions in the Bible, which we preach, pay lip-service to, but are unwilling to grasp. It can only be done with the grace of God. Saints are fearless people. They have the mettle that allows them to embrace change if it is called for by God. Today we honour the saints.

Feast Of All Saints

Has Liberation Theology Been Replaced By Prosperity Theology?

Readings: Apoc 7:2-4, 9-14; 1 Jn 3:1-3; Mt 5:1-12

Have we forgotten what Jesus came to do? The basic prophecy of Jesus is contained in the Gospel of today's Mass

The 'good news' that Jesus came to proclaim was not 'pie in the sky when you die'. He awakened hope in the poor and oppressed. The good news of the Kingdom of God was news about a future state of affairs on earth, when the poor would no longer be poor, the hungry would be satisfied and the oppressed would no longer be miserable. The activity of Jesus was so centred on the poor, the outcast, the sinners and oppressed that it is impossible to believe that the Church should not have the same priorities. The Church just is not credible if it is not working in the 'liberationist' tradition established by Jesus. It was not charity or healing that Jesus came to bring – it was freedom. The bound-up were promised freedom.

> The spirit of the Lord has been given to me,
> He has sent me to bring the good news to the poor,
> To heal the brokenhearted,
> To proclaim liberty to captives,
> Freedom to those in prison,
> To proclaim the Lord's year of favour' (Isaiah 61)

I can still remember the exciting, heady days when the emerging liberation theology seemed to align itself so closely to the ministry and preaching of Jesus. I had the privilege at that time to visit South

America and speak to such people as Gutierrez, Boff and Segundo. I saw in Chile how many small groups were struggling to make sense of the powerful moneyed and vested interests ranged against them. 'How do we respond in the light of the Gospel?' was the question on the lips of the poor. The liberation theologians aimed to dissolve the alliance of Church, State and military that had dominated Latin America for centuries. The 'preferential option for the poor' was a first premise of pastoral strategy.

It became politicised, the Vatican said. Indeed, it has to be admitted that had it become a truly significant grassroots movement, even the Vatican and a few powerful South American prelates would have had a lot more difficulty quenching the movement. 'It is not our job to change the structures, leave that to others' was the tenor of the Congregation of the Doctrine of the Faith's admonition. Who has replaced the Dom Helder Camaras? Here was a man who called upon Christians to go deep – deeper into community and deeper into solidarity with the poor. The 'Pax Americana' we now live under is driven mainly by big business and multinationals. Now we appear to have replaced liberation theology with prosperity theology. The Beatitudes in today's Gospel compel us to reconsider our priorities as individuals and as a Church.

How do we preach about need in a world of plenty? What are the obligations of the affluent? Grassroots movements like the Simon Community must seek volunteers from abroad. Even the Society of St Vincent de Paul must advertise extensively for helpers. All this at a time of unprecedented prosperity! In order for things to be different, something has to change. The only person I can change is myself. Change must mean conversion of heart to the strategy of Jesus. His ministry was predominantly with the poor and the outcast. This Gospel provides an opportunity for an examination of conscience.

The Feast Of All Souls

Readings: Isa 25:6-9; Rom 5:5-11; Mt 11:25-30

Today we remember the familiar faces, now gone. We intercede for all those who have gone before us. We pray that they may be purified in Purgatory, and that we, like them, will enjoy the presence of God's infinite love one day.

America has tried to anaesthetise itself against the reality of death. In 1993 I was doing a month's duty in a parish in Florida. My visits to the funeral parlours were rare moments of wonderment. The gentle piped music, the deep-tufted carpets, the armchairs, the beautifully embalmed body, cosmetically restructured, to look better than life itself, shouted out that death has been eliminated. No more death!

Such a scene is a million miles away from the traditional Irish familiarity with death. Tomás O'Crohan, in *The Islandman,* gives a wonderful description of a wake in the early years of the nineteenth century. 'The feet of the corpse were to the fire and its head to the door. On the other side, facing the door, was the whole set-out. There was a great flame of fire, a kettle on the hook above it, two kettles at the side of it and the gathering was beginning – men, women, and children up and down throughout the house. At this moment four people were arranging the corpse finely. "A dress for the journey to the other side," as one of the women said when they had done.' Later in the evening the festivities began: 'I saw a man come up towards me from the bottom of the house with a great white bucket, running over with porter in one of his hands, and an empty mug to hold about a pint in the other.' Apart from the drink the ritual of sharing a pipe of tobacco was important. 'I glanced over to where the candles were flaming at the end of the table, where the feet of the corpse were, and there were two men there, seated on chairs, who were busied over tobacco and pipes; and that was no pleasant job.' The wake, in the presence of the corpse, continued for twenty-four hours. Although Tomás himself didn't approve of the drink, the wake and the annual pattern day provided one of the few opportunities for socialising and for mingling between the sexes.

Somehow God reaches us through the culture and traditions that have been handed down to us. If we let go of these we allow ourselves to be 'robbed' of the spirit. This is what is happening in the twenty-first century. Globalisation is breaking down the distinct culture and traditions of indigenous peoples. Some years ago in the Samburu desert in Kenya I was amazed to see a young boy herding emaciated cattle, with a staff in one hand and a ghetto blaster blaring rock music in the other.

Thankfully in this country death is still celebrated as an occasion in which all the community participates. The long lines of people waiting to greet the bereaved after the removal of the remains to the church are a sign of solidarity and compassion. But it also conveys an intuitive understanding of the nature of death itself as a portal to something else. The many people, often at great inconvenience, who attends funerals, indicates an understanding of the intimacy between life and death.

Today we remember our dead – the joy that they have brought to our lives. The hugs, the words of comfort, the acts of kindness we received from the deceased brought succour to our lives. We pray for those who have died alone, emigrants in a foreign land. We pray in the belief that our prayer makes a difference. The purification of the soul being prepared to meet the glorious love of God is dependent in some mysterious way on our intercession.

Grief is good. Weeping is cleansing. The longing left behind by the dead creates an anxiousness and emptiness in our heart which may never be filled in this life. The longing for future things. The restlessness of the human heart, we believe, will never rest until it rests in infinity. On this day we look forward to that place where there will be no more weeping or gnashing of teeth – where all tears will be wiped away.

Sharing Our Faith With Others

Readings: Isa 2:1-5; Eph 4:11-16; Mt 28:16-20

Mission Sunday is a good day to remember that 'the Church exists in order to evangelise'. To know Christ and to make him known is at the heart of what it means to be a Christian.

For over twenty years I have had an interest in and concern for the activities of new religious movements, commonly called sects or cults. My first encounter was with a devotee of the Divine Light Mission in O'Connell Street in Dublin in 1975. He told me about the possibility of acquiring 'the knowledge' and of the inspired leadership of Guru Maharaji Ji. I accepted his invitation to visit their 'ashram' in Santry. I took off my shoes and entered the prayer room, one end of which was decorated by a massive picture of the Guru, to which everyone bowed on entering. This was the beginning of a long journey. One characteristic that all of these new religious groups have in common is a burning desire to share the 'light' or 'wisdom' that they have acquired with others. For the Moonies, this often means long hours on the streets confronting potential recruits. The Hare Krishna will be seen at rock festivals sifting through the youth like sleuths, to converse with likely converts. The Children of God tirelessly distributed the so-called 'letter of Mo' in cities across the world. New Age promoters, like film actress Shirley MacLaine, have written books and lectured worldwide to promote a philosophy that is sweeping the Western world. Meanwhile, the Christian missionary effort is listless and without the enthusiasm or zeal of former years. I accept that the truth subsists in some ways in some of these new groups, and that no one can doubt the sincerity of many of their adherents. But Christianity makes unique claims, which if we believe them to be true compel us to proclaim them by word and example.

From the beginning the desire to proclaim Jesus was integral to what it meant to be a Christian. Peter and John, having been arrested, were promised their liberty if they would not speak about Jesus. Their answer? 'We cannot but speak about what we have seen and heard.' For more than fifteen years after his call outside Damascus, Paul worked as a missionary far away from Jerusalem. Jesus had instructed his disciples 'to preach and to heal'. The great commission to 'go and teach all nations, baptising them in the name of the Father and of the Son and of the Holy Spirit' gives the Church its reason for existing.

The heart of the message is the person of Jesus Christ. 'This is eternal life, to know you the One true God, and Jesus Christ whom you have sent.' To know and experience the overwhelming love of God is the foundation of mission. To know him not only with the head but with the heart leads inevitably to a desire to make him known to others. For a Christian, to proclaim Jesus, whether by word or example, is not a choice. It is an imperative. We all share in the priesthood of Christ through our Baptism and Confirmation. It is in the nature of priesthood to 'bring God to people and people to God.'

I can recall the late Frank Duff, the founder of the Legion of Mary, saying, 'A Legionary is always on duty', indicating that, as Christians, our stance towards others ought to be motivated by a desire to allow the Christ in us, to reach out to the Christ in others, thereby sharing the great love that God has for both.

Mission Sunday

The Trinity – The Central Mystery Of The Christian Faith

Readings: Ex 34:4-6, 8-9; 2 Cor 13:11-13; Jn 3:16-18

* *The Trinity is the mystery of God's own inner life. The nucleus of this life is love, from which everything of God radiates.*

When Albert Einstein died in 1955, his brain remained, soaking for decades in a jar of formaldehyde. No one bothered to dissect the brain until the 1980s. By then bits of Einstein's brain began making the rounds of certain neurobiologists, who learned . . . absolutely nothing. It was just a brain. We talk as though humanity could be divided into two groups: Albert Einsteins and everybody else. Einstein's theory of relativity was shocking and revolutionary. The name of Einstein to this day has entered the English language as a series of clichés: 'it doesn't take an Einstein'; 'he's no Einstein'; 'a poor person's Einstein'. And yet, even to a person of the calibre of Einstein, the Holy Trinity would continue to remain a mystery of faith.

Is the Trinity really a living doctrine for the average Catholic? To be honest, I have a suspicion that many Christians deviate from it, to one side or the other. Some are virtually 'tritheists': the Father, the Son and the Holy Spirit are regarded practically as three separate Gods. Others are virtually unitarians: in the practice of their faith the Father alone is God, while Jesus Christ is seen as a special man who reveals the Father, and the Holy Spirit is for them a power rather than a divine Person.

* 'The mystery of the Most Holy Trinity', according to the *Catechism of the Catholic Church,* 'is the central mystery of Christian faith and life. It is the mystery of God in himself. It is the source of all other mysteries of faith, the light that enlightens them'. We know about the

Trinity through the revelation by God of his own inner life. We believe on the basis of a God revealing himself. But this mystery is inaccessible to reason alone and demands faith in the one who reveals.

Jesus revealed that God is Father, calling him 'Abba'. God is eternally Father in his relationship to his Son; 'No one knows the Son except the Father, and no one knows the Father except the Son and anyone to whom the Son chooses to reveal him.' (Matthew 11:27) Before his Passover Jesus announced the sending of 'another Paraclete, the Holy Spirit. This Spirit will guide us into all truth'. One God, three Persons equal and distinct.

The Godhead is a community of love. As I understand it, one way of trying to grasp the essence of the Trinity is to think of the Father eternally loving the Son, from which issues eternally the Holy Spirit. This love is eternally active. The Trinity is a community of love constantly in motion. We, through our Baptism and our participation in the life of Christ, through grace, are drawn up into the love of the Trinity.

St Catherine of Sienna describes the Trinity as the Father who holds and keeps all of his creation in his embrace, and mirrors the mystery of his own identity in the human power of remembering, while the Son, living image and Word of the Father and the Son, traces the uniqueness of his Person in our capacity for understanding. The Spirit, personal union of the Father and Son, images himself in our human ability to love.

We are made in his image + likeness
we are most authentic when we love.
we worship God, the undivided unity of F S + HS
by our prayer, but also by growing more
+ more in God's likeness.
We do all in the name of F S + HS.

The Dropouts

Readings: *Deut 4:32-34, 39-40; Rom 8:14-17; Mt 28:16-20*

Why do people leave the Church? Have those who are committed any obligations in that regard? The Gospel today gives us the answer.

I read somewhere that the largest single Christian denomination in the United States is Roman Catholics, and the second largest Christian denomination is of fallen-away Catholics. Could that be coming true in Ireland also? A deep and comprehensive study of lapsed Catholics was undertaken by Dean Hoge, in his book *Converts, Dropouts and Returnees,* a study he did for the United States bishops. He listed five types of dropouts. First are the weary dropouts. These are people who found the Church boring and uninteresting, where no motivation for Mass attendance exists. The median age of such a dropout is twenty-six. A lot of these were people who were just tired of the Church's 'hassle', particularly in cases of marriage, divorce and remarriage. Lifestyle dropouts were those who wanted something the Church couldn't give them. A lot of these people objected to the Church's teachings, particularly on sex and how it is to be used. A third class that Hoge mentions are 'spiritual need' dropouts, and these are those who were not getting enough from the Church, who felt that their spiritual needs were not being met. These are the sort of people who join other denominations or new religious movements. A fourth group leave the Church because of intermarriage. These people drift out of the Church or find attendance at church increasingly inconvenient. Family-tension dropouts left the Church for reasons other than religion or the Church. They did so as part of their rebellion against family pressure. These young people had never internalised their faith and therefore left at the first opportunity when parental authority was weakened. This last type were those who were most likely to return to Church later.

Today's Gospel is short but very focused in its instruction to the disciples. Jesus says, 'Go, therefore, make disciples of all nations....' This has been called the 'great commission'. It is addressed to you and me. We do not disciple people to the Church but to Jesus. The heart of evangelisation is the desire to lead others into the loving heart of Jesus, Lord and Saviour. God loves people. People are made in his image. Our finite minds can hardly grasp the love of God. To know love with the heart as well as the head affects the whole being. Can you remember your first love? You waited, tingling with excitement, for your boyfriend or girlfriend to arrive on a date. Just to be in the company of the one you loved was thrilling. You wanted the feeling to last for ever. Every page of the Gospel story assures us of God's love for us. We know this by faith but we can also experience its effect in our lives. The commission of today's Gospel is fulfilled by telling your friends, your acquaintances, about God's love and inviting them to explore the issues and make a commitment.

The commission is fulfilled by living a life of love in relationship with God. It is fulfilled by allowing our light to shine so that people know we witness to something greater than the world has to offer. We are not alone as we witness to God's love. The promise is 'I am with you always; yes, to the end of time'. Jesus will use our lips, our legs, our hands, to do his work. That work is to make him known and loved. The Church then is the sacrament or sign of the presence of Christ in the world. What a responsibility that places upon us! People need to see the Church as a sign of the compassion, forgiveness, healing, of Christ in the world. The Church is the mother, who protects us from evil, who guides us into the truth, who through the power of Christ 'missions' us to witness to Jesus.

Trinity Sunday

The Trinity:
A Community Of Love

Readings: Prov 8:22-31; Rom 5:1-5; Jn 16:12-15

In revealing the Trinity Jesus gives us a glimpse of the inner working of the Godhead.

A priest was sitting in an airport waiting for his plane. A man sat down beside him and began to give his opinions on religion. 'I just will not believe anything I cannot understand,' he boasted. 'Take this business of three Gods in one God, or whatever it is. I can't buy that. Nobody can explain it to me, so I will not believe it.'

Pointing to the sun streaming in the window, the priest asked, 'Do you believe in the sun?' 'Why, of course,' the man answered. 'All right,' the priest continued, 'the rays of the sun have travelled over 90 million miles to here. The heat we feel comes both from the sun and from its rays. The Holy Trinity is something like that. The sun is God the Father; the sun sends out its rays, God the Son. Then from both the sun and its rays, from the Father and the Son, proceeds or comes the Holy Spirit, the heat. Can you explain how that happens?' The doubter changed the conversation.

The Trinity is a community of love. Three Persons, one God. Through our sharing in the same life of the Godhead through Baptism we share in the life of the Trinity. In the Person of Jesus, God revealed the inner working of the Godhead. In the Gospel today we have the 'spirit of truth, everything that the Father has in mind'. The doctrine of the Trinity is of great importance for a proper understanding of the doctrine of creation. 'The world as creation is the work of his love.' Belief in the Trinity is essential for the doctrine of revelation; in fact, it is the basis for all revelation. In the revelation of the Father in the Son through the Spirit, we not only receive some external information about God, but we have the guarantee that God himself is speaking to us and opening his divine heart to us. Revelation is really and fully self-revelation.

None of this is bald theory. It is echoed in Christians' personal experience. Believers know by experience that they are children of the Father, that they are redeemed by the Son and that the Holy Spirit is present in their lives. And they also know that all three relationships have to do with the one and same God.

It is, as it were, a constant moving to and fro: from the Father through the Son to the Holy Spirit in our lives, and then again from the Holy Spirit in our lives, through the Son to the Father. Often the threefoldness in the relationship is more to the fore of our experience than the unity.

We cannot understand the mystery of the Trinity, let alone take it in. It is far beyond our human thinking. We can only end where we started: by worshipping God the three-in-one. In fact, this was and is the whole reason why the Church tries to penetrate this mystery: that we may worship God as he really is; bring him praise, not only for what he has done for us, but above all for what he is in himself. In their worship, believers will adore God for his incomprehensible greatness and glory.

The Athanasian Creed, the most theological of all ancient creeds, begins with these words: 'And the Catholic faith is this: That we worship one God in Trinity, and Trinity in Unity'. And at the end of the first section it repeats it emphatically: 'So that in all things, the Unity in Trinity, and the Trinity in Unity, is to be worshipped'.

Trinity Sunday

I Am The Bread Of Life

Readings: Gen 14:18-20; 1 Cor 11:23-26; Lk 9:11-17

Jesus made the crowds welcome and talked to them about the Kingdom of God; and he cured those who were in need of healing.

The story of Helen Keller is well known. She was born in 1880 in Alabama, USA. She lost her sight and hearing as a young child of only nineteen months. She had a life-long companion, Anne Sullivan, who taught her to speak, to read and to write. Such was the trusting relationship between herself and Anne Sullivan that she went on to obtain a degree in 1904, and become a distinguished lecturer and writer. Her biography, *The Story of My Life*, became a runaway bestseller. It was later dramatised by William Gibson, for which he won a Pulitzer Prize, and was made into a film entitled *The Miracle Worker*. Anne Sullivan was truly 'the bread of life' for Helen Keller.

Laurence Oates was an explorer, born in London in 1880. In 1910 he joined Scott's expedition to the South Pole, in charge of the ponies. He was one of the five to reach the South Pole in 1912. On the return journey the explorers became weatherbound. Lamed by severe frostbite, and convinced that his condition would fatally handicap his companions' prospect of survival, Oates left the tent and walked out into a blizzard, sacrificing his life. His last words became famous: 'I am just going outside, I may be some time'. Laurence Oates was truly the 'bread of life' for his companions.

Marie Curie was born in Warsaw in 1867. With her French husband, Pierre, she worked on magnetism and radioactivity and she discovered radium in 1903. They won the Nobel Prize for Physics for the discovery of radioactivity. She herself won the Nobel Prize for chemistry in 1910. Her discoveries had a profound and beneficial effect on the treatment of countless sufferers from cancer. She herself died of leukaemia, probably caused by long exposure to radiation in the course of her work. Who knows how many people Marie Curie was the 'bread of life' for, through her discoveries.

When Jesus said 'I am the bread of life' he was both promising to give us something and asking to receive something from us. Anne Sullivan was the 'bread of life' for her companion Helen Keller. Her presence, her encouragement, her skill, gave Helen a life she could hardly have dreamed of. Poor Laurence Oates, in an action of heroic sacrifice, was ready to give his life so that his companions might live. He thought that his sacrifice might be the 'bread of life' for them. Marie Curie was an indefatigable worker in the field of science, searching for a cure for cancer. She was the 'bread of life' for many. Jesus wants to be the 'bread of life' for me.

Jesus wants to be my friend. He knows me through and through. He knows my weaknesses, my sins and my fears and he wants to support me through and beyond them. Not content to be just a spiritual presence, he wants a closer relationship with me. That closer relationship comes about through the Eucharist, which is truly a 'meeting with Christ'.

The Eucharist is the source and summit of Christian life. Theologian Henri de Lubac said that 'the Church makes the Eucharist but the Eucharist makes the Church'. He also wrote that 'Christ in his Eucharist is truly the heart of the Church'. The *Constitution on the Liturgy* of the Second Vatican Council says that 'the most holy Eucharist holds within itself the whole treasure house of the Church'. One Protestant writer claimed that 'If I believed as you Catholics do I would go up the Church on my knees'.

The promise is that anyone who eats this bread and drinks this blood has eternal life and will live for ever. But by meeting with Christ, in some sense, we already have 'heaven on earth'.

Corpus Christi